# VENICE: A LITERARY COMPANION

# VENICE
*A Literary Companion*

# Ian Littlewood

JOHN MURRAY

© Ian Littlewood 1991

First published in 1991
by John Murray (Publishers) Ltd
50 Albemarle Street, London W1X 4BD

The moral right of the author has been asserted

*British Library Cataloguing in Publication Data*

Littlewood, Ian
    Venice: a literary companion.
    1. Venice. Literary associations. History
    I. Title
    945.31

ISBN 0-7195-4787-3


Typeset by Rowland Phototypesetting Ltd
Bury St Edmunds, Suffolk
Printed and bound in Great Britain
by Biddles Ltd, Guildford and King's Lynn

*For Ayumi*

# CONTENTS

# ILLUSTRATIONS

*(between pages 148 and 149)*

The author and publishers wish to thank the following for permission to reproduce the illustrations: Ancient Art and Architecture Collection, No. 3; Osvaldo Böhm, Venice, Nos. 17, 18; Bridgeman Art Library, No. 1; Mary Evans Picture Library, Nos. 5, 13, 14; Explorer, Paris, No. 6; *Illustrated London News*, No. 16; Mansell Collection, No. 12; National Gallery, No. 11; Scala, Nos. 2, 4; Scala and Ca' Rezzonico, No. 10; Scala and Biblioteca Querini Stampalia, No. 7; Duke of Bedford's Collection, Woburn Abbey, No. 8.

# PREFACE

'Abhorrent, green, slippery city,' D. H. Lawrence called it. Venice has never been loved by those who want to change the world. Prophets, moralists, people with missions and ambitions, tend to be impatient of its endless windings and quietly reflective surfaces. Its obsession with the past offends their sense of purpose. At once shabby and narcissistic, it attracts admirers of a different kind. 'The deposed, the defeated, the disenchanted, the wounded, or even only the bored,' observed Henry James, 'have seemed to find there something that no other place could give.'

Writers, many of them, they have served Venice well, and she has returned the compliment by remaining much as they described her. Plenty of cities have been preserved for us in literature; the eerie charm of Venice is that it has also, to a large extent, been preserved in reality. If James could again settle into his gondola, he would have no trouble in finding the polished steps of 'a little empty *campo* . . . with an old well in the middle, an old church on one side and tall Venetian windows looking down.' The shadowy buildings whose outlines were known to the young Casanova still rise around us as we walk by night through the Campo Sant'Angelo. Thomas Coryate, standing once more on the Rialto bridge, would recognize quite enough to bring back memories of his stay in 1608. Even a pilgrim like Felix Fabri would be able to renew acquaintance with churches he visited on his way to the Holy Land at the end of the fifteenth century.

For us, on the edge of a different millennium, it is still possible to sit outside a café in Venice, read their words, look up and nod in recognition. In this extravagant theatre we can with equal ease find settings for the murder of a Renaissance prince or the seduction of an eighteenth-century nun, the execution of a dissolute friar or the melancholy thoughts of a Victorian poet.

The range of material is vast. 'A man to visit Italy and not to write a book about it,' remarked Landor. 'Was ever such a thing heard of?' Not often, it seems. Readers will no doubt be dismayed by many omissions. Detailed accounts of processions, festivals and ceremonies have been kept to a minimum, as have descriptions of buildings. I have usually preferred byways to highways: there will be no tour of the Doge's Palace, no guide to the mosaics of St Mark's, no helpful words on the paintings in the Frari.

This is a guide-book, but it is only in part about the familiar city of churches, palaces and canals. From certain kinds of writing, often by the sort of people James had in mind, another Venice emerges – elusive, unwholesome, perhaps a little unsafe. This other Venice owes more to myth than to brick and stone. Tainted with past iniquity, sluttish under her regal garb, she invites a kind of surrender that can tempt even the most respectable. Today we scarcely notice, for the place is ill-adapted to the urgency of modern tourism; its first requirement is time. Only to those who linger here after they have seen the sights, knowing that they should have left, does it reveal itself. In putting the book together, I have tried to recover something of this ambiguous appeal.

The chapters are arranged in the form of six walks which will take the determined reader into every part of the city. The final chapter touches on a few of the neighbouring islands. For those who would like to follow the suggested routes, maps are provided. Alternatively, and delightfully, one can trust to luck. Anyone who stays in Venice long enough or goes back often enough will sooner or later stumble upon everything mentioned in these pages.

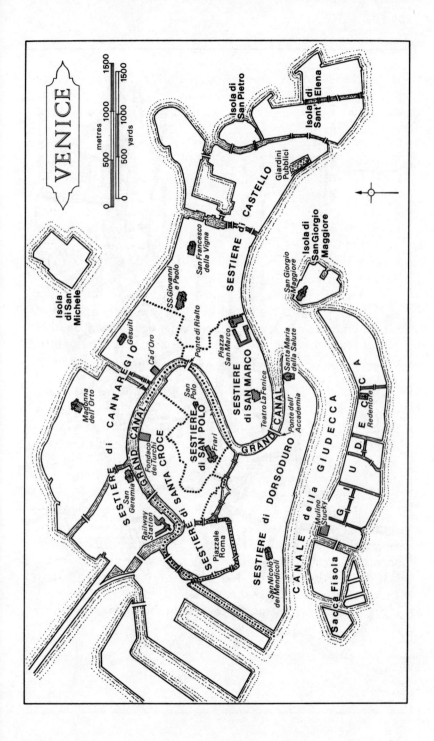

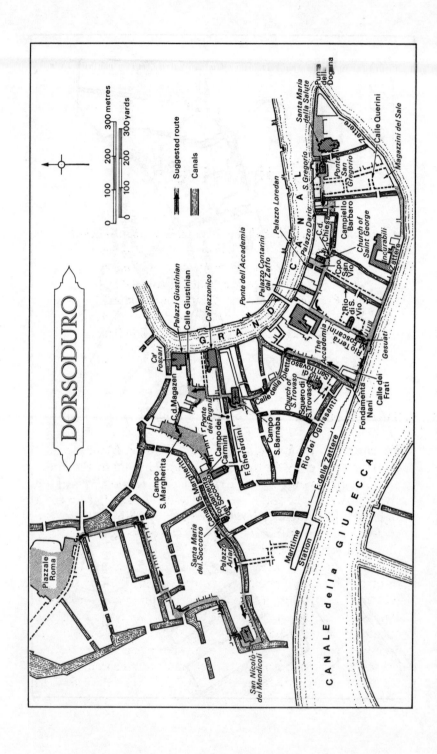

# 1
# DORSODURO

## SANTA MARIA DELLA SALUTE

To enter Venice by train, claimed Thomas Mann, is like
entering a palace by the back door. We shall enter by the front,
San Giorgio on our left, the Doge's Palace on our right, as we
sweep towards the mouth of the Grand Canal. Before us, a
sight that Coryate and Evelyn never saw: rising behind the
customs house at the eastern tip of Dorsoduro are the stately
domes of Santa Maria della Salute.

In the autumn of 1630 the plague receded, leaving almost a
third of the city's population dead. Among the survivors it
was an occasion for gratitude. The Republic commissioned
Baldassare Longhena to build a church in honour of the
Virgin. It was to be 'strange, worthy and beautiful,' the
architect declared, a building 'in the shape of a round
"machine", such as had never been seen, or invented either in
its whole or in part from any other church in the city.'[1] In
retrospect, Longhena's optimism seems wholly justified. His

design is an astonishing success. With its majestic cupolas and
baroque façade, the Salute has become so much a part of our
image of Venice that its absence from early illustrations leaves
us with a sense of something incomplete.

At the entrance of the city the church greets us, according to
Henry James, 'like some great lady on the threshold of her
saloon':

> She is more ample and serene, more seated at her door,
> than all the copyists have told us, with her domes and
> scrolls, her scolloped buttresses and statues forming a
> pompous crown, and her wide steps disposed on the
> ground like the train of a robe.[2]

Prominent among the statues, above the architrave of the
left-hand chapel, is a figure that caught the eye of the French
poet Théophile Gautier. He had arrived in Venice in the
summer of 1850 on a rainy night which allowed him to
glimpse only a tantalizing shadow of the city around him. In
the morning he ran to his balcony in the Hotel Europa and
looked out across the Grand Canal towards the Salute. There
'a figure of Eve in the most gallant state of undress smiled at us
from a cornice under a shaft of sunlight'.[3]

The interior of the church is dominated, as the terms of
Longhena's commission stipulated that it should be, by the
high altar. Horatio Brown, an Englishman who lived in
Venice from 1879 and was one of its most tireless chroniclers,
describes the scene at the annual festival of the Salute on 21
November, commemorating the city's salvation from the
plague:

> Inside the church, the devout light the candles they have
> carried, one taking the fire from another, and press
> forward after the priests up to the altar rails; there the
> tapers are handed over to the sacristans and placed beside
> the high altar, where Madonna stands, triumphing over a
> figure of the plague. Thousands and thousands of candles
> are passed over the rails until the whole space by the altar
> seems like one solid wall of embossed gold as the flames
> waver and flicker in the draught. In return for their

candles and some centesimi, the pious receive a picture of Madonna, which is devoutly kissed and put away inside their shirts or shawls . . .[4]

And when the religious business is done, the *festa* moves on to the neighbouring wine-shops and eating-houses. These occasions must have had their drawbacks for the church authorities. Henri de Régnier observed with pleasure a restrained notice in the Salute at the turn of the century: 'Out of respect for God and Saint Mary, you are requested not to spit on the ground, but to use, for preference, your handkerchief.' At night the area round the Salute has a charm increased by its silence. John Addington Symonds, the author of *Renaissance in Italy*, was a friend of Horatio Brown and another Englishman who found in Venice a congenial release from the rigidities of late Victorian England. A long love affair with his gondolier, Angelo Fusato, tied him to Venice through the 1880s until his death in 1893, and for part of each year he rented a small flat attached to Brown's house on the Zattere. In one of the essays in *A Venetian Medley* he describes a night-time stroll towards the Punta della Dogana:

Tonight . . . the waning moon will rise late through veils of *scirocco*. Over the bridges of San Cristoforo and San Gregorio, through the deserted Calle di Mezzo, my friend and I walk in darkness, pass the marble basements of the Salute, and push our way along its Riva to the point of the Dogana. We are out at sea alone, between the Canalazzo and the Giudecca. A moist wind ruffles the water and cools our forehead. It is so dark that we can only see San Giorgio by the light reflected on it from the Piazzetta. The same light climbs the Campanile of S. Mark, and shows the golden angel in a mystery of gloom. The only noise that reaches us is a confused hum from the Piazza. Sitting and musing there, the blackness of the water whispers in our ears a tale of death. And now we hear a plash of oars, and gliding through the darkness comes a single boat. One man leaps upon the landing-place without a word and disappears. There is another wrapped in a military cloak asleep. I see his face beneath mo, pale and quiet. The *barcaruolo* turns the point in silence. From the darkness they came; into the darkness they have gone.[5]

## CAMPIELLO BARBARO

From the Salute we can walk past the church and campo of San Gregorio and then on to the Ponte San Gregorio mentioned by Symonds. A short way beyond the bridge, ivy spills over the walls of the ancient Palazzo Dario, where Henri de Régnier lived in 1899 and 1901. In the beautiful little Campiello Barbaro, with its picture shops and its three gaunt trees, there is a plaque to his memory on the wall beside the curving bridge. Behind are the dark red walls of the palace. The inscription tells us that he wrote '*venezianamente*', 'Venetianly'. It is an apt expression. Certainly his novel *L'Altana* and the *Esquisses vénitiennes* are penetrated by the atmosphere of the place:

> As I write these words, the evening light thickens over the Grand Canal, the bells sound under a grey November sky. From my table by the window I see the gondolas glide over the water with their black Harlequins at the stern. Here and there a light goes up in the façade of a palace.[6]

Another time he will look out at the silent waters of the little canal that runs alongside the Campiello Barbaro and note the gondolas, stripped of their cushions and *felzi*, waiting idly for the spring to come again. Venice in general and the Palazzo Dario in particular offered a perfect context for the seductive mixture of melancholy and nostalgia which was his characteristic vein. When he catches sight through his window of a group of strangers, Baedekers in hand, asking directions of a policeman, he merely hopes that they won't seek out, through this tangle of streets, the traghetto San Gregorio; for it is here, 'in this district so melancholy and so solitary . . . that the house stands in which I live – happier than a Doge.'[7]

An earlier inhabitant of the Palazzo Dario, from 1838–1842,

was Ruskin's friend Rawdon Brown, a later one, in the 1970s, Kit Lambert, manager of the rock group The Who. Between the scrupulous antiquarian and the flamboyant, dope-ravaged Lambert there could scarcely have been a wider gap. But they were both lonely men to whom happiness did not come easily, and both of them were happy in Venice. While Florence was a natural resort in the nineteenth century for exiled couples, Venice became increasingly the haven of individuals. A string of writers and artists from the late nineteenth century onwards – men as different as Symonds, Brown, James, Proust, Corvo – seemed to find in its passivity and its decadence and its ambiguous femininity an atmosphere that allowed them to breathe more freely. Often, in spite of their sociability, they were solitary figures, often homosexual. Whereas other writers passed through Venice and admired what is to be admired, these were caught in her toils. And they wrote of the city with corresponding intensity – about the beauties she displays, but more particularly about the less familiar beauties that she half-conceals.

Rawdon Brown had come here in the summer of 1833 to look for the burial place of Thomas Mowbray (see p. 114), and for the next fifty years, until his death, he stayed:

> I scarcely wake in the morning but I thank God that he has let me spend my days in Venice; and sometimes of an evening, when I go to the Piazzetta, I am afraid to shut my eyes, lest when I open them I should find it had all been a dream.[8]

In the 'Sonnet to Rawdon Brown' Browning pictures him about to return to England for a last sight of it before he dies. On the point of leaving, he looks back at Venice: 'What a sky, / A sea, this morning! One last look! Good-by, / Cà Pesaro . . .'
He never leaves.

RIO DI SAN VIO

This eastern spur of Dorsoduro has a distinctive tone which is reflected in the absence of large hotels and the sprinkling of smaller, more discreet *pensioni*.[9] It has long been associated with foreign visitors, but not, for the most part, with those who travel on expense accounts or in troublesome groups. If E. M. Forster had set a novel in Venice, this would surely have been the place for his more sympathetic characters. The atmosphere of its quiet streets readily suggests the image of English visitors of a certain age, cultured and unassuming, setting off from rather spartan rooms for a serious morning's sight-seeing. Perhaps they would not themselves patronize the Anglican church of St George on the corner of the Campo San Vio and the Calle della Chiesa, but its presence in the area would seem a fitting legacy from a slightly earlier age.

The Campo San Vio is separated from the Palazzo Loredan and the recently established Cini collection[10] by the Rio di San Vio, a canal that is usually busy with barges transporting anything from eighteenth-century furniture to crates of coca-cola. It was here that Baron Corvo suffered the indignity described in 'On Cascading into the Canal'. Corvo, whose real name was Frederick Rolfe, had arrived in Venice in the summer of 1908. He was forty-eight years old and had so far enjoyed a life of almost unrelieved failure. He had failed to become a Roman Catholic priest, he had failed as a painter, and his careers as schoolmaster and photographer had been equally unremarkable. He was, however, the author of a brilliant, patchy work of fiction, *Hadrian the Seventh*. It was his literary talent, combined with a prickly sort of charm, that enabled him to find a series of patrons with whom he inevitably quarrelled. The most recent of these was the archaeologist Richard Dawkins, who had brought him to Venice. A decent man some ten years younger than Rolfe, Dawkins had private means and shared, from a timid distance, his companion's interest in the homosexual possibilities of a city full of gondoliers. They took rooms on the fourth floor of the Hotel Belle Vue et de Russie, at the corner of St Mark's Square, intending to settle down for a six-week holiday.

Rolfe believed that it was the part of a gentleman to spend lavishly, and his belief was if anything reinforced by the fact that it was Dawkins's money that he was spending. Within a month the two had parted company and Rolfe was on his own in Venice. Until his death in 1913 he was frequently advised, cajoled, and bribed to leave by other members of the English colony, but the place had taken possession of him. With an enormous Waterman fountain pen and a padlocked laundry basket which contained the rest of his possessions, he moved about Venice for the next five years, running up debts, feuding with the resident English, chasing gondoliers, and writing with lyrical passion about the city he had adopted.

Corvo's main enthusiasm was for the various craft that plied the narrow Venetian canals, and he himself became an accomplished oarsman. Late one cheerless autumn afternoon he had set off from the Bucintoro club with his gondolier, Emilio Sacripan – 'Emily'. The man was in disgrace at the time, Corvo explains, and had been threatened with dismissal:

> So he was on his best behaviour when we set forth that dull cold afternoon on the top of a high tide and a flowing sea, from the Club, up Canal Grande past La Salute, turning off at the Duchess of Madrid's red and yellow posted palace with the gilded Florentine lilies, to go up Rio di San Vio. And then, just after you pass the Erastian temple, the Rio di San Vio narrows, and is crossed by a bridge, before it widens again into a very decent canal with quays for pedestrians on both sides of it. We had swirled through the narrow part and under the bridge, when the calamity occurred. I was rowing at the prow, and Emily was steering at the poop, the pace being my usual swift and hectic one. A big unwieldy barea of firewood came suddenly towards us, rowed by two of my former gondoglieri, Piero Venerand and Ermengildo Vianel, who had gotten a better winter job than mine in the firewood business of the latter's father. To avoid collision Emily precipitately twitched my *barcheta* to one side without much judgement. I incontinently lost my balance; and, disliking the notion of crashing ignominiously inboard to sprawl among oars and *forcole*, I made no ado whatever, but just gripped my short pipe more tightly between my teeth, and took a neat header into the canal, passing right under the approaching wood barge.

As I shot through the air I saw all the hands of all the
people on the two *fondamente* being flung to heaven, and I
heard all their voices bawling, 'Ara, Ara! O Mariaver-
gine! For pleasure here is an English going to drown
himself fastidiously!' So as soon as I got under water, I
told myself that the said English had better give these
people something truly rare and wholesome to cough
about. Wherefore I swam, submerged, about thirty yards
up the Rio, passionlessly emerging (to a fanfare of yells) in
a totally unexpected place, with a perfectly stony face,
and the short pipe still stiff and rigid in an immovable
mouth.[11]

## THE ACCADEMIA

A hundred yards beyond Corvo's canal the calle runs up to the
side-wall of the Accademia. The most entertaining travellers
are rarely the best art critics. Dutiful comments prompted by a
morning in a famous gallery make dull reading, as countless
volumes of eighteenth- and nineteenth-century memoirs tes-
tify. Only occasionally do the paintings meet their match.
W. D. Howells describes a Victorian paterfamilias contem-
plating Titian's *John the Baptist* in Room 6, with his family in
respectful attendance. After a few moments, his verdict is
reached: '"Quite my idea of the party's character," he said;
and then silently and awfully led his domestic train away.'[12]

Théophile Gautier was one traveller who could bring an
element of poetry to his description of the paintings in the
Accademia. He was moved, in particular, by Titian's great
*Pietà* – 'this grave and melancholy canvas, whose subject
seems almost a foreboding':

> In truth, Titian never painted a body more lifeless. Under
> this green skin, in these bluish veins, there remains no
> drop of blood, the crimson pulse of life has stopped for
> ever. . . . For the first time the great Venetian has been
> abandoned by his old, unalterable serenity. The shadow
> of approaching death seems to struggle with the sunlight
> that was always on the painter's palette, and to envelop

the canvas in a crepuscular chill. The hand of the artist went cold before completing its task, as witnessed by the inscription in black letters traced at the corner of the painting: *Quod Tizianus inchoatum reliquit Palma reverenter absolvit Deoque dicavit opus.* 'The work which Titian left unfinished, Palma reverently completed and offered to God.'[13]

Of the anecdotes that have attached themselves to various pictures, one of the most revealing concerns Veronese's encounter with the Inquisition over the painting, then called *The Last Supper*, which he had executed for the refectory of SS. Giovanni e Paolo. What troubled the somewhat humourless Inquisitors was that Veronese seemed to have been more interested in the decorative and artistic possibilities of the scene than in its religious content. He was called to account on 8 July 1573:

*Question.* What is the meaning of those men dressed in the German fashion each with a halberd in his hand? . . .
*Answer.* We painters take the same licence that is permitted to poets and jesters. I have placed these two halberdiers – the one eating, the other drinking – by the staircase, to be supposed ready to perform any duty that may be required of them; it appearing to me quite fitting that the master of such a house, who was rich and great (as I have been told), should have such attendants.
*Q.* That fellow dressed like a buffoon, with the parrot on his wrist – for what purpose is *he* introduced into the canvas?
*A.* For ornament, as is usually done.[14]

And so it goes on. 'Were you commissioned by any person to paint Germans and buffoons, and such-like things in this picture?' 'No, my lord.' 'Does it appear to you fitting that at our Lord's last supper you should paint buffoons, drunkards, Germans, dwarfs, and similar indecencies?' 'No, my lord,' Veronese again answers prudently.

This was clearly not a meeting of minds. Veronese's freewheeling notions of subject-matter belonged to a more expansive age, when the Renaissance was in full flower. It was

his good fortune that the Counter Reformation had been
taken up with only moderate zeal by the Venetians. The
Inquisitors initially wanted the offending items repainted, but
a happier solution was found by simply retitling the picture.
As *The Supper in the House of Levi* it could comfortably
accommodate dwarfs, parrots, buffoons, and even heretical
Germans.

Attempts to improve the reader's acquaintance with paintings not present to the eye are a hazardous business for the
casual traveller. In *The Annunciation* by a follower of
Veronese, E. V. Lucas helpfully informs us that 'we find a
good vivid angel, but she has a terrific leg.'[15] Perhaps, on the
whole, it is better to take the line of the admirable Dr John
Moore, father of the hero of Corunna. Writing of his visit to
Italy in 1776 he eschews the usual banalities of connoisseurship
and offers instead a cautionary tale. Some years earlier, he tells
us, he had been going round a gallery with a group of five or
six other Englishmen, among them a gentleman who affected
an enthusiastic passion for the fine arts:

> From the moment we entered the rooms he began to
> display all the refinements of his taste; he instructed us
> what to admire, and drew us away with every sign of
> disgust when we stopped a moment at an uncelebrated
> picture. We were afraid of appearing pleased with any
> thing we saw, till he informed us whether or not it was
> worth looking at. He shook his head at some, tossed up
> his nose at others; commended a few, and pronounced
> sentence on every piece as he passed along, with the most
> imposing tone of sagacity. . . .
> We at length came to the St John, by Raphael, and here
> this man of taste stopped short in an extasy of admiration
> – One of the company had already passed it, without
> minding it, and was looking at another picture; on which
> the connoisseur bawled out – 'Good God, Sir! what are
> you about?' The honest gentleman started, and stared
> around to know what crime he had been guilty of.
> 'Have you eyes in your head, Sir?' continued the con-
> noisseur: 'Don't you know St John when you see him?'

'St. John!' replied the other, in amazement. 'Aye, Sir,
St. John the Baptist, *in propria persona*.'
   'I don't know what you mean, Sir,' said the gentleman,
peevishly.
   'Don't you?' rejoined the connoisseur; 'then I'll en-
deavour to explain myself. I mean St. John in the wilderness, by the divine Raffaelle Sanzio da Urbino, and there
he stands by your side. – Pray, my dear Sir, will you be so
obliging as to bestow a little of your attention on that
foot? Does it not start from the wall? Is it not perfectly out
of the frame? Did you ever see such colouring? They talk
of Titian; can Titian's colouring excel that? What truth,
what nature in the head! To the elegance of the antique,
here is joined the simplicity of nature.'
   We stood listening in silent admiration, and began to
imagine we perceived all the perfections he ennumerated;
when a person in the Duke of Orleans' service came and
informed us that the original, which he presumed was
the picture we wished to see, was in another room; the
Duke having allowed a painter to copy it. *That* which we
had been looking at was a very wretched daubing, done
from the original by some obscure painter, and had been
thrown, with other rubbish, into a corner; where the
Swiss had accidentally discovered it, and had hung it up
merely by way of covering up the vacant space on the
wall, till the other should be replaced.[16]


## ZATTERE

'And on the Zattere,' wrote Horatio Brown, 'the air is laden
with the perfume of honeysuckle and other creepers that trail
over the wall of Princess Dolgorouki's garden.'[17] To reach this
beautiful fondamenta we can walk up the broad, leafy Rio
Terrà M. Foscarini – Rio Terrà indicating that it was once a
canal – which runs alongside the Accademia and opens on to
the Zattere just beside the church of the Gesuati. Brown's own
house, with a relief of St George and Dragon above the door,
was nearby at no. 560. He was one of several resident and

visiting Englishmen who favoured this area towards the end of
the nineteenth century. In his later years Ruskin too stayed on
the Zattere, and Count Zorzi recalls coming upon him chop-
ping wood in the courtyard of what is now the Pensione
Calcina. For the diligent expatriate, *Murray's Handbook* for
1877 notes that Italian lessons can be had from Signora Michiel
at 420, Zattere gli Incurabili, close to where Brown was
living.

The Incurabili of this address is the massive building for
delinquent youth a short way along the Zattere towards the
Salute. It was established in 1522 in response to the spread of
syphilis, which had first appeared in Venice some thirty years
earlier – the Gallic disease, as it was firmly called. (This was
not merely an Italian quirk. Syphilis, like the Devil, always
comes from outside – practically every country in Europe
shuffled the responsibility on to one of its neighbours and
named the disease accordingly.) On 22 February 1522 a proclamation was addressed to the increasing numbers afflicted by
the French pox, 'some of whom in their impotence loiter on
the streets and in the passageways of churches and public
buildings both at Rialto and at San Marco to beg for their
living'. They were ordered to repair to the hospital without
delay.

Among the first to work here were members of the newly
founded Society of Jesus. Along with Loyola himself, they
spent the spring and summer of 1537 in Venice waiting for
papal permission to make a pilgrimage to the Holy Land.
Forty years later the Portuguese Simon Rodriguez, who had
been one of their number, set down an account of these
months. At a time when syphilis and leprosy were popularly
thought to be transmissible merely by the infected breath of
the sufferer,[18] it must have required strong convictions to turn
to this sort of work with any enthusiasm. To overcome their
repugnance, it was not enough for these early Jesuits to
undertake the routine business of caring for the sick:

> In the hospital of The Incurabili, a leper, or one suffering
> from a form of skin disease, covered all over by a kind of
> pestilential mange, called one of the fathers and asked him

to scratch his back. The father diligently performed this service, but whilst he was doing so he was suddenly struck with horror and nausea, and with the terror of contracting the contagious disease. But since he wanted to master himself and to suppress his own rebellious spirit rather than take thought for the future, he put into his mouth a finger covered with pus and sucked it. . . . For this father, who had done the act in good faith and fervour in order to conquer himself, the words of our Lord Jesus Christ were fulfilled: 'And if they drink any deadly thing, it shall not hurt them.'[19]

This was excellent in its way, but the Venetians were never quite comfortable with religious fervour. For most of the city's history the Jesuits were kept at a cautious distance.

More congenial, at least according to Corvo, was the ancient order of the Poveri Gesuati, founded in the late fourteenth century and suppressed in 1668. Their church, which was built after the order had been taken over by the Dominicans, is one of the landmarks passed by Corvo's hero, Nicholas Crabbe, as he wanders through the city. Like Corvo himself, he is obliged by poverty to spend long nights sleeping in his *sandolo* on the lagoon or tramping the streets:

The whole quay of the Zattere extended itself before him. He set himself to pace it from end to end. The drizzle ceased, and a warm haze bloomed on the darkness. He kept moving, to dry his drenched clothes.

Midnight sounded, and the stroke of one. The last ferries left the pontoons by the church of the Gesuati. He thought it a pity that that order of Gesuati, which is three centuries older than the Gesuiti, should have become extinct. The Jesuats always had a most respectable reputation . . .

On the distant bank of the wide canal of Zuecca, the lengthy line of lights along Spinalonga fluttered like little pale daffodils in a night-mist coloured like the bloom on the fruit of the vine. Great quiet reigned. He prayed, to comfort the minutes as they fled by. Holy thoughts

were his, and ardent yearnings, in his unhoused
loneliness . . .[20]

On his way from the church of the Gesuati to the tip of the
Zattere Nicholas Crabbe would have passed not only the
Incurabili but also the imposing wall of the old salt warehouse
just beyond. Not a sight much regarded by tourists, it was
singled out by the art critic Adrian Stokes in his discussion of
the beauty of Venetian brick. One thinks of Venice as a city of
stone, he remarks, 'because stone is the final material, the head
and the fruit of walls of brick and stucco. Emergent from
duller surfaces, the white stone glows. Istrian stone is nearly
always the boundary as well as the relevant mark upon the
wall.'[21] But the unhidden brick in Venice has an attraction of
its own:

> Some of the early Gothic and Renaissance Gothic palaces
> from which the stucco has peeled are remarkably charm-
> ing. Such rosy brick, like the occasional greenness of
> enclosed gardens that appears over walls, or like huge
> Venetian red sails and blinds, suggests an islanded peace,
> an earth substance matured by the sun, an aged country
> warmth. Another instance is the Abbazia San Gregorio
> on the Grand Canal or the huge wall of the salt warehouse
> on the Zattere, the warmest pitch in Venice on many days
> of winter.[22]

## SAN TROVASO

The Rio di San Trovaso is one of the main highways between
the Giudecca Canal and the Grand Canal. If we turn off the
Zattere and walk beside it along the Fondamenta Nani, we can
see across the canal, just before the church of San Trovaso, a
relic of earlier times. On the corner of the Rio dei Ognissanti,
sloping into the water, is a ramp usually occupied by half a
dozen gondolas, hulls to the air, waiting to be planed and
painted. Behind them is the open workshop where they
are built and overhauled. At the end of the sixteenth
century there were ten thousand gondolas in Venice,

today a few hundred at most. Even this boatyard of San Trovaso survives partly by subsidy from an international committee.

There are shelf-loads of books – histories, anthologies, picture books, academic studies – devoted solely to the gondola. We do not have to read far to stumble on at least one explanation for this: it is the gondola which focuses most sharply the intriguing association between Venice and death. The sumptuary laws which stripped the gondola of colour and left it bare of all but the most austere form of decoration were in the end responsible for its enduring hold on our imagination. The Romantics were quick to respond: 'Just like a coffin clapt in a canoe,' wrote Byron. And Shelley, 'I can only compare them to moths of which a coffin might have been the crysalis.' Arriving in Venice for the first time James Fenimore Cooper notes their 'solemn and hearse-like look'. Twenty years later, Wagner, already fearful of cholera, had to force himself to get into one, so disagreeably did it suggest the idea of taking part in a funeral procession. 'Black as nothing else on earth except a coffin' is Gustave von Aschenbach's prophetic thought in Thomas Mann's novella.

Venice is traditionally a city of pleasure and fantasy; but an equally powerful tradition links it with images of what is sinister – with pestilence and decay, the assassin's hand and the secret ways of Venetian justice. There is always the sense both of the carnival and the dungeon, the mask and what the mask conceals, of a city that is, in Mann's words, 'half fairy-tale, half snare'. And as Mann realized, it is the peculiar fascination of the gondola that it enshrines both these elements. The point had already been made in characteristic fashion by Henry James:

> The little closed cabin of this perfect vehicle, the move-
> ment, the darkness and the plash, the indistinguishable
> swerves and twists, all the things you don't see and all the
> things you do feel – each dim recognition and obscure
> arrest is a possible throb of your sense of being floated to
> your doom, even when the truth is simply and sociably
> that you are going out to tea. Nowhere else is anything as

innocent so mysterious, nor anything as mysterious so
pleasantly deterrent to protest.[23]

As so often, James's imagery brushes the dangerous edge of
the sexual before declaring itself respectably social. More
lightly, less respectably, Byron had put the same perception
into verse:

> And up and down the long canals they go,
>   And under the Rialto shoot along,
> By night and day, all paces, swift or slow,
>   And round the theatres, a sable throng,
> They wait in their dusk livery of woe, –
>   But not to them do woeful things belong,
> For sometimes they contain a deal of fun,
>   Like mourning coaches when the funeral's done.[24]

It is hard to feel anything but regret for the passing of such a
graceful and romantic vehicle as the gondola. The one positive
consequence was perhaps that it forced lethargic tourists to
their feet. In former times walking had been firmly discour-
aged. It was the sort of thing that a few dubious expatriates
might get up to, but not the readers of *Cook's Handbook* for
1875:

> A long residence is necessary to enable any one to find his
> way through the labyrinthine streets. Besides which,
> nobody ever thinks of walking in Venice. It is poor policy
> to do so. Gondolas are very cheap, and very comfortable.
> Museums, churches, and picture galleries are very tiring.
> And much valuable time is lost in wandering north,
> south, and east, in order to find a place in the west.[25]

As the gondolas and boatyards have disappeared, so ro-
mance has accrued to the survivors – which receive cor-
respondingly more attention from writers, painters, and
photographers. The *squero* opposite the Fondamenta Nani
already had an honourable tradition. It was here that Nicholas
Crabbe rented lodgings for the beautiful and ambiguous Zildo
in *The Desire and Pursuit of the Whole*, securing a room 'which
gave a view of the rio in front flanked by the lovely old squero

with the trees and green and church, and the Rio di Ognisanti
with the Long Bridge and the Zuecca canal, to right, and left,
respectively.'[26]

Just a year before Crabbe, the slightly less fictional figure of
Ezra Pound had turned up in the same place. He had arrived in
Venice in the spring of 1908, twenty-two years old with a
broken engagement and an abortive academic career behind
him, and dreams of literary fame ahead. At first, he took a
room a short distance away near the Ponte San Vio 'by the
soap-smooth stone posts where San Vio/meets with il Canal
Grande'. At the end of June he moved from there to lodgings
on the corner of the Fondamenta Nani and the Calle dei Frati,
overlooking the *squero*, which he blithely claimed to be 'probably an exact replica of what it was in the sixth century'. It was
while he was living here that his first volume of poems, *A
Lume Spento*, was privately printed in Venice. The city, and
particularly this part of it, became for him, as it has for others,
a focus of nostalgia and a source of images of past happiness. In
a darker future these lines were written for the *Pisan Cantos* but
later omitted:

> San Giorgio, San Trovaso . . .
> Will I ever see the Giudecca again?
> or the lights against it or Ca Foscari?
> or Ca Giustinian . . .
> or the boats moored off le Zattere . . .

Perhaps no city but Venice lends itself so powerfully to
nostalgia because no other city resists time so faithfully or
marks its passage so clearly. Everywhere one turns, the stones
of Venice record the wearing, transforming effects of successive centuries; and yet the stones themselves have survived.
Released in 1958 from the madhouse where his sympathies
with Italian fascism had landed him after the war, Pound
returned to this part of Venice a few years later to spend much
of his last decade living in the nearby Calle Querini. As he
walked through the Piazzetta in sad old age and saw the
unfettered young of the late sixties sprawled on the steps of the
column where St Theodore stands with his crocodile, he must
have thought back to the months he had spent in Venice sixty

years earlier, when his life seemed able to take whatever
direction he chose:

> And
> I came here in my young youth
>    and lay there under the crocodile
> By the column, looking East on Friday,
> And I said: Tomorrow I will lie on the South side
> And the day after, south west.
> And at night they sang in the gondolas
> And in the barche with lanthorns;
> The prows rose silver on silver
>    taking light in the darkness.[27]

No other place can hold one's youth in amber quite so
perfectly.

## SOTTOPORTICO DEL CASIN

Just before the end of the Rio San Trovaso a left turn across the
bridge and into the Calle della Toletta will take us towards the
Campo San Barnaba, which we enter through the Sottoportico del Casin. Surmounted by handsome old chimney-
pots, this passageway takes its name from the *casino* that was
once situated here. When public gambling halls were closed in
1774, the business simply went private, and the spread of
*casinos* was the immediate result. They could be used as places
of rendezvous when occasion offered, but their main function
is indicated by Mutinelli's thundering denunciation in his
*Annali Urbani*:

> This was where, amid gossiping, gaming and sneering,
> debauchery called itself gallantry, impudence urbanity,
> and vice pleasure; where the lustful behaviour of the
> women was brought to new heights by the rivalry of
> others who sought to replace them; where, almost to a
> man, the winners laughed in the face of the losers; where
> the losers yelled in vexation at every card, some blaming
> themselves, others someone else, and so loudly and with

such violence that they were sometimes on the edge of coming to blows.[28]

## PONTE DEI PUGNI

If we bear left across the Campo San Barnaba, we shall come almost at once to a small bridge with a barge of brightly coloured fruit moored beside it. This is the most famous of the city's Ponti dei Pugni. The opposing pairs of footprints set into the top of the bridge mark the place where battles once took place between the ancient factions of the Castellani and the Nicolotti. The rivalry between these two sections of the Venetian populace dated back to a parish feud in the fourteenth century and was based on a geographical division between the eastern side of the city, which was the territory of the Castellani, and the western, which was inhabited by the Nicolotti. (According to tradition, the two façades of the church of San Trovaso were due to its site on the borderline between the hostile groups; the Castellani could use the south door and the Nicolotti the west.) The enmity between the two factions periodically broke out in street brawls, but for the most part it was channelled into set-piece battles that usually took place in the autumn and early winter, originally with clubs, later with fists. To add to the interest of these occasions, the various bridges were left without parapets, so that the combatants could get drenched as well as bruised.

An abrupt end was put to the tradition of the Guerra dei Pugni at the beginning of the eighteenth century. On 30 September 1705 the combatants on this bridge in San Barnaba progressed from fists to knives and stones. The result was a bloodbath. Thereafter they had to make do with the less dangerous rivalry of the regattas.

## CAMPANILE OF THE CARMINI

To the left of the Ponte dei Pugni, rising above the buildings on the other side of the canal, is the campanile of Santa Maria dei Carmini. Before crossing the bridge, we can take a slightly closer look by walking alongside the canal up the pretty Fondamenta Gherardini. From the far end of it we get the best view available of the enclosed campanile. It looks in less than perfect shape today, but it is probably safer than it used to be. Built in the early seventeeth century, the campanile rapidly developed an alarming list. The details of how it was ingeniously straightened by Giuseppe Sardi in 1688 are given in Hugh A. Douglas's excellent guide-book *Venice on Foot*:

Holes were bored in the brickwork about 70 feet from the ground, on three sides, omitting the side to which it inclined. Into these holes wedges of wood were driven, and then more holes were made and more wood inserted, until there was a complete stratum of wood on these three sides. A strong acid was then applied to the wood, which, being gradually consumed, the whole structure settled down into the vacant space and so resumed its upright position, which it has practically retained ever since. The scars of the operation can be clearly seen in the interior of the building, where there is also a Latin inscription recording the operation.[29]

In his somewhat deadpan manner Captain Douglas, as he then was, goes on to mention the time in 1756 when the campanile was struck by lightning, 'on which occasion the monks, who were ringing the bells, fled in such haste that one of them ran his head against the wall and killed himself'.

## CA' REZZONICO

On the far side of the Ponte dei Pugni the fondamenta leads down to the Ca' Rezzonico, described by Henry James as 'thrusting itself upon the water with a peculiar florid assurance, a certain upward toss of its cornice which gives it the air of a rearing sea-horse'.[30] It was in this great seventeenth-century palace that Robert Browning spent his final days. After a long break he had started visiting Venice again in the summer of 1878, usually as the guest of Katharine de Kay

Bronson (see p. 77). Hankering for a palace of his own, he tried to buy the Palazzo Contarini dal Zaffo near the Accademia. The failure of this attempt was a blow to which he was only reconciled some years later when his son Pen, on the strength of a rich American wife, bought the Ca' Rezzonico. Suddenly the feckless Pen, who had otherwise proved rather disappointing, revealed an unsuspected talent. Under his direction the palace was transformed. Again Henry James was on hand to comment, giving the business a malicious gloss in a letter to his sister from the Palazzo Barbaro:

> What Pen has done here, through his American wife's dollars, with the splendid Palazzo Rezzonico, transcends description for the beauty, and, as Ruskin would say, 'wisdom and rightness' of it. It is altogether royal and imperial – but 'Pen' isn't kingly and the *train de vie* remains to be seen. Gondoliers ushering in friends from pensions won't fill it out.[31]

By this time the splendours of the Ca' Rezzonico were no longer of consequence to Browning himself. He had only had six weeks to marvel at his beloved son's achievements. On the evening of 12 December 1889, cheered by news of *Asolando*'s successful publication in England, he died. After lying in state in the ballroom of the palace, his body was transported with due pomp to the chapel of San Michele and thence, two days later, to Westminster Abbey.

Today the palace houses a museum devoted to the attractions of eighteenth-century Venice. Browning's apartment is usually locked, but a plaque beside the land entrance of the palace reminds the visitor of its association with the English poet:

A
## ROBERTO BROWNING
MORTO IN QUESTO PALAZZO
IL 12 DICEMBRE 1889
VENEZIA
POSE
'Open my heart and you will see
Graved inside of it, "Italy."'

## PALAZZI GIUSTINIAN

From the upper windows of the Ca' Rezzonico, we can just see the roofs of the Palazzi Giustinian a few yards further down the Grand Canal. It was in the middle one of these three palaces that Wagner completed the second act of *Tristan and Isolde*. He had arrived in Venice at sunset on 29 August 1858. After a night at the Danieli he moved into an imposing room here, overlooking the canal, redecorated it with dramatic red wallpaper and curtains, and set to work. The daily life he describes in his autobiography follows a scrupulous routine: work till two, a meal in St Mark's Square, a walk along the Riva degli Schiavoni to the Public Gardens, then at nightfall back by gondola along the darkening canal until he sees the glow of his lamp, 'the only point of light in the nocturnal façade of the Palazzo Giustinian'.

Wagner's finances on this first visit were sometimes stretched. Unable to pay the landlord on one occasion, he applied for help to Suski, the commissionaire. This enterprising man later appeared with the rent, having borrowed it from the landlord himself, who was also in business as a moneylender.

A slightly later resident of the Palazzi Giustinian was W. D. Howells, who lived for a time in the palace nearest the Salute, tenant of six huge rooms and a magnificent hall on the *piano signorile* at a rent of one dollar a day. He had come to Venice in 1861 as American consul – a reward for his flattering biography of Lincoln. The job was unclouded by any obligation to work, and for the next four years he was free to potter about the city collecting material for a number of books, among them the amiable reminiscences published in *Venetian Life* (1866). Much of the average day at the Palazzo Giustinian seems to have been spent on the balcony, starting with an agreeable breakfast – 'a cup of coffee, with a little bread and butter, a musk-melon, and some clusters of white grapes, more or less':

After our breakfast we began to watch for the gondolas of the tourists of different nations, whom we came to

distinguish at a glance. Then the boats of the various
artisans went by, the carpenter's, the mason's, the plas-
terer's, with those that sold fuel, and vegetables, and
fruit, and fish, to any household that arrested them. From
noon till three or four o'clock the Canal was comparatively deserted; but before twilight it was thronged again
by people riding out in their open gondolas to take the air
after the day's fervour.[32]

One pleasure that Howells enjoyed, denied to most modern
visitors, was the view of a Venetian garden at the back of the
palace. This was owned by an aged artist who lived on the
floor below:

It was full of oleanders and roses, and other bright and
odorous blooms, which we could enjoy perfectly well
without knowing their names; and I could hardly say
whether the garden was more charming when it was in its
summer glory, or when, on some rare winter day, a
breath from the mountains had clothed its tender boughs
and sprays with a light and evanescent flowering of snow.
At any season the lofty palace walls rose over it, and shut
it in a pensive seclusion which was loved by the old
mother of the painter and by his elderly maiden sister.
These often walked on its moss-grown paths, silent as the
roses and oleanders to which one could have fancied the
blossom of their youth had flown; and sometimes there
came to them there, grave, black-gowned priests, – for
the painter's was a devout family, – and talked with them
in tones almost as tranquil as the silence was, save when
one of the ecclesiastics placidly took snuff, – it is a dogma
of the Church for priests to take snuff in Italy, – and
thereafter, upon a prolonged search for his handkerchief,
blew a resounding nose.[33]

## CALLE DEL MAGAZEN

From the Calle Giustinian, which runs alongside the palace, a
series of twisting alleys lead to the Calle del Magazen. The

name of the street suggests the working-class associations of
the area. The *magazen* was a curiously Italian brand of pawn-
shop. For the goods you gave in pawn you would receive
two-thirds of their value in money and one-third in cheap
wine, allowing you to drink away your family's substance
with more than usual convenience. The appearance and
atmosphere of these places is described by Casanova in a
paragraph of his memoirs which evokes an interesting corner
of contemporary working-class life:

> In each of the seventy-two parishes of the city of Venice,
> there is a big tavern called a *magazzeno*, where wine is sold
> at retail, which stays open all night, and where one can
> drink more cheaply than at the other taverns in the city,
> where food is also provided. One can also eat at the
> *magazzeno* by sending out for what one wants to the pork
> butcher's shop, which is also regularly to be found in each
> parish and which is open all night. The pork butcher also
> keeps a cook shop, where he prepares execrable food; but
> since he sells everything cheaply his establishment is of
> great use to the poor. In the *magazzeno* itself one never
> sees either members of the nobility or citizens in good
> circumstances, for cleanliness is not to be found there.
> These places are frequented only by the common people.
> They have small rooms containing only a table sur-
> rounded by benches instead of chairs.[34]

For nineteenth-century tourists, as for their modern
counterparts, the ready flow of wine was one of the attractions
of European travel. Thomas Cook was himself a teetotaller,
and the enthusiasm with which some of his early tourists took
to Continental ways plainly distressed him:

> Wine drinking in Italy was then, as it was in France and
> Switzerland, one of the prevailing torments of the people,
> though it was thought that the common wines of Italy
> were less potent than those of France and Switzerland,
> and I was sometimes grieved to see my parties . . .
> purchase large quantities of common drinks, the merits of
> which they were utterly unacquainted with. I had such a

strong feeling in reference to this, and the evils that were already beginning to be manifested in the shape of prevalent diarrhoea amongst some of the weaker of the party, that I remonstrated with them, and said to them on going to the rooms, 'Gentlemen, do not invest your money in diarrhoea.'[35]

To judge from the number of streets which still bear the name Calle del Magazen, this was not a cry that would have touched the Venetians.

## AN UNNAMED COURTYARD

The Calle del Magazen opens into the spacious Campo Santa Margherita. On sunny days this is a cheerful spot, animated by market stalls and the usual supply of children. On the far side a series of alleys branch confidently out of the square, all but two of them leading straight into the Canal Santa Margherita. To miss one's way from time to time is inevitable, but these detours are no hardship. A lucky chance might bring you upon the little courtyard which the Irish writer Sean O'Faolain found one day during the hot August weeks of 1948 recorded in *A Summer in Italy*. Venice is prodigal of such unexpected gifts:

I remember one day taking a wrong turning near the Campo Santa Margherita. I should not now be able to find it if my life hung on it. I found myself in a *calle* that ended up in a dead end, a tiny *corte*, and was about to turn back when my eye fell on an old carved block of Verona marble through which a wall has been built in the most cavalier indifference to the craftsman's art. I now know it to be of Verona marble, and an ancient well-head, because I have found out since that, as one might expect, the tireless John [Ruskin] – he who knew all, saw all, told all – also found it in his day, when searching for the land-entrance on the Rio San Pantalon to the house whose Byzantine arches he had spotted from the Ca' Foscari. I cannot believe that one out of ten thousand visitors, or for that matter Venetians, has ever laid eyes on that old Verona well-head.[36]

At its south-western corner the Campo Santa Margherita narrows to a point a few yards from the bare space of the Campo dei Carmini, where tradition once placed the home of Shakespeare's Othello. He was reputed to have lived in the house at the corner of the campo, overlooking the canal. All that remains of the original building is the thoroughly un-Moorish statue, niched in the wall, of an epicene page-boy supporting a shield and looking down the canal. This was confidently identified with Othello himself. 'Indeed,' remarks Howells, 'what can you say to the gondolier, who, in answer to your cavils, points to the knight, with the convincing argument, "There is his statue!"'[37]

## SAN NICOLÒ DEI MENDICOLI

A left turn out of the Campo dei Carmini will take us along the fondamenta past the slightly austere cream-coloured façade of Santa Maria del Soccorso at no. 2590. Now an institute for female students at the university, this was earlier the site of a home for fallen women founded at the end of the sixteenth century by the celebrated courtesan Veronica Franco. Even at the time it must have been rare for a courtesan's client to be offered a couple of sonnets in addition to a night of love. Small wonder, perhaps, that Henri III of France carried home a portrait of her in enamel. Later, when poetry and penitence had led her into retirement, she made contact with Montaigne during his visit to Venice in 1580.

Directly in front of Santa Maria del Soccorso we cross over to the fondamenta on the other side of the canal and walk up past the splendid Palazzo Arian, distinguished by its fourteenth-century Gothic windows and the swirl of students who now enliven its courtyard. A short way from here the fondamenta comes to an end beside the ancient campanile of San Nicolò dei Mendicoli, an appealing church restored by the Venice in Peril fund. It was here that the ill-fated hero in the film of Daphne Du Maurier's *Don't Look Now* was working.

The story itself is a modest affair, but out of it Nicholas Roeg created a succession of crisp, lonely images which reflect the atmosphere of Venice in winter with loving delicacy.

In front of the church we can pause in a charming little campo, lapped on both sides by the Rio di San Nicolò. Near the canal is a stone pillar topped by a somewhat weather-beaten lion of St Mark. This reminder of the column in front of the Doge's Palace is not accidental. The flagstaff nearby memorializes, according to the inscription, 'the favours and privileges granted by the Republic to the Nicolotti and their Doge'. What this refers to is the election of a sort of Doge of the Poor, chosen from among the Nicolotti to preside over them and to represent their interests. It was one advantage at least that the Nicolotti could claim over their rivals, the more prosperous Castellani. George Sand records the popular taunt: '*Ti, ti voghi el dose, et mi vogo col dose.*' ('You row for the Doge, but I row with the Doge.')[38]

## The Docklands

This outer rim of the city, skirting the docklands, is not a popular destination. Tourists with only a few hours to spend will turn elsewhere. For Corvo, however, it had one abiding attraction:

> Today I have had adventures. This morning I bought a pair of boots and a kilogramme of tobacco. Lunched here, stewed celery, dry toast, water. Afterwards went to the Bonvecchiati, had a steak and a litre of red wine (the new vintage which is just in and very heady); and then, feeling up to any devilry, went smoking for a long walk through Cannareggio into the Ghetto to look for Jews. For mind you, a satisfactory Jew is worth a dozen Gentiles. They have more spunk about them somehow. I saw one whom I am going to watch as likely to be ready next spring. From here I got over to the station bridge and by a long round to the harbour end of the Zattere. A Sicilian ship was lying alongside the quay and armies of lusty youths

were dancing down long long planks with sacks on their
shoulders which they delivered in a warehouse ashore.
The air was filled with a cloud of fine white floury dust
from the sacks which powdered the complexions of their
carriers most deliciously and the fragrance of it was
simply heavenly. As I stopped to look a minute one of the
carriers attracted my notice. They were all half naked and
sweating. I looked a second time as his face seemed
familiar. He was running up a plank. And he also turned
to look at me. Seeing my gaze he made me a sign for a
cigarette. I grabbed at my pockets but hadn't got one; and
shook my head. He ran on into the ship. I ran off to the
nearest baccy shop and came back with a packet of cigs
and a box of matches to wait at the foot of his plank.
Presently he came down the plank dancing staggering
under a sack. I watched him. Such a lovely figure, young,
muscular, splendidly strong, big black eyes, rosy face,
round black head, scented like an angel. As he came out
again running (they are watched by guards all the time) I
threw him my little offering. 'Who are you?' '*Amadeo
Amadei*' (lovely mediaeval name). The next time, 'What
are you carrying?' '*Lily-flowers for soap-making.*' The next
time, 'Where have I seen you?' '*Assistant gondolier one day
with Piero last year*' – then – '*Sir, Round Table* [a homosexual fraternity] –' My dear F. I'm going to that ship
again to-morrow morning. I want to know more . . .[39]

PIAZZALE ROMA

From San Nicolò a short walk through the neglected western
fringe of the city will bring us to the Piazzale Roma. It is
perhaps not possible to step into the Piazzale itself without a
lowering of the spirits – which is why it makes such a suitable
point of departure from the city. With its waiting coaches, its
smell of diesel, and the ugly mass of its prematurely dilapidated air terminal building, this dismal creation of the 1930s
perfectly matches one's mood as one prepares to go back into
the world.

Fortunately, our stay in Venice has only just begun. We have merely wandered out here to gloat, or perhaps returned from a brief excursion to what the seventeenth-century traveller James Howell refers to as 'the dainty Townes' of the plain. Standing at the edge of the Piazzale Roma, one has a sharper sense than anywhere else in Venice of all the disagreeable things that are left behind on stepping into the vaporetto or crossing the Rio Nuovo. To return by bus from a long day in Padua or Vicenza, to be dropped at this noisy terminus, and then simply to step away, leaving it behind, is a wonderful pleasure. A few seconds are all it takes to slip through one of the narrow openings that lead back into the city's fabulous cocoon.

Max Beerbohm catches exactly the sense of relief one feels on being returned to the embrace of Venice after contact with the harsher world outside. Having stayed in the city for some weeks, he begins to feel the edge of his appreciation dulled. It is time to leave, he thinks, before he runs the risk of surfeit.

One afternoon in Padua is enough to persuade him of his error. He wanders restlessly around the unfamiliar town: 'I turned down a side-street, under an arcade. All the side-streets seemed to be arcaded; and yes, they were picturesque; but how heavy, how coarse, in comparison with – no; it was not fair to make that comparison.' But the comparison keeps forcing itself upon him. He tries in vain to kill time. Finally, he seeks distraction at a theatre, and there his attention is caught by the struggles of a captive bird to escape the auditorium. It is a parable he takes to heart:

> The manager of the hotel was very sorry I had to leave so soon; oh yes, there was a train for Venice: I should just have time to pack; he would have my bill made out at once.
>
> It was a very slow train. My heart outran it a thousand times on the way. No lover was ever more impatient than I. No one had ever been more in love than I was. To think there were people who did not know Venice – people who had never yet lived! And those who did know her – did they know her as I did? No, she had told the secrets of

her heart to me alone. She was waiting for me. I was on the way. . . .

I laughed aloud to myself, remembering my solemn academic theory about the dangers of sufficiency. I laughed to think that I had solemnly acted on this theory – prig and fool that I had been! Well, I had come to my senses. I could afford to laugh now. But why *wouldn't* the train go faster?

At last we were crossing the lagoon. And presently I was quit of the railway station, and out on the canal. There were scarves of cloud across the moon, and Venice looked more than ever visionary in that faint twilight. I felt not as though I had come to her in her sleep, but as though she, a vision, had come to me in mine; as though she, not I, were the 'revenant.' Was I truly awake? Yes, it was Venice that was sleeping. And *'Piano, gondoliere,'* I said. *'Lentamente . . . Piano . . .'*[40]

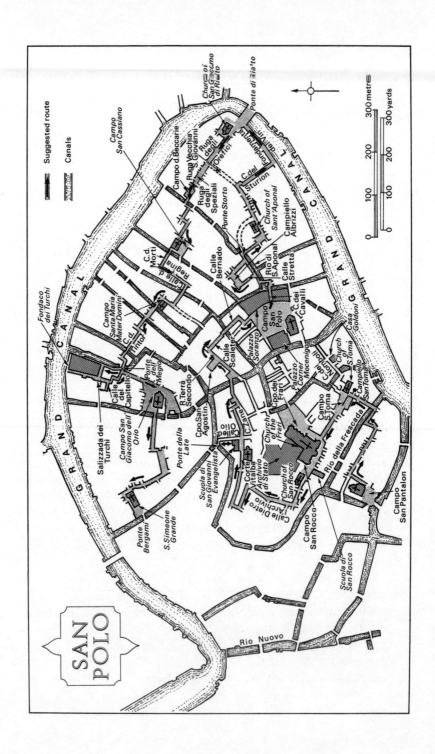

SAN
POLO

Suggested route

Canals

0   100   200   300 metres
0   100   200   300 yards

Fondaco
dei Turchi

Campo
San Cassiano

Campo d.Beccarie

Ruga Vecchia
S. Giovanni

Campo Santa Maria
Mater Domini

C. d.
Tintor

C.d.
Morti

Calle d.
Regina

Ruga
degli
Speziali

Ponte Storto

Ruga degli
Orefici

C.del
Sturion

Church of
Sant'Aponal

Church of
San Giacomo
dei Ri__to

Ponte di __ia'to

Calle
Bernado

Calle
della
Madonetta

Campiello
Albrizzi

Rio di
S.Aponal

Calle
Stretta

C. dei
Cavalli

Campo
San Polo

Salizzada dei
Turchi

Campo San
Giacomo dell'Orio

Ponte dell'
Megio

Calle del
Capitello

R.Terra
Secondo

Calle
Scaleter

Palazzo
Soranzo

Palazzo
Corner
Mocenigo

Cpo.dei
Frari

Church of
S.Tomà

Casa
Goldoni

Ponte della
Late

CpoSan
Agostin

Calle
dell'
Olio

Church
of the
Frari

Campo
S.Tomà

Campiello
San Tomà

Scuola di
San Giovanni
Evangelista

Corte
dell'Albero

Calle Dietro
l'Archivio

Archivio
di Stato

Church of
San Rocco

Rio della Frescada

Campo
San Pantalon

S.Simeone
Grande

Ponte
Bergami

Campo
San Rocco

Scuola di
San Rocco

Rio  Nuovo

# 2
# SAN POLO

*San Tomà—Casa Goldoni—Santa Maria Gloriosa dei
Frari—Scuola Grande di San Rocco—Ponte della
Late—The Aldine Press—Campo San Polo—Murder
of Lorenzino—Palazzo Corner Mocenigo—Rio di San
Aponal—Ponte Storto—Calle del
Sturion—Rialto—San Cassiano—Palazzo
Gozzi—Fondaco dei Turchi—Calle del Capitello to
Ponte Bergami*

## SAN TOMÀ

'Sinking, Shadowed and Sad – The Last Glory of Europe' was
the title of a short newspaper piece on Venice which Evelyn
Waugh wrote in 1960. That the city was gradually and ineluct-
ably returning to the sea had by then become part of every
visitor's response to its melancholy beauty. Six years later the
November floods brought a devastating reality to this graceful
image.

Wherever one walks in Venice, wherever one lives, the
threat of encroaching water is never far away. There are days
in winter when the *diretto* which brushes past the stark façade
of San Pantalon on its way to the Grand Canal slops an angry
little wave across the paving-stones towards the church. And
on the other side of the Rio della Frescada, the Campo San
Tomà yields quickly to the rising waters at times of *acqua
alta*. When autumn winds bank up the waves beyond the
lagoon and the canals begin to swell, the local population has

learnt what to expect. Horatio Brown describes the familiar
sequence as he observed it at the end of the last century:

> Steadily the tide flows faster and faster under the bridge,
> and the market-men and gondoliers secure their boats to
> the posts. So it goes on for an hour or more, till the
> jade-coloured flood has nearly brimmed to the edge of the
> *fondamenta*, but not yet overflowed it. Then the water
> begins to appear in the calle; it comes welling up through
> every drain-hole and between the flags of the pavement,
> bubbling like a little geyser and making a low gurgling
> noise; for the sea begins to flood Venice under pavements,
> and not over the *fondamente*, which are usually higher than
> the streets. Presently the baker puts out a board to serve as
> a bridge for his customers; but soon the water from the
> canal has joined that in the calle; the bridge ceases to be of
> use, and floats idly away. . . . Then the first boat passes
> down the calle stopping at the shop doors to pick up fares,
> and bare-legged men offer their services as porters from
> the high bridge steps to the upper end of the street, which
> is still dry. Indeed, the flood is the excuse for the display of
> bare legs, and half the population of the quarter are tucked
> above the knee. All the windows are full of women and
> children, laughing at the traffic below. . . . Then sud-
> denly, without a moment's warning, there is a dazzling
> flash of lightning, a rattling peal; every face disappears
> from the windows, and all the green shutters go to with a
> bang.[1]

In a later age the disreputable artist who is the hero of one of
Malamud's stories makes a few lire by acting as a porter on
these occasions. It was perhaps here in the Campo San Tomà,
with its line of modest shops and its church full of relics, that
Fidelman took his stand, ferrying pedestrians piggy-back
across the underwater square:

> Fidelman waded in hip boots through high water glinting
> like shards of broken mirror in the freezing winter sun-
> light, and deposited his customers on dry ground whence
> they proceeded hurriedly along narrow streets and alleys.

Occasionally while transporting a female he gave her a modified feel along the leg, which roused no response through winter clothing; still it was good for the morale. One attractive, long-nosed, almost oriental-eyed young Venetian woman who mounted his back, began at once to giggle, and laughed, unable to control it, mirthfully as he slowly sloshed across the pond. She sat on Fidelman, enjoying the ride, her rump bumping his, cheek pressed to his frozen ear, hugging him casually, a pair of shapely black-stocking legs clasped in the crooks of his arms; and when he tenderly set her down, his penis erect, athrob, she kissed him affectionately and hastily went her way. As Fidelman watched she turned back, smiling sadly, as though they had once been lovers and the affair was ended. Then she waved goodbye and walked on. He wished she hadn't, for he was after a while in love with her.

When the water receded as the bora roared, drying the city, uncovering here and there a drowned cat, the winter light sprang up crystal clear as Fidelman, once more jobless, holding onto his hat – you can't chase them on the canals – sought his lady, to no avail. He searched from the Public Gardens to the Slaughter House and on both sides of the humpbacked Grand Canal. And he haunted the little square of blessed memory where he had once carried her across the wet water, chain smoking used butts from a pocketful in his overcoat as he watched a steam-breathed sweeper sweeping at the mud with a twig broom; but she never appeared.[2]

Fidelman does at length catch sight of his elusive passenger again, through a shop window in the Mercerie, but their subsequent affair, its course diverted by her husband, turns out to be less orthodox than he expects.

CASA GOLDONI

Beside the bridge which leads from the neighbouring Campiello San Tomà into the Calle dei Nomboli is a plaque

indicating that this was the birthplace of the playwright Carlo
Goldoni. 'I was born at Venice,' he writes in the opening
sentence of his *Memoirs*, 'in the year 1707, in a large and
beautiful house between the bridges of Nomboli and Donna
Onestà, at the corner of the street Cà Centanni, in the parish of
St Thomas.'[3]
Venice has attracted many writers from outside but produced few of its own. Even the Italians who are associated
with it, like Aretino and d'Annunzio, tend to be settlers rather
than natives. Goldoni is duly prized, and in a city that has
never done much to honour its individual citizens his statue in
the Campo San Bartolomeo is an unusual tribute. The Palazzo
Centanni is in a picturesque area and is itself a handsome
building. From a small courtyard with its own well-head an
attractive stone staircase leads up to the first floor, where a
room has been given over to the Goldoni Museum. Next to an
entrance hall decorated with pictures of eighteenth-century
Venice the main room houses a couple of costumes, some first
editions, some commemorative medals, and a variety of
engravings. As writers' museums go, the collection is unremarkable, but the fine setting and the scarcity of other
visitors make it an agreeable spot to pass a few moments.

## SANTA MARIA GLORIOSA DEI FRARI

The advice handed down to generations of tourists has been to
do the churches in the morning. You stand a chance of seeing
what is inside them while the light is adequate and you sit
down to lunch with a clear conscience. There is also the fact
that certain churches close at midday and do not reopen. It
may therefore seem perverse to recommend the winter evenings. But to walk through this part of Venice at about six
o'clock, when the streets and campi are crowded with evening
shoppers wrapped against the cold, can be a pleasure as keen as
any that Venice offers. Dark alleys open into brightly lit
squares, narrow canals catch patches of light from windows in
the flaking walls, simple shops acquire a seductive glow that
transforms their daytime ordinariness.

It is not just the bridges and canals and the dream-like architecture that create this atmosphere. The shops themselves belong in part to an earlier age. Many of them have no names or only the discreetest lettering above the door. Their windows are recessed, sometimes under eaves, often set in thick walls. It is the sort of display that in England can only be found on a tiny scale in villages bypassed by the march of neon.

This time of evening lends a curious thrill to what might otherwise be the routine business of visiting another church. The smoking candles and the softness of the light on the other side of the church-door offer the giddy experience of slipping from one world to another.

This is especially true of the Frari. Those who find it hard to love the church by day should try it now. There are disadvantages, of course. Here, as elsewhere, the statuary recedes, its outlines muffled in shade; details of art and architecture become harder to distinguish. But such drawbacks are partial. Against them it might be urged that much ecclesiastical sculpture can only benefit from a little kindly shade. Canova's tomb in the north aisle is a case in point – at least according to Ruskin: 'The tomb of Canova, *by* Canova, cannot be missed; consummate in science, intolerable in affectation, ridiculous in conception, null and void to the uttermost in invention and feeling.'[4] After which, the wretched sculptor might well wish it in perpetual shade.

Directly to the right of the main door is the attractive sixteenth-century monument to Pietro Bernardo, an otherwise undistinguished scion of the patrician family which gave its name to a number of the city's streets. Rising in stately marble tiers, it looks to most visitors a fairly handsome memorial, but Pietro himself, who died in 1538, would hardly have been satisfied. The terms of his will, drawn up well in advance on 30 October 1515, make it quite clear what he had in mind:

His instructions were that as soon as he was dead his body should be washed in the finest vinegar and then anointed with musk to the value of 40 ducats by three of the most renowned doctors, each of whom would receive in

payment 3 fine, newly minted zecchini; that he should then
be laid with aloes and other spices in a coffin of lead which
had room enough for his body to lie at ease. This should
then be enclosed in another, extremely large coffin of
cypress wood, so well sealed and fastened that it could not
be opened without being broken into. This to be then
placed in a marble tomb to the value of 600 ducats, on the
front of which should be carved 8 verses rehearsing his
deeds in capital letters large enough to be read at a distance
of 25 feet, the poet to be paid a zecchino for every two
verses. Above the tomb should be carved the Eternal
Father and a likeness of Pietro Bernardo himself kneeling,
the image to be large enough for him to appear, at a
distance of 25 feet, a man of tall stature. Finally, it was
prescribed that the glories of his family should be celebrated in a book of 800 verses. In addition, seven psalms
should be composed in imitation of the Psalms of David,
together with other prayers, these to be sung by twenty
friars on the first Sunday of every month, at day-break, in
front of his sepulchre.[5]

Before moving on to San Rocco, note the monastery buildings beside the main door of the Frari. In over three hundred
rooms they house the voluminous archives of State. It was
here that Rawdon Brown spent the last twenty years of his life,
examining, it is said, some twelve million packets of docu-
ments in order to calendar the state papers that related to
British history.

## SCUOLA GRANDE DI SAN ROCCO

The attractions of the Scuola di San Rocco, a few yards from
the Frari, were bluntly summed up by Gilbert Burnet at the
end of the seventeenth century: 'The School of Sant. Roch,
and the Chappel, and Hall are full of great pieces of Tintorets.'
On the young John Ruskin their effect was more dramatic. 'I
have been quite overwhelmed today,' he wrote to his father on
23 September 1845, 'by a man whom I never dreamed of –

Tintoret.' Next day he went back to study the paintings in more detail:

> I have had a draught of pictures today enough to drown me. I never was so utterly crushed to the earth before any human intellect as I was today, before Tintoret. Just be so good as to take my list of painters, & put him in the school of Art at the top, top, top of everything, with a great big black line underneath him to stop him off from everybody – and put him in the school of Intellect, next after Michael Angelo. He took it so entirely out of me today that I could do nothing at last but lie on a bench & laugh. . . . Tintoret don't seem to be able to stretch himself till you give him a canvas forty feet square – & then, he lashes out like a leviathan, and heaven and earth come together. M Angelo himself cannot hurl figures into space as he does, nor did M Angelo ever paint space itself which would not look like a nutshell beside Tintoret's. Just imagine the audacity of the fellow – in his massacre of the innocents one of the mothers has hurled herself off a terrace to avoid the executioner & is falling headforemost & backwards, holding up the child still. And such a resurrection as there is – the rocks of the sepulchre crashed all to pieces & roaring down upon you, while the Christ soars forth into a torrent of angels, whirled up into heaven till you are lost ten times over. And then to see his touch of quiet thought in his awful crucifixion – there is an *ass* in the distance, feeding on the remains of strewed palm leaves. If that isn't a master's stroke, I don't know what is.[6]

That tourists now stream through San Rocco on their round of the city's sights is partly due to these two days in September 1845. For the modern visitor the paintings are reasonably lit, but the experience is perhaps a little comfortless. Less than one might wish remains of the atmosphere described by Henry James in 1882:

> The interest, the impressiveness, of that whole corner of Venice, however melancholy the effect of its gorgeous

and ill-lighted chambers, gives a strange importance to a
visit to the Scuola. Nothing that all travellers go to see
appears to suffer less from the incursions of travellers. It is
one of the loneliest booths of the bazaar, and the author of
these lines has always had the good fortune, which he
wishes to every other traveller, of having it to himself. I
think most visitors find the place rather alarming and
wicked-looking. They walk about a while among the
fitful figures that gleam here and there out of the great
tapestry (as it were) with which the painter has hung
all the walls, and then, depressed and bewildered by the
portentous solemnity of these objects, by strange
glimpses of unnatural scenes, by the echo of their lonely
footsteps on the vast stone floors, they take a hasty
departure, finding themselves again, with a sense of
release from danger, a sense that the *genius loci* was a sort
of mad white-washer who worked with a bad mixture, in
the bright light of the *campo*, among the beggars, the
orange-vendors and the passing gondolas. Solemn indeed
is the place, solemn and strangely suggestive, for the
simple reason that we shall scarcely find four walls elsewhere that inclose within a like area an equal quantity of
genius. The air is thick with it and dense and difficult to
breathe; for it was genius that was not happy, inasmuch as
it lacked the art to fix itself for ever. It is not immortality
that we breathe at the Scuola di San Rocco, but conscious,
reluctant mortality.[7]

St Roch himself, a Frenchman who devoted the last part of
his life to nursing victims of the Black Death, had originally
been venerated in Montpellier, until one of the Republic's
pious thefts brought him to Venice. His sarcophagus now
rests in the church.

PONTE DELLA LATE

From San Rocco it is worth a short detour via the Calle Dietro
l'Archivio and the Corte Vitalba to the enticing Scuola di San
Giovanni Evangelista. 'Beautiful it is, even in its squalid

misery,' writes Ruskin. 'As long as it is let alone, in its shafts
and capitals you will see on the whole the most characteristic
example in Venice of the architecture that Carpaccio, Cima,
and John Bellini loved.'[8]

Since we are now heading for San Agostin, it is no more
than a whim that makes us turn left up the Calle dell'Olio to
the Ponte della Late. This is not a celebrated bridge, and there
is no reason why it should be. It is merely the site of one
of those bizarre incidents with which Venetian history is
crammed – the sort of thing that in most places is forgotten but
that in Venice is preserved in the literary byways of its diarists
and antiquarians. While Carpaccio's languid courtiers strolled
at large through the city, Marin Sanudo, a learned patrician
salaried by the Council of Ten, was compiling an
extraordinary survey of the world that passed before their
eyes. In the fifty-eight volumes of his diary he recorded the
minutiae of Venetian life, both public and private, with a sharp
eye for the dramatic, the scabrous, and the grotesque. On
31 August 1505 he notes:

> Today the execution took place of the Albanian who
> treacherously murdered Zuan Marco. First, his hand was
> cut off at the Ponte della Late. And mark that this gave rise
> to a curious incident; to wit, while his wife was taking
> leave of him, he made as if he wanted to kiss her and bit
> her nose off. It is said that she was responsible for
> bringing his crime to light.[9]

## THE ALDINE PRESS

Opposite the gateway of the Scuola, the Calle Zane, entered
through a narrow archway, leads us towards the slightly
battered, quiet little square of San Agostin. This was once the
site of the palace of Baiamonte Tiepolo. In 1310 Baiamonte
had been at the head of an uprising to depose the Doge. When
it failed, his palace was destroyed and replaced by a *colonna
d'infamia*, which was later removed to the Correr Museum.
Beside the clothes shop on the corner of the Calle della Chiesa,

you will see in the place where the column once stood a cracked paving-stone bearing the inscription *Loc. Col. Bai. The. MCCCX.*

We can leave the square by the Rio Terrà Seconda. At no. 2311, a few yards along on the right-hand side, stands a small Gothic palace with a pleasant balcony round the three central windows on the second floor. This was the home of one of the great printing presses of the Renaissance.

By the end of the fifteenth century, Venice's two hundred printers had issued more works than Rome, Florence, and Milan put together. Although the press here was not entirely free, it was at least protected from the worst of the Church's meddling. Most famous of the Venetian presses was that of Aldus Manutius. Under the imprint of the dolphin and anchor, it quickly became known for its fine editions of the classics, and when Erasmus wanted a publisher for his enlarged edition of the *Adagia*, it was to Aldus that he turned.

Having reached Venice in the spring of 1508, Erasmus spent the rest of the year in the home of Aldus's father-in-law, Andrea Torresani. The resulting collaboration was successful enough from a literary point of view, but in other respects Erasmus found life in the Torresani household something of an ordeal. Twenty years later, in 'Opulentia Sordida', he produced a rancorous satire on the family's domestic arrangements. What dismayed him most, apart from the bugs and fleas, was the miserly provision of food: watered wine, mouldy bread, small leaves of lettuce swimming in vinegar, cheese as hard as stone, soup fit for sows. In the end, Erasmus claims, he was forced to fend for himself:

> I employ'd a certain Friend to buy me every Day three Eggs with my own Money, two for my Dinner, and one for my Supper: But here also the Women put their Tricks upon me; for instead of my new-laid Eggs that I paid a good Price for, they would give me rotten ones, that I thought I came well off, if one of my three Eggs prov'd eatable. I also at last got a small Cask of good Wine bought for my own drinking, but the Women broke open my Cellar-Door, and in a few Days drank it all up,

and my Landlord *Antronius* did not seem to be much displeas'd at the Matter.[10]

Fortunately, perhaps, by the time this sketch of Venetian hospitality appeared in print, Aldus himself was long dead.

## CAMPO SAN POLO

Just beyond the Aldine Press, the Calle del Scaleter leads down towards the vast Campo San Polo, the biggest square in Venice after St Mark's. Its size has made it a natural site for festivities, from bull-fights in the seventeenth century to open-air discothèques in the modern carnival. In earlier times one of the more notable episodes was the great bonfire of vanities held here on 26 July 1450 at the urging of a Franciscan friar who was a follower of Bernardine of Siena. Fripperies, fine clothes, and false coils of hair all went up in flames at a jamboree that anticipated the efforts of Savonarola in Florence forty years later. But these displays of religious enthusiasm were not really to the Venetians' taste, and they soon returned to a preference for more secular entertainments of the sort described by John Evelyn in 1646. Deep snow had kept him in Padua through January, but he managed to leave in time for Shrove Tuesday, 'when all the world repair to *Venice* to see the folly & madnesse of the *Carnevall*':

> The Women, Men & persons of all Conditions disguising themselves in antique dresses, & extravagant Musique & a thousand gambols, & traversing the streetes from house to house, all places being then accessible, & free to enter: There is abroad nothing but flinging of Eggs fill'd with sweete Waters, & sometimes not over sweete; they also have a barbarous costome of hunting bulls about the Streetes & Piazzas, which is very dangerous, the passages being generally so narrow in that Citty: Likewise do the youth of the severall Wards & parrishes contend in other Masteries or pastimes, so as tis altogether impossible to recount the universal madnesse of this place during this time of licence: Now are the greate banks set up for those

who will play at Basset, the Comedians have also liberty
& the *Operas* to exercise: Witty pasquils are likewise
thrown about, & the Mountebanks have their stages in
every Corner.[11]

The festive traditions of the Campo San Polo have not been
without problems for the church at the south-west corner. If
you walk round to the wall of the apse, you will see an early
bas-relief of the Madonna with saints and angels. Under it is a
square stone plaque set there in 1611, of which Captain
Douglas offers a rough translation:

> MDCXI. 10th August. All games whatsoever are pro-
> hibited: as also the sales of goods, or the erection of shops,
> round this church, by order of the most excellent
> 'esecutori contra la biastema' [magistrates appointed for
> the suppression of blasphemy, swearing and kindred
> offences]: with the penalty of prison, the galleys, exile,
> and also 300 lire de' piccoli, to be divided between the
> accuser and captors.[12]

Noble festivities were perhaps viewed with a different eye.
It was a private celebration in the Palazzo Soranzo, at the east
end of the square, that marked a turning point in the career of
Giacomo Casanova. Educated to a profession in the church, he
had slipped into a life of hectic dissipation, making what
money he could as a hired musician and living by night in wild
and vicious company. It was at this point, around the time of
his twenty-first birthday, that he met the man who was to
become his principal friend and protector in Venice. Senator
Matteo Giovanni Bragadin was a decent, rather gullible patrician whose name would have been long forgotten if a brush
with death had not brought him into contact with Casanova.
In the spring of 1746 Casanova was one of the musicians
playing at the celebrations for the marriage of Girolamo
Cornaro with a daughter of the Soranzo family:

> On the third day, when the festivities were nearly over, I
> leave the orchestra an hour before dawn to go home, and
> as I go downstairs I notice a senator in his red robe about
> to get into his gondola. I see a letter drop to the ground

beside him as he is drawing his handkerchief from his pocket. I advance and pick up the letter and, catching up with the imposing Signore just as he is going down the steps, I hand it to him. He thanks me, he asks me where I live, I tell him, he insists upon taking me home, I accept the courtesy he was kind enough to offer me, and take a place on the bench beside him. Three minutes later he asks me to shake his left arm: 'I feel,' he said, 'such a numbness that I seem not to have this arm at all.' I shake it with all my might, and I hear him tell me, in ill-articulated words, that he felt as if he were losing his whole leg too and that he thought he was dying.

Greatly alarmed, I open the curtain, take the lantern, look at his face, and am terrified to see that his mouth was drawn up towards his left ear and his eyes were losing their lustre.

I call to the gondoliers to stop and let me get out to find a surgeon who will come at once and bleed His Excellency, who had certainly been struck by apoplexy.

I disembark. It was at the bridge by the Calle Bernardo, where three years earlier I had given Razzetta a cudgeling. I run to the coffeehouse, someone shows me where a surgeon lives. I knock loudly, I shout, the door opens, the man is wakened, I urge him to hurry, I will not let him dress, he takes his case and comes with me to the gondola, where he bleeds the dying man, and I tear up my shirt to make him a bandage.

We quickly reach his palace in Santa Marina; the servants are awakened, he is removed from his gondola, carried to his apartment on the second floor, undressed, and put to bed almost dead. I tell a servant to run for a physician, he goes, the physician arrives and bleeds him again. I station myself beside the bed, considering it my duty not to leave.[13]

Bragadin survived to be grateful. It was for Casanova the start of a valuable friendship.

MURDER OF LORENZINO

Almost exactly two hundred years earlier the square had
witnessed a murder which was both elaborately planned and
extravagantly rewarded. At the far end of the campo, just
between the campanile and the southern doorway of the
church, is the spot where Lorenzino de' Medici was assassinated in 1546. It is an intriguing episode that gives a sharp edge
of reality to some of the traditional clichés about life in
Renaissance Italy.

The story is graphically told by J. A. Symonds from
the record left by one of the murderers. Nine years earlier
Lorenzino had himself been responsible for the murder of his
cousin Alessandro, who was then Duke of Florence. As the
next Duke of Florence, Cosimo de' Medici was concerned that
this should not become a precedent. He was a serious man, and
the price he put on Lorenzino's head was vast.[14] Before long
two soldiers of fortune called Bebo and Bibboni had managed
to track Lorenzino to Venice. Symonds takes up the narrative,
using Bibboni's own account:

> In the carnival of 1546 Lorenzo meant to go masked in the
> habit of a gypsy woman to the square of San Spirito,
> where there was to be a joust. Great crowds of people
> would assemble, and Bibboni hoped to do his business
> there. The assassination, however, failed on this oc-
> casion, and Lorenzo took up his abode in the palace he had
> hired upon the Campo di San Polo. This Campo is one of
> the largest open places in Venice, shaped irregularly, with
> a finely curving line upon the western side, where two of
> the noblest private houses in the city are still standing.
> Nearly opposite these, in the south-western angle, stands
> detached, the little old church of San Polo. One of its
> side-entrances opens upon the square; the other on a lane
> which leads eventually to the Frari. There is nothing in
> Bibboni's narrative to make it clear where Lorenzo hired
> his dwelling. But it would seem from certain things
> which he says later on, that in order to enter the church his
> victim had to cross the square. Meanwhile Bibboni took
> the precaution of making friends with a shoe maker,

whose shop commanded the whole Campo, including Lorenzo's palace. In this shop he began to spend much of his time; 'and oftentimes I feigned to be asleep; but God knows whether I was sleeping, for my mind, at any rate, was wide-awake.'[15]

After weeks of observation the assassins finally get their chance. On 28 February 1546 Lorenzo and his bodyguard cross the square in company with a third man, Alessandro Soderini, and enter the church. Bebo, on watch at the southern door, opposite the campanile, sees them push aside the thick leather curtain and signals to Bibboni. When Lorenzo emerges from the southern door, Bibboni is waiting:

> I saw him issue from the church and take the main street; then came Alessandro Soderini, and I walked last of all; and when we reached the point we had determined on, I jumped in front of Alessandro with the poignard in my hand, crying, 'Hold hard, Alessandro, and get along with you, in God's name, for we are not here for you!' He then threw himself around my waist, and grasped my arms, and kept on calling out. Seeing how wrong I had been to try to spare his life, I wrenched myself as well as I could from his grip, and with my lifted poignard struck him, as God willed, above the eyebrow, and a little blood trickled from the wound. He, in high fury, gave me such a thrust that I fell backward, and the ground beside was slippery from having rained a little. Then Alessandro drew his sword, which he carried in its scabbard, and thrust at me in front, and struck me on the corslet, which for my good fortune was of double mail. Before I could get ready I received three passes, which, had I worn a doublet instead of that mailed corslet, would certainly have run me through. At the fourth pass I had regained my strength and spirit, and closed with him, and stabbed him four times in the head, and being so close he could not use his sword, but tried to parry with his hand and hilt, and I, as God willed, struck him at the wrist below the sleeve of mail, and cut his hand off clean, and gave him then one last stroke on his head. Thereupon he begged for God's

rake spare his life, and I, in trouble about Bebo, left him in
the arms of a Venetian nobleman, who held him back
from jumping in the canal. . . .
     When I turned, I found Lorenzo on his knees. He raised
himself, and I, in anger, gave him a great cut across the
head, which split it in two pieces, and laid him at my feet,
and he never rose again.[16]

There follows a breathless chase across Venice until the two
assassins finally take refuge in the Spanish embassy, from
which some days later they are smuggled out to the mainland
via the Cannaregio canal. Once at Pisa they are safe. As
Bibboni smugly remarks, 'We were now able for the whole
time of life left us to live splendidly, without a thought or
care.' Renaissance Italy knew little of the code by which evil
fails to prosper. Bibboni concludes his narrative with the
words: 'Bebo from Pisa, at what date I know not, went home
to Volterra, his native town, and there finished his days; while
I abode in Florence, where I have had no further wish to hear of
wars, but to live my life in holy peace.'

PALAZZO CORNER MOCENIGO

At the far end of the square from the church, at nos 2128 and
2128a, stands the massive Palazzo Corner Mocenigo. Since
the eighteenth century two doors from it have opened on to
the Campo San Polo, an arrangement ordered by Giovanni
Cornaro so that the dead and the living might never pass
through the same doorway. Corvo stayed here from the
summer of 1909 to the spring of the following year as a guest
of the Van Someren family, and it was from here that he wrote
most of the notorious Venice letters, detailing his exploits, real
or imagined, with the lithe gondoliers for whom he pined. His
memories of the palace were not happy. Looking at the rather
bleak face of the Campo San Polo on a December afternoon,
one can imagine something of the rigours of a bad winter:

    The fact is this last fortnight has been absolutely Devilish.
    No tobacco, Alps covered with snow, *bora* blowing up
    Adriatic one day and wind from Alps bringing simply

perishing cold. And here I live and work and sleep on an *open landing* of this palace on the side which never sees the sun with *stone* floor, walls, ceiling and stairs, no privacy (it's the servants' stair) and *no heating arrangements whatever*. My dear, *I'm simply dying of cold and hunger*. The doctor is a dear. If he didn't give me this hospitality I should be on the streets and that would be the end of all my hopes.[17]

This charitable view of Dr Van Someren did not last. On 28 December Corvo writes:

As for me, things have gone from bad to worse. I have never had such an unchristian Christmas in my life. Never! Neither beef nor turkey nor plum-pudding nor mince-pie have passed my lips, and I ADORE them all. Not a single soul said or sent a single Christmas word to me excepting the servants here and the boys. No, not one. . . . Our dear pious Plymouth Brother of a doctor dismissed three of his six servants when I last wrote to you, the man and two maids: and shunted on to me their work which I have been doing ever since. This gets me up at 5.30 to light fires, fill cisterns, work the cream-making machine, and get up wood for the stoves. It's devilish hard work. . . . Of course my book is at a standstill. How can I possibly write when I'm toiling upstairs bent double with a load of wood, much less think out what I'm going to write with my mind raging in agony and disappointment?[18]

Hospitality to Rolfe was always likely to earn mixed rewards. The book in question was *The Desire and Pursuit of the Whole*. When the Van Somerens discovered it to be a scarcely veiled attack on their friends in the English colony, the troublesome author was asked to leave.

RIO DI SAN APONAL

To get from the Campo San Polo to the Campiello Albrizzi takes only a couple of minutes, but it is one of the most

fascinating walks in the city. The succession of twisting alleys,
empty canals, dark corners, and crumbling arcades offers one
in the space of a few yards a stretch of quintessential Venice.
Late in the afternoon, beside the lonely Rio di San Aponal, the
air seems haunted – perhaps by the romantic couple who pass
this way in Carlo Gozzi's autobiography.

Gozzi himself, the only serious rival of Goldoni on the
eighteenth-century stage, was if anything a somewhat moral-
istic figure, different from Casanova in almost every way; and
yet the Venice that emerges from their memoirs is in some
respects uncannily similar. As a young man Gozzi had become
acquainted with the attractive girl who lived opposite him in
the Calle della Regina (see p. 59). From time to time her
melancholy songs had drifted through his study window and
the two had moved from exchanging bows to exchanging
words – no further. But she was the young wife of an impotent
old aristocrat and this acquaintance with Gozzi was seized on
by her husband's unscrupulous lodgers as a means of extorting
money from her. In desperation she turned to Gozzi for help:

> She had obtained her husband's permission to go that day
> after dinner to visit an aunt of hers, a nun, on the
> Giudecca. Therefore she begged me to repair at twenty-
> one o'clock to the *sotto portico* by the *ponte storto* at S.
> Aponal. There I should see, waiting or arriving, a gon-
> dola with a white handkerchief hung out of one of its
> windows. I was to get boldly into this gondola, and I
> should find her inside. 'Then you will hear all about the
> circumstances in which my want of caution has involved
> me.' . . .
> I took my dinner in haste, nearly choked myself, and
> alleging business of the last importance, flew off to the
> *ponte storto*. The gondola was in position at a *riva*, with the
> flag of the white handkerchief hung out. I entered it in
> haste, impelled perhaps by the desire to join the lovely
> woman, perhaps by curiosity to hear her explanation.
> When I entered, there she was, resplendent with gems of
> price at her ears, her throat, her fingers, underneath the
> *zendado*. She made room for me beside her, and gave

orders to the gondolier that he should draw the curtain, and row toward the Giudecca to a monastery which she named.[19]

Gozzi manages to extricate her from the blackmailers but in the process becomes himself entangled with her. Their affair ends unhappily, though not the rest of the girl's story. In time her ailing husband dies and she can marry a respectable merchant, making thereafter, Gozzi informs us, a model wife.

A short way along the arcaded fondamenta beside the Rio di San Aponal we can turn left down the narrowest street of all, the Calle Stretta, into the Campiello Albrizzi. Just opposite the calle, between the ground floor windows of no. 1491, is a fragment of Austrian shell with beside it d'Annunzio's ringing declaration, one of his many:

This fragment of barbarism is lodged in the noble stone as testimony of the perpetual enmity which adds shame to their shame, glory to our glory. 10 August 1916.

PONTE STORTO

At the far end of the campiello the Calle Albrizzi leads back to the lovely Ponte Storto. On the left, facing the canal, is the splendidly dilapidated old house which was the home of Bianca Cappello. It was from one of these balconies that in 1563 she made the acquaintance of a Florentine bank-clerk who was living in a nearby house. She was only fifteen at the time and the youth was well below her in rank. Their subsequent elopement caused her father enough dismay for him to have them both declared outlaws.

Life in Florence with the clerk and his family quickly proved tiresome, but Bianca had the good fortune to come to the notice of Francesco de' Medici, son of the Grand Duke of Tuscany. Over the next few years the deaths of Bianca's husband, Francesco's father, and finally, in 1578, Francesco's wife left the outlaw from Venice in the position of Grand Duchess of Tuscany. Pragmatic as ever, the Venetians pronounced her a 'true and particular Daughter of the Republic',

and for the next eight years she repaid the courtesy by doing
all she could to forward Venetian interests. Sadly, when she
and Francesco died within a couple of days of each other,
either from poison or disease, Venice left her unmourned and
made no attempt to recover the body which the hatred of
Francesco's brother had consigned to a common grave.
Popular legend has been kinder, and today her house is marked
by a plaque.

The place is a match for its romantic history. With crumbling stonework eaten away around the windows and a few
simple plants overhanging the balcony, it looks altogether in
keeping with its past. The atmosphere of this charmed region
of the city is caught by George Sand in the second of her *Lettres
d'un voyageur*:

> Do you remember the little light that glimmers at the far
> end of the canal and is reflected and multiplied in the
> shining weather-worn marble of Bianca Cappello's
> house? There is not a more mysterious and melancholy
> little canal in all of Venice. That single light shining on all
> things and lighting none, dancing on the water and
> seeming to play in the wake of a passing boat like a
> will-o'-the-wisp bent on pursuing it, reminded me of that
> long row of street-lamps quivering in the Seine and
> tracing fiery zigzags upon its waters.[20]

## CALLE DEL STURION

From the Ponte Storto we can carry straight on to the church
of Sant'Aponal and then turn left along the Ruga Vecchia San
Giovanni in the direction of the Rialto. About a hundred yards
before the bridge, an opening on the right leads into the Calle
del Sturion. The street takes its name from a celebrated inn, the
Sturgeon, which for many years stood here on the corner of
the Fondamenta del Vin. By 1398 it is already mentioned in the
city records for watering its wine.

The commercial importance of the Rialto made it a prime
site for inns. Through the fourteenth and fifteenth centuries a
stream of pilgrims stayed in this district on their way to the

Holy Land (see p. 183). In 1436 the Spanish traveller Pero
Tafur notes arriving in Venice and going straight to worship in
St Mark's, 'after which we went to an inn called the *Sturgeon*, a
very notable hostelry, where we lodged the day and night
following'.[21] By chance this is the same inn which found its
way into Carpaccio's painting of the *Miracle of the Holy Cross*
about sixty-five years later. If you look closely at the left-hand
side of the picture, you can see its sign, with a silver fish on a
red background, just above the projecting porch in front of the
old Rialto bridge.

The annual rent paid by a landlord in this favoured area
could be as much as 800 ducats, 250 more than for some of the
best palaces in the city. The inn had to make a corresponding
profit, and landlords were not always scrupulous about how
this was achieved. As long as the State was overseeing the
pilgrim trade, foreigners could expect to be reasonably well
treated, but later visitors had harsh things to say of the
standards of Italian inns, and Venice was not excepted. Samuel
Sharp, a surgeon from Guy's Hospital, delivered what had
become by the middle of the eighteenth century a familiar
broadside:

There are, by the bye, no such things as curtains, and
hardly, from *Venice* to *Rome*, that cleanly and most useful
invention, a privy; so that what should be collected and
buried in oblivion, is for ever under your nose and eyes.
Take along with you, that in all these inns the walls are
bare, and the floor has never once been washed since it
was first laid. One of the most indelicate customs here, is,
that men, and not women, make the Ladies beds, and
would do every office of a maid servant, if suffered. To
sum up, in a word, the total of *Italian* nastiness, your
chamber, which you would wish to be the sweetest, is by
far the most offensive room in the house, for reasons I
shall not explain. I must tell you, that except in two or
three places, they never scour their pewter, and unless
you were to see it, you will not conceive how dirty and
nauseous it grows in thirty or forty years. Their knives
are of the same colour as their pewter, and their table-

cloths and napkins such as you see on joint-stools, in
*Bartholomew-Fair*, where the mob eat their sausages. In
these inns they make you pay largely, so much a head, and
send up ten times as much as you can eat. For example,
this is almost constantly the fare. – A soop like wash, with
pieces of liver swimming in it; a plate full of brains, fried
in the shape of fritters; a dish of livers and gizzards; a
couple of fowls (always killed after your arrival) boiled to
rags, without any the least kind of sauce, or herbage;
another fowl, just killed, stewed as they call it; then two
more fowl, or a turkey roasted to rags. . . . The bread all
the way is exceedingly bad, and the butter so rancid, it
cannot be touched, or even borne within the reach of our
smell.[22]

Venice is still not a wonderful place for food, but things
have improved.

## RIALTO

From whatever direction one approaches the Rialto, the press
of people on the streets increases. Four centuries before
Shylock it was already the commercial heart of the city, and
four centuries later it is still the most crowded place in Venice.
The Ruga degli Orefici, at the centre of this district, is the old
street of goldsmiths, whose business was confined to the
Rialto by a law of the fourteenth century. In 1594, at about the
time Shakespeare's thoughts were turning to Venice, Fynes
Moryson was making his way through Italy on the last leg of
his long European journey. A surprising amount of what he
observed around the Rialto will be familiar to the modern
visitor:

> The foure square market place of Rialto, is compassed
> with publike houses, under the arches whereof, and in the
> middle part lying open, the Merchants meet. And there is
> also a peculiar place where the Gentlemen meet before
> noone, as they meet in the place of Saint Marke towards
> evening. . . . The Gold-smiths shoppes lie thereby, and
> over against them the shoppes of Jewellers, in which Art

the Venetians are excellent. There is the Pallace of a Gentleman, who proving a Traytor, the State (for his reproch) turned the same into a shambles, and some upper chambers to places of judgement. The fish market lies by this shambles, a great length along the banke of the great channell, and in the same shambles and fish market, as also in the like of Saint Marke, great plenty of victuals, especially of fish, is daily to be sold.[23]

It was here, amid a scene which impressed itself on generations of English writers, that Antonio walked in *The Merchant of Venice* and Otway's conspirators plotted revolution in *Venice Preserved*.

The bridge of the Rialto has had a mixed press. In the judgement of the Venetians, says Moryson, it 'deserves to be reputed the eighth miracle of the world'. Coryate, while deploring 'the vicious and licentious varlets' who worked the traghetto underneath it, was in agreement – 'the fairest bridge by many degrees for one arch that ever I saw, read, or heard of.' But then both Moryson and Coryate were there within a few years of the bridge's completion. Others have since been less charitable, condemning it as top-heavy and ungraceful. The dispute is academic. Like the Eiffel Tower, the Rialto has acquired a symbolic status that puts it well beyond the reach of aesthetic judgements.

Walking back from the bridge, we pass Venice's oldest church, San Giacomo di Rialto, now almost entirely obscured by sellers of trinkets, vegetables, and the inevitable Murano glass. Some way further on, the Ruga degli Speziali runs into the little Campo delle Beccarie. The Beccarie are the shambles referred to by Moryson, created in the early fourteenth century as a reprisal against the Quirini family for their part in the revolt of Baiamonte Tiepolo. The vengeance of the Republic has been long-lasting: today the lively square is still pervaded winter and summer by the smell of fish. For the enthusiast, of course, the proximity of the market is not necessarily a penance. The light of a Venetian dawn, writes Elizabeth David, 'is so limpid and so still that it makes every separate vegetable and fruit and fish luminous with a life of its own, with unnaturally heightened colours and clear stencilled outlines':

> In other markets, on other shores, the unfamiliar fishes may be vivid, mysterious, repellent, fascinating, and bright with splendid colour; only in Venice do they look good enough to eat. In Venice even ordinary sole and ugly great skate are striped with delicate lilac lights, the sardines shine like newly-minted silver coins, pink Venetian *scampi* are fat and fresh, infinitely enticing in the early dawn.[24]

## San Cassiano

A couple of minutes from the Campo delle Beccarie, on the far side of the adjacent canal, is the Campo San Cassiano. We are now in the midst of what was for long the most notorious area of the city. From the fifteenth century onwards it was a rare traveller who could return without commenting on the number and beauty of the Venetian courtesans. 'The best flesh-shambles in Italy', Venice was called in John Day's *Humour out of Breath*, and the city's name, with its mingled suggestions of the exotic and the erotic, has graced brothels across the world from sixteenth-century Whitefriars to twentieth-century Bangkok.

Tradition has long outlived reality; if people wish to sin in Venice today, they take their own company. By contrast, provision for earlier travellers was often felt by the authorities to be excessive. In 1439 an attempt had been made to confine women of the town to the area called Castelletto, allowing them by day to ply their trade around the streets and inns towards the Rialto; but gradually they began to colonize the district of San Cassiano, and it is with this part of the city, known at the time as Carampane, that they came to be associated.

The reputation of the area can be judged by the dispassionate details of the State archives on prostitution. It matters little which page one opens: 'Elena, Courtesan, lives in San Cassiano in the Corte della Ruosa, fined 30 ducats, 5 May

1581.' The entry is typical. Today the square itself is in every way a modest enough spot, though if you glance down the Calle dei Morti or pause before the somewhat dissolute buildings which front the canal on the far side of the campo, it is not difficult to imagine the world that Thomas Coryate stepped into in 1608.

Stepped is the appropriate word. An eccentric Englishman from Odcombe in Somerset, Coryate had made a good part of the journey to Venice on foot. He paid his respects to the British ambassador, Sir Henry Wotton, and also, at some length, to the courtesans:

> As for the number of these Venetian Cortezans it is very great. For it is thought there are of them in the whole City and other adjacent places, as Murano, Malamocco, & c. at the least twenty thousand, whereof many are esteemed so loose, that they are said to open their quivers to every arrow. A most ungodly thing without doubt that there should be a tolleration of such licentious wantons in so glorious, so potent, so renowned a city. For me thinks that the Venetians should be dailie affraid least their winking at such uncleannesse should be an occasion to draw down upon them Gods curse and vengeance from heaven, and to consume their city with fire and brimstone, as in times past he did Sodome and Gomorrha.[25]

But the Venetians were a practical lot, and the fear of divine retribution was held at bay by more pressing concerns. The number and variety of prostitutes made Venetian husbands feel more secure against the danger of being, in Coryate's phrase, 'capricornified' and also supplied the State with enough tax revenue to maintain a dozen galleys.

In spite of a succession of sumptuary laws, the luxury with which the more successful Italian courtesans surrounded themselves was a subject of frequent comment by contemporary travellers. So overwhelmed was a Spanish ambassador in the sixteenth century that rather than soil the rugs and hangings around him, he chose, with a delicacy that did him credit, to spit on to the face of one of his valets.[26]

Coryate was plainly entranced:

For so infinite are the allurements of these amorous Calypsoes, that the fame of them hath drawen many to Venice from some of the remotest parts of Christendome, to contemplate their beauties, and enjoy their pleasing dalliances. And indeede such is the variety of the delicious objects they minister to their lovers, that they want nothing tending to delight. For when you come into one of their Palaces . . . you seem to enter into the Paradise of Venus. For their fairest roomes are most glorious and glittering to behold. The walles round about being adorned with most sumptuous tapistry and gilt leather . . .[27]

But pleasure must be paid, and the Venetian courtesan had a sharp way with defaulters:

Moreover I will tell thee this newes which is most true, that if thou shouldest wantonly converse with her, and not give her that salarium iniquitatis, which thou hast promised her, but perhaps cunningly escape from her company, shee will either cause thy throate to be cut by her Ruffiano, if he can after catch thee in the City, or procure thee to be arrested (if thou art to be found) and clapped up in the prison, where thou shalt remaine till thou hast paid her all thou didst promise her.[28]

The pragmatic attitude of the Venetian State towards its prostitutes is nicely illustrated by one of the more bizarre edicts of the fifteenth century, reported by Gallicciolli. In an effort to wean the youth of Venice from sodomy, it was decreed that the city's courtesans, when sitting at the window to attract clients, should leave their breasts uncovered. (Hence the name of the nearby Ponte delle Tette.) How much success the measure enjoyed is doubtful; the logic of the situation might suggest that it would have been better to keep everything covered for as long as possible. Indeed, some of the more enterprising courtesans had the wit to improve their chances by dressing as young men.

At all events, the problem was one which continued to exercise the Senate, as a series of other edicts in the fifteenth

and sixteenth centuries make clear.[29] (The portico of Santa
Maria Mater Domini was noted by the authorities as a place of
particular iniquity.) In each parish two nobles were appointed
to root out the practice and all doctors or barbers called on to
treat either man or woman, '*in partem posteriorem confractam per
sodomiam*', were obliged by a law of 1467 to report the incident
within three days. Retribution was sometimes severe. In the
cause of sexual purity more than one poor fellow was burnt to
death between the columns of the Piazzetta.

Among other means used to punish unnatural vice was the
*cheba*, a sort of cage, primarily intended for delinquent priests,
in which the culprit was suspended from the campanile in St
Mark's Square. Bread and water could then be let down to him
from the bell-chambers. This curious punishment left the
condemned man with one unusual expedient that was adopted
by a certain Agostino, a priest in the parish of Santa Fosca.
Sentenced to the *cheba* in 1518 for gambling and blasphemy, he
became the subject of a popular poem in which he expressed
his sense of ill-usage, complaining that the urchins on the
ground below harassed and ridiculed him with such im-
pudence that to relieve his indignation he was obliged 'to piss
on them from above' ('*pissarli adosso*').

At least today's visitors need guard only against the pigeons.

## PALAZZO GOZZI

A left turn just beyond the Campo San Cassiano will take us
down the Calle della Regina. At the far end of the street,
opposite the turning to the Calle de Ca' Bragadin al Cristo,
stands no. 2269, the somewhat decrepit palazzo that was the
home of Carlo and Gaspar Gozzi. (For a more attractive view
of it we can stand on the bridge into the Campo Santa Maria
Mater Domini and look at the façade it presents to the square.)
In this passage from his memoirs Gozzi describes his return to
the house with an army friend after his period of military
service:

We reached the entrance, and my companion gazed with
wonder at the stately structure of the mansion, which has

really all the appearance of a palace. As a connoisseur of architecture, he complimented me upon its fine design. I answered, what indeed he was about to discover by experience, that attractive exteriors sometimes mask discomfort and annoyance. He had plenty of time to admire the façade, while I kept knocking loudly at the house-door. I might as well have knocked at the portal of a sepulchre. At last a woman, named Eugenia, the guardian-angel of this wilderness, ran to open. To my enquiries she answered, yawning, that the family were in Friuli, but that my brother Gasparo was momently expected. Our luggage had now been brought from the boat, and we began to ascend a handsome marble staircase. No one could have expected that this fine flight of steps would lead to squalor and the haunts of indigence. Yet on surmounting the last stair that was what revealed itself. The stone floors were worn into holes and fissures, which spread in all directions like a cancer. The broken window panes let blasts from every point of the compass play freely to and fro within the draughty chambers. The hangings on the walls were ragged, smirched with smoke and dust, fluttering in tatters. Not a piece remained of that fine gallery of pictures which my grandfather had bequeathed as heirlooms to the family. I only saw some portraits of my ancestors by Titian and Tintoretto still staring from their ancient frames. I gazed at them; they gazed at me; they wore a look of sadness and amazement, as though enquiring how the wealth which they had gathered for their offspring had been dissipated.[30]

## Fondaco dei Turchi

The Fondaco dei Turchi, overlooking the Grand Canal, is about five minutes from Gozzi's house, along the Calle della Chiesa and the Calle del Tintor, then over the Ponte del Megio. (Notice beside the bridge the yellow house at the corner of the Calle del Spezier. It was here that Marin Sanudo, whose diaries furnish several of the details given in these pages, died in 1536.) The Fondaco only acquired the function of warehouse for Turkish merchants in the seventeenth century. Formerly it was a private residence, where the poet Tasso had stayed in 1562 as a guest of the Duke of Ferrara. Its history from the seventeenth century onwards was one of steady decline, to the point where Ruskin, studying it in the early 1850s, could take it as a symbol of all that was decadent and neglected in modern Venice. His words invest its dilapidation with a kind of splendour. It is, he says, a ghastly ruin. The covering stones have been torn away from it like the shroud from a corpse; its walls are rent into a thousand chasms:

> Soft grass and wandering leafage have rooted themselves in the rents, but they are not suffered to grow in their own wild and gentle way, for the place is in a sort inhabited; rotten partitions are nailed across its corridors, and miserable rooms contrived in its western wing; and here and there the weeds are indolently torn down, leaving their haggard fibres to struggle again into unwholesome growth when the spring next stirs them: and thus, in contest between death and life, the unsightly heap is festering to its fall.[31]

After undergoing one of the nineteenth century's more brutal restoration jobs, it became the home first of the Correr Museum and now of a Natural History Museum which displays among other items a crab of such monstrous size that it might have ambled straight out of a science fiction film. The curious may also see, under the arcade beside the Grand Canal, the sarcophagus of Marin Falier. In 1355 the aged Doge, prompted by senile resentments, became embroiled in a murderous plot to overthrow the State. The nobility of Venice were to be slaughtered in the Piazza and Falier himself proclaimed Prince. In the event, details of the conspiracy were betrayed to the Council of Ten. Falier's sarcophagus tells the rest. When it was opened in the nineteenth century, it revealed the old man's skeleton, with the skull, neatly severed by the headsman's axe, resting between the knees. In the place of his portrait in the Ducal Palace there is just a black curtain inscribed with the words. '*Hic est locus Marini Faledri decapitati pro criminibus.*'

## CALLE DEL CAPITELLO TO PONTE BERGAMI

At the far end of the Salizzada which runs past the entrance to the Natural History Museum is the Calle del Capitello. Its towering, lightless walls are forbidding even by Venetian standards, and the name is an indication of at least one murder which took place in this narrow street. *Capitelli* are small shrines, and the lamps which burned before them were the first form of street-lighting that Venice enjoyed. They were placed in the dark corner where murder had been done, partly, as Douglas tells us, that their light should make such secret acts more difficult, partly to awaken kinder thoughts in those who were bent on violence. By the time Felix Fabri visited the city in the late fifteenth century the use of these lights was widespread:

> In every corner, where the ways are twisting and crooked, a lamp is hung, which is lit at night, and lest the light should seem to burn to no purpose, they place against the wall, behind the lamp, an image of the Blessed Virgin, and the lamp burns as much for the honour of the Virgin as for the convenience of wayfarers.[32]

It may well have been the invitation to murder offered by winding alleys and black canals that led the Venetian State to institute general street-lighting as early as the 1730s.

The agreeable streets around this western curve of the Grand Canal have little in the way of monuments to tempt the visitor, but we should at least pass through the distinctive Campo San Giacomo dell'Orio. This is where the hero of L. P. Hartley's *Eustace and Hilda* ends up, as he tries to dash back to Lady Nelly's palazzo on hearing of his sister's illness. When time is short, the pleasant frustrations of finding one's way across Venice can turn to nightmare:

> He looked up. What was this campo with the terra-cotta-washed, round-apsed church, and the trees and the

sweeping crescent of houses that ended in a restaurant covered with a vine? San Giacomo dell'Orio, the street sign told him. He was out of his way, much too far to the left. A panic seized him, an access of train-fever intensified a thousand-fold. He started to run . . .[33]

Before ending our walk opposite the railway station, it is worth pausing a moment at the Ponte Bergami just beyond the church of San Simeone Grande. Look to your left and you will see on the far side of the canal, a short way down, the crumbling façade of the Palazzo Cappello. The palace, for the moment, is derelict, its garden wild and overgrown. A hundred years ago Henry James seems almost to have foreseen their decline when he took this palace for the setting of *The Aspern Papers*:

> It was not particularly old, only two or three centuries; and it had an air not so much of decay as of quiet discouragement, as if it had rather missed its career. But its wide front, with a stone balcony from end to end of the *piano nobile* or most important floor, was architectural enough, with the aid of various pilasters and arches; and the stucco with which in the intervals it had long ago been endued was rosy in the April afternoon. It overlooked a clean, melancholy, unfrequented canal, which had a narrow *riva* or convenient footway on either side.[34]

'Our house is very far from the centre,' Miss Bordereau remarks, 'but the little canal is very *comme il faut*.'

The famous garden, which James's narrator busily cultivates to ingratiate himself with Miss Bordereau and her niece, also plays its part in Gabriele d'Annunzio's novel *Il Fuoco*. The scents of fruit and jasmine that permeate the evening air in the garden of the Palazzo Cappello have a peculiar vividness, because the garden itself, 'enclosed like an exiled thing by its girdle of water, becomes all the more intense from its banishment, like the soul of the exile'.[35]

Gardens have a special importance in Venice. In a city whose buildings are everywhere lapped by the sea, there is, as d'Annunzio realized, something both exotic and slightly poignant about the few that have been allowed to survive.

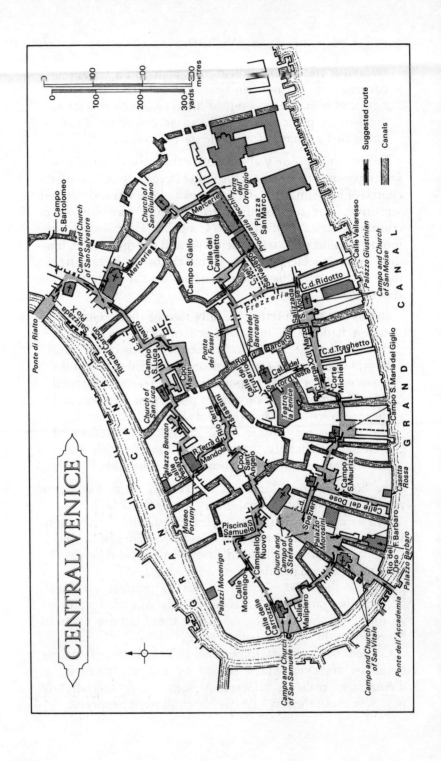

# CENTRAL VENICE

Suggested route
Canals

Ponte di Rialto

Campo S. Bartolomeo

Campo and Church of San Salvatore

Church of San Giuliano

Mercerie

Mercerie

Torre dell' Orologio

Procuratie Vecchie

Piazza San Marco

Calle del Cavalletto

Campo S. Gallo

Calle Vallaresso

Palazzo Giustinian

Campo and Church of San Moisè

C.d. Ridotto

Frezzeria

X old Spezieria

Salizzada

Salizzada

Rivadel Carbon

Campo Teatro S. Luca

Cpo Manin

Ponte dei Fuseri

Rio del

Ponte dei Barcaroli

Calle d. Frutariol

Barcaro

Sal. S. Moisè

C.d. Traghetto

Church of San Luca

Calle del

Sartor d'Veste

Larga XXII Marzo

C.d.

Corte Michiel

Campo S. Maria del Giglio

Palazzo Benzon

R. Terrà Rio Terrà d. Assassini

Teatro la Fenice

Calle della Mandola

Calle Pesaro

Cpo Santo Angelo

Campo S. Maurizio

Museo Fortuny

C.d. Spezier

Palazzo Morosini

Caseta Rossa

Piscina S. Samuele

Campiello Nuovo

Church and Campo of S. Stefano

Calle del Dose

Palazzi Mocenigo

Calle Mocenigo

Calle delle Carrozze

Calle Malipiero

Rio del Orso

R. F. Barbaro

Palazzo Barbaro

Campo and Church of San Samuele

Campo and Church of San Vitale

Ponte dell' Accademia

GRAND CANAL

G R A N D   C A N A L

0   100   200   300 yards
metres

# 3

# CENTRAL VENICE

*Harry's Bar—Frezzeria—Ridotto—Church of San
Moisè—Spies in San Moisè—Lodgings in San
Moisè—Hotel Regina—La Fenice—Ponte dei
Barcaroli—Corte Michiel—Campo Santa Maria del
Giglio—Calle del Dose—Calle del Spezier—Campo
San Stefano: Palazzo Barbaro—Calle
Malipiero—Palazzo Mocenigo—Campo Sant'
Angelo—Palazzo Benzon—Campo Manin—Teatro
Goldoni—Campo San Salvador—Campo San
Bartolomeo—Mercerie—Campo San Gallo*

## HARRY'S BAR

The area round San Moisè has long been favoured by tourists.
As the vaporetto makes its way across from San Marco to the
Salute and then swings back towards Santa Maria del Giglio,
we can look out at a line of palaces that includes many of the
city's most celebrated hotels – among them the Monaco, the
Europa and Regina, the Bauer Grünwald and the Gritti Palace.
But for the homesick American, returning wearily from
another encounter with the tangled streets beyond the Piazza,
a more welcome sight than any of these is a discreet doorway
in the nearby Calle Vallaresso.

Like St Mark's or the Doge's Palace, Harry's Bar has
become a place of pilgrimage. Frequented by the fictional
characters of writers from Hemingway to Patricia Highsmith,

it has an association with America which, as Gore Vidal explains, goes back to its origins:

> In 1931, an American lamented with his favourite hotel bartender, the late Giuseppe Cipriani, that what Venice lacked was a good bar. The American, whose name was Harry, probably was not the first refugee from American Prohibition to make that observation, although the lengthy Venetian chronicles of two other Americans, Henry James and William Dean Howells, carry no mention of the city's lack of saloons. But Harry was the first to follow the inbred American tradition of wanting to set right a wrong. This was done in the form of financial backing to Cipriani, who found a rope storeroom next to St Mark's *vaporetto* stop and there opened what he called Harry's Bar.
>
> Even without knowing the origin of its history, some American visitors today consider Harry's Bar as being almost extra-territorially *theirs*. Since the closing of the American consulate in the 1970s, it is indeed sometimes the only place for Americans in acute distress to go for comfort and advice. However, Harry's bar was and remains an entirely Venetian operation, though the babble of barbaric voices on summer days and nights is predominantly American. Most important, it is an innovation, perhaps the only one in the ancient city, which has been accepted by the Venetians. It has become one of their own monuments. Like most natives everywhere, they may shy away from actually visiting their monuments (call it the Grant's Tomb or Tower of London syndrome), but they like to know that it is there, and that it is appreciated and frequented by foreign visitors.[1]

## FREZZERIA

The other end of the Calle Vallaresso opens into the Salizzada San Moisè almost opposite the Frezzeria. It was at nos 1673–1674 in the Frezzeria, on the corner of the Calle di

Piscina, that Byron took rooms when he arrived in Venice. Above a suitably fashionable clothes shop, the building is beginning, like many in Venice, to look its age; but then the same may well have been true when Byron first saw it in November 1816. He had left England some six months earlier, after his marriage to Annabella Milbanke had ended in separation and scandal. Pursued by evil rumours about his treatment of his wife and his relationship with his half-sister Augusta, he had made first for Geneva and then for Venice. It was here that he settled. A letter to his friend Tom Moore, dated 17 November, explains some of the attractions of the city, and also of this particular house in the Frezzeria:

It is my intention to remain at Venice during the winter, probably, as it has always been (next to the East) the greenest island of my imagination. It has not disappointed me; though its evident decay would, perhaps, have that effect upon others. But I have been familiar with ruins too long to dislike desolation. Besides, I have fallen in love, which, next to falling into the canal, (which would be of no use, as I can swim) is the best or the worst thing I could do. I have got some extremely good apartments in the house of a 'Merchant of Venice,' who is a good deal occupied with business, and has a wife in her twenty-second year. Marianna (that is her name) is in her appearance altogether like an antelope. She has the large, black, oriental eyes, with that peculiar expression in them which is seen rarely among *Europeans* – even the Italians – and which many of the Turkish women give themselves by tinging the eyelid, – an art not known out of that country, I believe. This expression she has *naturally*, – and something more than this. In short, I cannot describe the effect of this kind of eye – at least upòn me.[2]

Marianna was the first, and one of the most enduring of Byron's Venetian loves, and his letters keep up a diverting commentary on the progress of their affair. A couple of months after the letter quoted above, he was writing to Moore again to give an account of a turbulent evening which

elsewhere might have ended badly. The letter is revealing in
what it tells both of Byron and of Venice:

> Now for an adventure. A few days ago a gondolier
> brought me a billet without a subscription, intimating a
> wish on the part of the writer to meet me either in gondola
> or at the island of San Lazaro, or at a third rendezvous
> indicated in the note. 'I know the country's disposition
> well' – in Venice 'they do let Heaven see those tricks they
> dare not show,' &c. &c.; so, for all response, I said that
> neither of the three places suited me; but that I would
> either be at home at ten at night *alone*, or at the ridotto at
> midnight, where the writer might meet me masked. At
> ten o'clock I was at home and alone (Marianna was gone
> with her husband to a conversazione), when the door of
> my apartment opened, and in walked a well-looking and
> (for an Italian) *bionda* girl of about nineteen, who in-
> formed me that she was married to the brother of my
> *amorosa*, and wished to have some conversation with me.
> I made a decent reply, and we had some talk in Italian and
> Romaic (her mother being a Greek of Corfu), when lo! in
> a very few minutes, in marches, to my very great aston-
> ishment, Marianna S, *in propria persona*, and after making
> polite courtesy to her sister-in-law and to me, without a
> single word seizes her said sister-in-law by the hair, and
> bestows upon her some sixteen slaps, which would have
> made your ear ache only to hear their echo. I need not
> describe the screaming which ensued. The luckless visitor
> took flight. I seized Marianna, who, after several vain
> efforts to get away in pursuit of the enemy, fairly went
> into fits in my arms; and, in spite of reasoning, eau de
> Cologne, vinegar, half a pint of water, and God knows
> what other waters beside, continued so till past midnight.
> . . . After about an hour, in comes – who? why, Signor
> S, her lord and husband, and finds me with his wife
> fainting upon the sofa, and all the apparatus of confusion,
> dishevelled hair, hats, handkerchiefs, salts, smelling-
> bottles – and the lady as pale as ashes without sense or
> motion. His first question was, 'What is all this?' The lady

could not reply – so I did. I told him the explanation was the easiest thing in the world; but in the meantime it would be as well to recover his wife – at least, her senses. This came about in due time of suspiration and respiration.

Youneednot be alarmed–jealousyisnottheorder ofthe day in Venice, and daggers are out of fashion; while duels, on love matters, are unknown – at least, with husbands.[3]

The busy Frezzeria was originally the main centre for shops selling arrows (*frecce*) – an important commodity in a city where, during the fourteenth century, all males between the ages of sixteen and thirty-five were obliged to present themselves for weekly practice with the cross-bow. Returning towards the Salizzada, you might glance down the sotto-portico a few yards along on the other side of the street. It leads to the somewhat uninviting Corte del Luganegher, where Casanova lived in 1774.

From the Salizzada a turning to the left takes us down the Calle del Ridotto, at the end of which, on the right, stands the Palazzo Giustinian. It is now the headquarters of the Biennale, but in the nineteenth century, as the Hotel Europa, it was patronized by a range of literary figures, including Gautier, Proust, and de Musset. It was here that George Eliot came with her husband in May 1880, just a month after their marriage. A couple of weeks into their holiday, the bridegroom, John Cross, jumped from the balcony of their room into the Grand Canal and had to be fished out by gondoliers. The episode shook George Eliot and their visit was cut short. Within a few days the unstable Cross had been removed to Verona and thence back to England. In the circumstances it is perhaps not surprising that George Eliot had little of interest to say about the sights of Venice.

RIDOTTO

The Calle del Ridotto takes its name from the famous gambling-house, or *ridotto*, which stood on the other side from

the Palazzo Giustinian, at no 1361. This was the old Palazzo
Dandolo, just behind what is now the Hotel Monaco. The
State had given permission for Marco Dandolo to open a
public gaming-house in his palace in 1638, but when it was
expanded and embellished in the middle of the following
century, the effects were too devastating to be ignored. Within
twenty years the toll of ruined families had forced the Maggior
Consiglio to take action. On 27 November 1774, 'in order to
stamp out the vice in its principal seat', it decreed the closing of
the Ridotto.

In its heyday the Ridotto was one of the centres of Carnival
Venice, where huge sums were nightly won and lost. Its
appearance in the mid-eighteenth century has been described
by Pompeo Molmenti in his social history of Venice:

> The entrance hall was hung with stamped leather, and
> here the maskers would walk and talk, or would pass
> thence into two little neighbouring chambers with buf-
> fets: at one they sold chocolate, coffee, and tea; at the
> other, wine, cheese, sausages, and fruit. From the en-
> trance hall opened ten large rooms in which the gaming
> tables . . . were set out. At each table sat a nobleman, in
> robe and wig, with piles of sequins and of ducats before
> him ready to hold the bank against all comers provided
> they were either patricians or masked.[4]

One of those who frequented the Ridotto in the last year or
two before it closed was Lorenzo da Ponte, later to become
Mozart's librettist. At the time he was in his early twenties and
in love with a woman whose brother was a furious gambler. A
striking episode in his memoirs begins with a typical scene at
one of the gaming tables. The brother has taken da Ponte's
own recent winnings, promising to double them:

> It was already past midnight, and all the other bankers had
> put down the cards. But play began again now for
> desperate stakes. In the first two games his luck was
> wonderfully good. He soon had a little mountain of gold
> in front of him. I sat on one side of him and his sister on
> the other. We did not dare speak, but we made signs to

him with our eyes and hands and feet to make him stop playing. But all was in vain. He began a third game but did not finish it: about half way through all his money was gone. With wonderful coolness he then put down the cards, 'looked at me with a mocking laugh and a toss of the head,' and taking his sister by the hand, bade me good-night and went away.

I need not say what my feelings were. I withdrew into the 'chamber of sighs,' a room so called because it was frequented by unfortunate lovers or gamblers, for talk or sighing or sleep. After some time I fell asleep and did not wake till broad daylight, when all the company had gone, except a few who, like myself, had slept there.

A man in a mask sitting near me, seeing me awake, begged a couple of *soldi* of me. After having felt in my pockets in vain, I put my hand into the fob of my coat, and what was my surprise and joy to find some sequins there, which, as they were underneath a handkerchief, had not been noticed and so had not been taken out of my pockets with the rest of the money when my mistress's brother arrived home. It was only with difficulty that I concealed my joyful surprise. However, having no other change, I offered my neighbour one of the sequins. At first he refused to take it, but afterwards, looking hard at me, said, 'I will take it only on condition that you allow me to return it to you in my own house.' So saying, he took a playing card and on the back wrote the name of the street and the number of his house, saying as he gave it to me that he was sure I should not regret paying him a visit. But just then I was thinking only of my mistress and the fact that some of the money was saved, so I put the card into my pocket without paying attention to it and hurried home at once. [5]

It is some time later, on the first Sunday in Lent, that da Ponte comes across the card again and is driven by curiosity to visit the address. The masked man from the Ridotto turns out to be a native of Leghorn whom hardship had forced to the life of a professional beggar. In a curious scene, which da Ponte

insists is a truthful record of events, the old man reveals how
well he has prospered over the years and shows the bemused
visitor his horde of money. To da Ponte's astonishment the
details of his life are already well known to the man, who has
displayed his wealth for a purpose:

> 'There are five thousand *zecchini* there, and I will give
> them to you the day you marry my daughter. Afterwards
> at my death, or before if you need it, you will have
> another four thousand, which is all I possess, but you
> must promise me always to remember the poor, and that I
> believe you will do. I have had you in my eye for about
> two years. I liked your appearance immediately I saw
> you. For some years I sat begging at the foot of the Ponte
> San Gregorio where you passed by every day, and your
> repeated acts of charity to me there won my good-will
> and respect for you. It always seemed marvellous to me
> that you should give me alms for I knew the state you
> were in, and it made me feel that you must have a
> kindly-disposed heart, and that, I think, is the sum of all
> the virtues and the soul of true religion.'[6]

Obsessed by his current mistress, who later does what she can
to get him killed, da Ponte refuses the old man's offer and after
a pleasant day with him and his daughter leaves the house.
Within a few months the daughter marries someone else and
da Ponte is left with his regrets.

In any other city it would be impossible to take the story for
more than a fairy-tale, but eighteenth-century Venice is itself
so close to fairy-tale that what would elsewhere be the stuff of
fantasy seems almost the texture of daily life. Perhaps the
future librettist of *Don Giovanni* and *Cosi Fan Tutte* really did
pause from time to time as he crossed the Ponte San Gregorio
to drop a coin into this unlikely beggar's hand.

## CHURCH OF SAN MOISÈ

So absorbingly ugly is the modern façade of the Hotel Bauer
Grünwald that if one enters the Campo San Moisè from the

Piazza, the church can almost escape notice. Only the defiant have had anything very charitable to say about San Moisè since Ruskin passed judgement: 'one of the basest examples of the basest school of the Renaissance', was his characteristically firm assessment. The wilder flights of the baroque are not always a happy sight, but one can feel a certain sympathy with the hero of L. P. Hartley's *Eustace and Hilda* in his hesitant refusal to be intimidated by the art historians:

> Not for the first time the crumbling, florid front of the church of San Moisè claimed his attention. Ruskin had loaded it with obloquy: in his eyes it was frivolous, ignoble, immoral. Eustace was determined to like it: half one's pleasure in Venice was lost if one could not stomach the rococo and the baroque. But this evening, as he stood on the little bridge and watched the pigeons strutting to and fro, hardly visible among the swags, cornucopias, and swing-boat forms whose lateral movement seemed to rock the church from side to side, his interest was not in the morality or otherwise of the tormented stonework, but in the state of mind of people to whom such exuberance of spirit was as natural as the air they breathed. Never a hint, in all that aggregation of masonry, of diffidence or despondency, no suggestion of a sad, tired mind finding its only expression in a stretch of blank wall.[7]

Less anxiously, Sean O'Faolain observes the life of the campo on an August day in 1948:

> This torrid morning I am passing out of the dimness of San Moisè, idly wondering if it was the Oriental influence that sanctified Moses as I look back again at the carnal clusters on the façade that threw Ruskin into such a spluttering rage. I lean over a humped bridge beneath whose shade a gondolier lies fast asleep in his gondola. I pass on and pause beside an entirely modern chemist's window, packed with nostrums, glittering with feminine war-tackle. Then I stroll a few feet beyond and come on one of those eloquent obituaries that Italian piety pastes

on dead walls, or hangs in shop-windows, or inserts in the newspapers to show the world that dead friends are not forgotten . . . As I read this pious memorial, behind me are the chaffering black-marketeers, offering tobacco, scents, foreign money. The crowds float past unheeding. I can just see the feet of the sleeping gondolier, sticking out into the sun that burns his soles. In the flickering miasma of the heat the statues on the church seem to sway.[8]

## SPIES IN SAN MOISÈ

In the days of the Republic a bystander might occasionally have seen furtive passers-by pausing a few yards from the church's extravagant façade to slip a note into the *bocca di leone* of San Moisè, the lion's mouth which acted as a post-box for secret denunciations. It was here that in May 1779 an unknown hand posted the denunciation which drove da Ponte from the city.[9] In his case the accusations of various kinds of sexual and financial misconduct were probably well justified, but in spite of safeguards, the system was open to abuse, and it engendered widespread fear. An eighteenth-century satirical work, in which Casanova probably had a hand, makes the point with some bitterness: 'A foreigner who travels to this Republic should leave his tongue at Fusina and arrive in Venice mute. Silence is the emblem of this government: everything is secret and cloaked in mystery. Political doings are covered by a thick veil of darkness. In Venice those who talk are buried alive in a tomb covered with lead.'[10]

As this implies, the State's concern was primarily political. Its attitude is summed up by Charles de Brosses, President of the Burgundian Parliament, writing in 1739: 'I will tell you that nowhere on earth do liberty and licence have a more complete empire than in Venice. Stay clear of politics and for the rest do what you will.'[11]

Whether true or not, the story of how Lord Chesterfield unsettled the philosophical calm of Montesquieu conveys something of the atmosphere of the time. The Frenchman had merely been taking in the sights and trying to make a study of Venetian laws. On a whim, Chesterfield gave him to understand that he had come under the eye of the State Inquisitors. The effect on Montesquieu was dramatic: he burned his notes, packed his bags, and headed for Holland.

Historians have long been sceptical about the myths that lie behind this sort of story, but it is nonetheless true that spying was something of a Venetian speciality. It was the province of the so-called Council of Ten, which had been established in the wake of Baiamonte Tiepolo's conspiracy and from which the three State Inquisitors were drawn. The ten Senators who made up this Tribunal were elected annually from the larger Maggior Consiglio. Acting in concert with the Doge, they exercised wide executive powers, and from the start they had developed a brilliant intelligence network, both inside the city and out. By the eighteenth century its scope had been much reduced, but even so, those luckless figures who came to the attention of the Ten were likely to be scrutinized down to the smallest details of their daily lives. We know, for example, that on 30 June 1791 a patrician named Pietro Giacomo Foscarini passed close to the spot where we are now standing on his way to visit a tailor. The report was made out by a certain Gerolamo Mazzucato who had dogged his footsteps throughout the day. When Foscarini emerged from his house, he went first to the Della Nave, a café in the Calle Larga San Marco:

Ordered a coffee. Stayed half an hour or so, but spoke to no one. Went to the Vecchie Procuratie, to the snuff-merchants, for an ounce of snuff. Walked in the Mercerie for perhaps fifteen minutes, and then home. About one o'clock came out again; to the Delle Rive, the café under the Padaglione. There till two, spoke to no one. Then to the tailor on the San Moisè bridge, and spent half an hour talking to the owner. Owner and he came out together and proceeded to the Piazza, where they strolled until nearly three, talking. Parted. The Noble Gentleman went to the Della Nave and met some people there. Said little, drank a barley-water and left at four-thirty. Back to the

Piazza, walked under the Vecchie Procuratie and greeted someone I did not recognize. Went to the Arco Celeste, said very little and nobody addressed him. Strolled once more until five o'clock or so; back home.[12]

If this was an average summer's day, the Ten probably had good reason to fear that men's minds might turn to intrigue.

## LODGINGS IN SAN MOISÈ

To leave the Campo San Moisè we cross the bridge into the Calle Larga over what Corvo described as 'that dreadful little ditch of a canal by Sanmoise which is lined on both sides with the gondole of the most disagreeable extortionate nasty-tempered gondolieri in Venice'. A writer who remembered the area more kindly was Théophile Gautier. For him San Moisè was '*le coin où nous avons passé un mois si heureux*'. After an initial stay at the Hotel Europa, he took lodgings just beside the canal in rooms recently vacated by a Russian prince. Not, he adds, that the word prince should mislead people: 'In Venice one can treat oneself to the luxury of a palace at friendly prices. A jewel from the hand of Sansovino or Scamozzi is cheaper to rent than a garret in the Rue de la Paix, and our lodging was part of a simple house with pink rendering, like most of the houses in Venice.'[13] His only complaint was one shared by the majority of travellers to Venice before the twentieth century:

The great business before going to bed is the hunt for insects, vicious mosquitoes that particularly torment foreigners, on whom they hurl themselves with the sensual appetite of a gourmet savouring some rare and exotic dish. The grocery shops and pharmacies sell a fumigating powder which you burn on a small stove with all the windows closed, and which sees off or suffocates the terrible insects. This powder seems to be more obnoxious to people than to mosquitoes, and the number of bumps on our hands and face each morning were an indication of how ineffective it was as a remedy. The

most sensible course is not to put any light near the bed
and to seal yourself hermetically inside the veils of the
mosquito net.[14]

Gautier's experience might make one doubtful of the claims
of local pharmacists, but the *Cook's Handbook* for 1875 helpfully lists an 'English chemist', albeit with a rather un-English
name: 'Dr Zampironi, S. Moisè, near Piazza S. Marco. Pre-
scriptions carefully prepared – patent medicines – special
pastilles for killing mosquitoes.'

## HOTEL REGINA

A few yards along the Calle Larga XXII Marzo, on the other
side of Corvo's 'dreadful little ditch', the Calle del Traghetto
leads down to the Grand Canal almost exactly opposite the
Salute. At the end, a convenient jetty enables one to walk out
and survey the Hotel Regina, formerly the Casa Alvisi, home
of Katharine de Kay Bronson. Originally from New York,
Mrs Bronson became known in Venice for her hospitality to a
long succession of English and American visitors. In the 1880s
she provided a base for both Browning and Henry James,
lodging them in the Palazzo Giustiniani-Recanati, just behind
the Casa Alvisi. As Mrs Prest in *The Aspern Papers*, it is she
who shepherds the narrator through the canals and brings him
to the house of Miss Bordereau and her niece. Earlier, James
had paid a pleasant tribute to life at the Casa Alvisi in the
closing lines of his best known essay on Venice:

> If you are happy you will find yourself, after a June day in
> Venice (about ten o'clock), on a balcony that overhangs
> the Grand Canal, with your elbows on the broad ledge, a
> cigarette in your teeth and a little good company beside
> you. The gondolas pass beneath, the watery surface
> gleams here and there from their lamps, some of which
> are coloured lanterns that move mysteriously in the
> darkness . . .[15]

LA FENICE

Back on the Calle Larga, we are at a convenient point from
which to turn aside for a look at the Fenice, just a short walk
along the Calle del Sartor da Veste. It was not one of Venice's
earliest theatres, but since it opened in 1791 it has always
been the most celebrated, scene of the opening nights of
both *Rigoletto* and *La Traviata* as well as, more recently,
Stravinsky's *The Rake's Progress*.

At the heart of the city the Fenice has a symbolic importance
that outweighs its actual function, for it is an elaborate shrine
to one of Venice's most striking characteristics. For centuries
the rulers of this theatrical city, cheerfully aided by the people,
made calculated use of its dramatic possibilities. In 1177 they
staged the great reconciliation scene between Frederick Bar-
barossa and Pope Alexander III, when the Emperor knelt to
the Pope in the vestibule of St Mark's, and thereafter the
diplomatic advantages to be gained from putting on an im-
pressive show were rarely missed. Now that Venice has
grown old, it is easy for us to see in its handsome, flaking
façades the elegiac appeal of an abandoned stage-set. Or
perhaps, as Henry James suggests in *The Aspern Papers*, the
theatre has merely taken on a more domestic tone. The city, he
says, is like an immense collective apartment, furnished with
palaces and churches:

> And somehow the splendid common domicile, familiar,
> domestic and resonant, also resembles a theatre, with
> actors clicking over bridges and, in straggling pro-
> cessions, tripping along fondamentas. As you sit in your
> gondola the footways that in certain parts edge the canals
> assume to the eye the importance of a stage, meeting it at
> the same angle, and the Venetian figures, moving to and
> fro against the battered scenery of their little houses of
> comedy, strike you as members of an endless dramatic
> troupe.[16]

By the time Ruskin and his bride visited the Fenice, it had
acquired a genuine right to the name of Phoenix, having been
destroyed by fire in 1836 and rebuilt shortly afterwards. It had

also by then become a focus for protests against the Austrian occupation. Not that this was of great concern to Effie Ruskin, who found the manners and dress of the Austrian officers beyond reproach. Even for her, however, the social demands of an evening at the Fenice could be oppressive. She went there for Rossini's opera *Semiramide* two days after Christmas, 1851:

> We came away before the end as it was so long. I wish they did not talk so much in the Theatre for it is imposs- ible to pay any attention to the Opera, for first came Nugent talking English as fast as he could, at the same time the Princess talking her Venetian and General Duodo replying – then came Falkenhayn with his German & Wrbna with his French making your box a sort of Babel, and as it would be considered quite contrary to etiquette that Ladies should ever be left alone in their box, whenever one gentleman has paid his visit of a quarter of an hour or so another arrives to take his place and you never have a chance of being alone a minute. I complained of it last night to Mdme. Pal. and they were all against me; they said that the Theatre was public property and every body had a right to call upon any body that they knew, and as most people went every night for an hour it was economical as it saved them lighting their rooms at home, and that having a box at the Opera was the cheapest way for all to see people & society.[17]

## PONTE DEI BARCAROLI

Before returning to the Calle Larga, devotees of George Sand might like to walk a few yards down the Calle del Frutariol as far as the pretty bridge that crosses the Rio dei Barcaroli. Writing the Preface to a new edition of *André* in 1851, Sand recalled: 'It was in Venice that I dreamed up and wrote this novel. I was living in a little low house alongside a narrow strip of water which was green and yet limpid, close to the Ponte dei Barcarolli . . .'[18] She could not have asked for a more ex- quisitely Venetian setting. It was here that she had come in the spring of 1834 with Pietro Pagello, the young doctor whose appearance on the scene had put an end to her tortured relationship with Alfred de Musset. The 'little low house' was the Ca' Mezzani, now no. 1880 in the Corte Minelli, which the couple shared with Pagello's brother and stepsister. Glimpses of this ménage, sketched with ironic affection, can be found in Sand's *Lettres d'un voyageur*, the first three of which she wrote while she was living here.

## CORTE MICHIEL

Just before the Calle Larga veers round to the left, a street beside the consulate of Monaco leads off in the other direction to the secluded little Corte Michiel, where Countess Isabella Teotocchi Albrizzi lived. It was on a visit to her house, one of the great literary salons of the time, that Byron first made the acquaintance of the nineteen-year-old Countess Teresa Guiccioli. The Countess's recent marriage was not of a kind to inconvenience her social life, and when she met Byron again the following year, she was happy to accept him as her *cavalier servente*. This genial institution available to married women of the day cast the man in the role of courtier, attendant, general dogsbody and, if he was lucky, lover. English writers tended to take a dim view of it. Samuel Sharp, travelling to Venice in the previous century, had commented:

> Gallantry is so epidemical in this city, that few of the Ladies escape the contagion. No woman can go into a public place, but in the company of a Gentleman, called here, a *Cavaliere Servente*, and in other parts of *Italy*, a *Cicesbeo*. This Cavaliere is always the same person; and she not only is attached to him, but to him singly; for no other woman joins the company, but it is usual for them to sit alone in the box, at the opera, or play-house, where they must be, in a manner, by themselves, as the theatres are so very dark that the spectators can hardly be said to be in company with one another. . . . On the other hand, the husband has his revenge; for he never fails to be the *Cavaliere Servente* of some other woman; and, I am told, it would be so ridiculous for a husband to appear in publick

with his wife, that there is no instance of such a phe-
nomenon; and, therefore, it is impossible for a woman to
bear up against the torrent of this fashion.[19]

Given its various constraints, it is a somewhat startling role for
Byron to have accepted. As he wrote to his friend Hobhouse:

> I like women – God he knows – but the more their sys-
> tem here developes upon me – the worse it seems – after
> Turkey too – here the *polygamy* is all on the female
> side. – I have been an intriguer, a husband, and now I am
> a Cavalier Servente. – by the holy! – it is a strange
> sensation.[20]

The account of it he gives in *Beppo* conveys even less
enthusiasm:

> But 'Cavalier Servente' is the phrase
>   Used in the politest circles to express
> This supernumerary slave, who stays
>   Close to the lady as a part of dress,
> Her word the only law which he obeys.
>   His is no sinecure, as you may guess;
> Coach, servants, gondola, he goes to call,
>   And carries fan and tippet, gloves and shawl.

But in spite of occasional backsliding, Byron seems to have
taken to the job readily enough. In something close to respect-
ability he and his mistress settled down to grow plump
together in Ravenna, until domestic and political upheavals
drove them first to Pisa and then to Genoa. It was perhaps
surprising – not least to Byron himself – that the relationship
was still unbroken when the affairs of Greece called him away
to his death.

## Campo Santa Maria del Giglio

At the end of the Calle Larga a small bridge crosses the canal,
and then the Calle delle Ostreghe takes us into the Campo
Santa Maria del Giglio. For those who travel in comfort this is

a square of blessed memory, since it houses the Gritti Palace hotel, whose guests in recent years have included Hemingway, Graham Greene, and Somerset Maugham. It is here that Hemingway's Colonel Cantwell stays in *Across the River and into the Trees* – as the author himself had done while writing the book.

Before it became a modern hotel the Gritti provided lodgings for Ruskin and Effie during their visit to Venice in 1851–2, when Ruskin wrote the second volume of *The Stones of Venice*. His letters in the early days of their tenancy show a certain anxiety to stress the diligent, respectable, and economical nature of their life, probably because when the idea of looking for a place of their own was first mooted the response of Ruskin's father had been a masterpiece of Victorian foreboding:

> . . . would it either morally or religiously harmonize with your feelings or strengthen your minds or Character? . . . Mama deems it a duty to beseech of you to pause before you plunge too far into the fascinations of Continental Life – They never yet I fancy did much good to either man or woman – Woman especially . . . I cannot at once say I entirely approve of hiring House or Palace abroad yet – It sounds Byronish or Shelleyish . . . how few of our best men have dwelt in Foreign Land? – Gibbon is the most known after Byron & neither would we like you to resemble . . .[21]

In spite of the vistas of expatriate debauchery which suggested themselves to Ruskin père, the couple went ahead and secured a comfortable suite of rooms at the Gritti (then called the Casa Wetzlar after its current owner), where they stayed for some eight months. It might have added a certain piquancy to their defiance of parental fears to know how close the palace had come to being the scene of Byron's excesses. He had bargained for it before moving to the Palazzo Mocenigo but was unable to agree terms with the owner.

At the other end of the square from the Gritti – and one more source of dismay to Ruskin – stands the church of Santa Maria del Giglio, built in the late seventeenth century. Quite without religious significance, its confidently pagan façade stands as a monument to the man who paid for it, Antonio Barbaro. His statue, looking suitably imperial, dominates the centre, while on the left Fame trumpets his deeds towards the square. The rest is given over to allegorical virtues, statues of his relations, and flattering memorials of his rather inglorious military career.

Serious tourists might prefer to be spared the sort of episodes that Marin Sanudo liked to record in his diary, but for the more frivolous they are an engaging aspect of the city's life. Venetian youth were reckoned to be among the most unruly in Italy and the hapless boy who met his end here on 24 January 1518 must have been one of a familiar breed:

> It happened that a madcap youth, dressed as an old man, had a sort of cage with a phallus inside, which he went around showing to the women; but it seems that at Santa Maria del Giglio, when he showed it to a young woman at a certain balcony there, someone who had an interest in her came out, stabbed him with a dagger and killed him. He was 16 years old.[22]

## CALLE DEL DOSE

A couple of attractive bridges away, continuing in the direction of the Accademia, is the Campo San Maurizio. At no. 2760, on the corner of the Calle del Piovan, we pass the imposing Palazzo Bellavite, which was the home in the eighteenth century of the vernacular poet Giorgio Baffo and also, for the winter of 1803–4, of Alessandro Manzoni, author of *I Promessi Sposi*. It was in fact the house of Manzoni's uncle, to whom the eighteen-year-old had been sent on a visit, probably to cure him of an unfortunate liaison in his native Milan. He stayed just long enough to pick up a venereal infection and become a habitué of the salon of the Countess Benzon (see p. 94), though there is no suggestion that the two achievements were related. In old age, Manzoni looked back on his winter in Venice with pleasure. He is said to have talked of the city to one Venetian lady with such vividness that she asked if he had been there recently. 'About sixty-seven years ago,' was the reply.[23]

From the left-hand side of the campo it is worth following the Calle del Dose down to the Grand Canal for the view it offers of the far bank, across to the low white stones of the Guggenheim Museum and the beautiful façade of the Palazzo Dario. Just to the left of this vantage point is the little Casetta Rossa, where Canova had his studio. Later it was the head-quarters of Gabriele d'Annunzio, who lived here during the First World War. Invisible from the fondamenta, it can be reached via an alley off the Calle del Dose; but the best view, as usual, is from the Grand Canal. Hemingway's Colonel takes it in on his way to the Gritti, accompanied by his army driver:

'Jackson,' he said, 'that small villa on the left belonged to Gabriele d'Annunzio, who was a great writer.'

'Yes, sir,' said Jackson, 'I'm glad to know about him. I never heard of him.'

'I'll check you out on what he wrote if you ever want to read him,' the Colonel said. 'There are some fair English translations.'

'Thank you, sir,' said Jackson. 'I'd like to read him any time I have time. He has a nice practical looking place. What did you say the name was?'

'D'Annunzio,' the Colonel said. 'Writer.'

He added to himself, not wishing to confuse Jackson, nor be difficult, as he had been with the man several times that day, writer, poet, national hero, phraser of the dialectic of Fascism, macabre egotist, aviator, com-mander, or rider, in the first of the fast torpedo attack boats, Lieutenant-Colonel of Infantry without knowing how to command a company, nor a platoon properly, the great, lovely writer of *Notturno* whom we respect, and jerk.[24]

## CALLE DEL SPEZIER

The street which leads from the Campo San Maurizio to the Campo San Stefano is one of a number in Venice called the Calle del Spezier. The name indicates that it was a street of *spezieri* or pharmacists. In ancient Venice pharmacy was a highly regarded craft whose practitioners had, among other privileges, the right to marry a Venetian noblewoman. From the Middle Ages the city was famous for its *triaca*, sometimes rather misleadingly translated as treacle. This was a concoction of aromatic herbs, amber, and other ingredients imported from the East, which was reckoned to be a cure for more or less anything. There was consternation when it failed to cope with the plague in the fourteenth century, but in spite of this its reputation continued to grow. In 1646 John Evelyn made sure to pack some along with his books, pictures, and Murano glass, before returning to England, and in our own times both H. V. Morton and James Morris have managed to purchase some from what must now be a greatly depleted stock.

The ceremony of preparing *triaca*, which Evelyn had gone to the trouble of observing, 'for tis extremely pompous & worth seeing', took place at specific times of the year. The drugs to be powdered were placed in a mortar outside the pharmacy, where men in a special costume and chanting a special refrain carried out the pounding. The Calle del Spezier still opens into the Campo San Stefano just beside a pharmacy, and in front of it can be seen a number of hollowed paving stones in which the bronze mortars were set.

## CAMPO SAN STEFANO: PALAZZO BARBARO

In earlier times the pharmacy on this corner of the spacious Campo San Stefano must have enjoyed a particularly lucrative trade. Like San Polo, the square was much used for public entertainments. It was here that the last Venetian bull-fight took place in 1802. A disaster in which one of the stands in front of the Palazzo Morosini collapsed, killing a number of spectators, hastened the end of the sport in Venice. As at San

Polo, this aspect of Venetian life was not always welcome to the clergy. On the church at the far end of the square another of the plaques prohibiting games can still be seen. The church itself is a handsome Gothic building which invites a visit. 'For sheer comfort and pleasure,' writes E. V. Lucas, 'I think that S. Stefano is the first church in Venice.' The burial place of the eighteenth-century composer Giovanni Gabrieli, it is a church that was once more notable for acts of desecration than of piety. Tassini tells us that between 1348 and 1594 it had to be reconsecrated six times because blood had been shed on its stones.

At the other end of the square the main thoroughfare takes us past the church of San Vitale to the Accademia bridge. But first walk down the little fondamenta to the left, which leads to the edge of the Palazzo Barbaro. A bell beside the door has the name Curtis inscribed on a stone inset. This is the family who have owned the palace since 1885. Amongst those who enjoyed their hospitality in the early years was Henry James. It was in the summer of 1887 that he first came here, in the course of an extended Italian tour following the publication of *The Princess Casamassima*. Fond as he was of Mrs Bronson, the accommodation she offered in the Palazzo Giustiniani-Recanati, where he had stayed earlier in the year, was not really to his taste. He felt that the damp winter air had combined with the 'insalubrious' apartment to give him an attack of jaundice, and he was grateful, when he came back in May, for the more lavish appointments of the Palazzo Barbaro. Later the kindness of the Curtis family was returned when their home became the Palazzo Leporelli in *The Wings of the Dove*. It was exactly what the dying heroine required:

'no dreadful, no vulgar hotel; but if it can at all be managed – you know what I mean – some fine old rooms, wholly independent, for a series of months. Plenty of them, too, and the more interesting the better: part of a palace, historic and picturesque, but strictly inodorous, where we shall be to ourselves, with a cook, don't you know? – with servants, frescoes, tapestries, antiquities, the thorough make-believe of a settlement.'[25]

Here, 'with the fine old faded palaces opposite and the slow Adriatic tide beneath', Milly Theale lives out the final weeks of her life. Sketching only the lightest details, as in the scene where Milly receives one of her suitors in the *sala*, James manages to suggest the outlines, clear and yet mysterious, of the classic Venetian fantasy: 'The casements between the arches were open, the ledge of the balcony broad, the sweep of the canal, so overhung, admirable, and the flutter towards them of the loose white curtain an invitation to she scarce knew what.'[26]

Looking back from the Accademia bridge, we have a fine view of the palace, just to the right of the Rio del'Orso – more delicate than its neighbour, crumbling a little above the water, with a charming balcony and round marble insets in red and green above the window arches.

## CALLE MALIPIERO

Instead of walking back through the Campo San Stefano, we can turn left immediately after the church of San Vitale and carry on until we pass under the sagging beams of the house across the end of the calle. Just beyond is the Calle Malipiero, a narrow street with windows heavily barred on the ground floor and shuttered above. On the lower stretches of the wall the plaster has flaked off to reveal the usual decomposing brickwork. Half-way down, there is a solitary shop that specializes in carnival masks – a lingering echo of the eighteenth-century world described by the modern historian and art critic Marcel Brion:

> The carnival opened, in fact, on the first Sunday in October and went on until Lent, with a short interval from Christmas Day till Epiphany. In other words, for six months every year the people abandoned their regular avocations, and, protected by the anonymity of the mask, threw themselves into the lighthearted pastimes which immediately became their main preoccupation. . . .

The mask most usually worn by ladies and gentlemen of rank was an extraordinary white face, adorned with a huge nose shaped like the beak of a bird of prey, through which the wearer breathed. When we come across the mask today in museums or collections of old customs, there seems to be something disconcerting, frightening, almost ghostly about it. For the 18th-century Venetians, however, it had the advantage of covering the face completely. Furthermore, it was always worn with a long black cloak which hid the entire body.[27]

That a carnival shop should survive here in the Calle Malipiero seems entirely appropriate when we read the plaque at the end of the street: it was in this calle that Giacomo Casanova was born on 2 April 1725. The church of San Samuele, which we have just reached, was where he was baptized.

## PALAZZO MOCENIGO

The district of San Samuele has more than its share of Venetian dead ends, some of them marvellously perverse, but if we leave the campo by the Calle delle Carrozze, with the campanile on our right, we can walk in a more or less straight line for about a hundred and fifty yards until we pass the Calle Mocenigo. At the end of this street are the four Palazzi Mocenigo, which can best be seen by standing at the vaporetto stop of San Tomà and looking across from the other side of the Grand Canal.

Of the four palaces the first (nearest St Mark's) was the one in which the philosopher Giordano Bruno was staying when he was arrested by agents of the Inquisition. He had come to Venice in the autumn of 1591 at the request of Giovanni Mocenigo, who wanted the sage to teach him 'the art of memory and invention'. At a time when religious orthodoxy was enforced by the rack, Bruno's journey to Italy was an act of extraordinary foolhardiness. Mocenigo gave him hospitality, listened to his teachings, and then betrayed him – constrained, he said, by a pious conscience and the urgings of his confessor. On the night of 22 May 1592 Bruno was taken from his bed and locked in a room of the palace until the following evening, when Mocenigo handed him over to the officers of the Inquisition. It took a long time to arrange his death. After eight years of imprisonment and cross-examination, he was finally consigned to the flames in the Campo de' Fiori in Rome on 17 February 1600.

The most imposing of the Mocenigo palaces is the third in line as one moves down the Grand Canal towards the station. Between the two windows on the right of the entrance a plaque records Lord Byron's residence here from 1818–19. The chaotic household in which he managed to write the first two cantos of *Don Juan* was the subject of numerous pages of contemporary gossip, and scenes from this period of his life have continued to mould our image of him: the restless, romantic figure staving off boredom with a string of mistresses, riding on the Lido, swimming the length of the Grand Canal, talking till dawn in the company of Shelley, prowling through the vast rooms of a palace inhabited by a shifting population of servants, acquaintances, hangers-on, and half-tamed animals. The author of *Childe Harold* was fast expending his youth. In an uncharitable moment Shelley wrote home to the novelist Thomas Love Peacock:

> The fact is, that first, the Italian women are perhaps the most contemptible of all who exist under the moon; the most ignorant, the most disgusting, the most bigotted, the most filthy. Countesses smell so of garlick that an ordinary Englishman cannot approach them. Well, L[ord] B[yron] is familiar with the lowest sort of these women, the people his gondolieri pick up in the streets. He allows fathers & mothers to bargain with him for their daughters, & though this is common enough in Italy, yet for an Englishman to encourage such sickening vice is a melancholy thing. He associates with wretches who seem almost to have lost the gait & phisiognomy of man, & who do not scruple to avow practices which are not only not named but I believe seldom even conceived in England. He says he disapproves, but he endures.[28]

The dominating presence of these years, apart from the poet himself, is that of the baker's wife Margharita Cogni, La Fornarina. She was tall and dark, with fine black eyes, 'a thorough Venetian in her dialect – in her thoughts – in her countenance – in every thing'.

Byron had met her in the summer of 1817 as he rode one evening along the banks of the Brenta. They soon came to an agreement:

> She said that she had no objection to make love with me – as she was married – and all married women did it – but that her husband (a baker) was somewhat ferocious – and would do her a mischief. – In short – in a few evenings we arranged our affairs – and for two years – in the course of which I had more women than I can count or recount – she was the only one who preserved over me an ascendancy – which was often disputed & never impaired. – As she herself used to say publicly – 'It don't matter – he may have five hundred – but he will always come back to me'.[29]

Of all the stories of La Fornarina's passion and violence, the most striking is Byron's image of her stormswept figure on the steps outside the Palazzo Mocenigo:

> In the autumn one day going to the Lido with my Gondoliers – we were overtaken by a heavy squall and the Gondola put in peril – hats blown away – boat filling – oar lost – tumbling sea – thunder – rain in torrents – night coming – & wind increasing. – On our return – after a tight struggle: I found her on the open steps of the Mocenigo palace on the Grand Canal – with her great black eyes flashing through her tears and the long dark hair which was streaming drenched with rain over her brows & breast; – she was perfectly exposed to the storm – and the wind blowing her hair & dress about her tall thin figure – and the lightning flashing round her – with the waves rolling at her feet – made her look like Medea alighted from her chariot – or the Sybil of the tempest that was rolling around her – the only living thing within hail

at that moment except ourselves. – On seeing me safe –
she did not wait to greet me as might be expected – but
calling out to me – 'Ah! Can' della Madonna xe esto il
tempo per andar' al Lido?' (ah! Dog of the Virgin! – is this
a time to go to Lido?) ran into the house – and solaced
herself with scolding the boatmen for not foreseeing the
'temporale'. – I was told by the servants that she had only
been prevented from coming in a boat to look after me –
by the refusal of all the Gondoliers of the Canal to put out
into the harbour in such a moment and that then she sate
down on the steps in all the thickest of the Squall – and
would neither be removed nor comforted. Her joy at
seeing me again – was moderately mixed with ferocity –
and gave me the idea of a tigress over her recovered
Cubs.[30]

Although Byron is the only British resident honoured with
a plaque, he was by no means the first to be associated with the
Palazzo Mocenigo, which had been the home in the early
seventeenth century of the formidable Alathea Talbot, Countess of Arundel. A hundred years later the palace was occupied
by another Englishwoman of similarly forceful character.
Lady Mary Wortley Montagu had come to Venice in the
summer of 1739. Famous as a traveller and an intellectual, she
was also famous, less happily, as the butt of some of Alexander
Pope's most vitriolic satire. Amicably separated from her
diplomat husband, she found in Venice an atmosphere of
tolerance which encouraged her to make it her home for two
extended periods over the next twenty years. The one perma-
nent vexation was the stream of brainless and boorish English
youths descending on Venice in the course of their Grand
Tour:

Here are inundations of them broke in upon us this
carnival, and my apartment must be their refuge, the
greater part of them having kept an inviolable fidelity to
the languages their nurses taught them. Their whole
business abroad (as far as I can perceive) being to buy new
cloaths, in which they shine in some obscure coffeehouse, where they are sure of meeting only one another;

and after the important conquest of some waiting gentle-
woman of an opera Queen, who perhaps they remember
as long as they live, return to England excellent judges of
men and manners.[31]

## CAMPO SANT' ANGELO

From the Calle Mocenigo we can make our way via the Piscina
San Samuele and the Campiello dei Morti (now tactfully
renamed Campiello Nuovo) to the Campo Sant'Angelo.
Lined with handsome palaces, the square is distinguished by
two well-heads, in one of which a widow's corpse was
discovered in the summer of 1716. Although it lies midway
between the Accademia and the Rialto, the Campo Sant'-
Angelo often seems curiously empty by comparison with
other large squares on the main city routes. It has few shops
and no large cafés. Especially at night, one's footsteps seem to
send back a lonelier echo than usual. The camp is not well lit
and the outline of the listing campanile of San Stefano makes a
strange presence behind the buildings of the square. It is a place
easy to people with figures from the past. In his early twenties,
when he was making a precarious living as a professional
musician, Casanova fell in with one of the rowdy gangs for
which Venice was famed:

> We often spent our nights roaming through different
> quarters of the city, thinking up the most scandalous
> practical jokes and putting them into execution. We
> amused ourselves by untying the gondolas moored be-
> fore private houses, which then drifted with the current to
> one side of the Grand Canal or the other, and making
> merry over the curses the gondoliers would call down
> on us the next morning when they did not find their
> gondolas where they had moored them.
> We often woke midwives and made them dress and go
> to deliver women who, when they arrived, called them
> fools. We did the same to the most celebrated physicians,
> whose slumbers we interrupted to send them to noble-
> men who, we told them, had suffered an apoplexy, and

we routed priests from their beds and packed them off to pray for the souls of people in perfect health who, we said, were at death's door.

In every street through which we passed we relentlessly cut the bell cord hanging at every door; and when we happened to find a door open because someone had forgotten to shut it, we groped our way up the stairs and terrified all the sleeping inmates by shouting at their bedroom doors that the street door of the house was open. And then we decamped, leaving the house door as open as we had found it.

One very dark night we decided to overturn a big marble table which was a sort of monument. The table stood almost in the middle of the Campo Sant'Angelo. In the days of the war which the Republic had fought against the League of Cambrai, so the story ran, it was on this big table that the commissaries had counted out their pay to the recruits who enrolled in the service of St Mark.[32]

The sort of practical joking that Casanova records was a common enough feature of eighteenth-century life, but in a Venice given over to carnival and pleasure-seeking it seems to have flourished with peculiar ferocity.

The building on the right as we enter the Campo Sant'-Angelo is the sixteenth-century cloister of San Stefano, now taken over by the Finance Offices. It is accustomed to such invasions. In the mid-nineteenth century, when W. D. Howells took to passing through the courtyard on his way to the American consulate, it was occupied by the engineer corps of the Austrian army. Today it can still be visited during office hours, but we shall look in vain for the frescos that excited Howells; the few surviving fragments have been removed to the Correr Museum:

> On one wall of this court are remains – very shadowy remains indeed – of frescos painted by Pordenone at the period of his fiercest rivalry with Titian; and it is said that Pordenone, while he wrought upon the scenes of scriptural story here represented, wore his sword and buckler, in readiness to repel an attack which he feared from his

competitor. The story . . . gave a singular relish to our
daily walk through the old cloister . . .[33]


PALAZZO BENZON

From the Campo Sant'Angelo another Calle del Spezier leads
towards the Campo Manin. Before long it meets on the right
the Rio Terrà degli Assassini, whose name carries its own
warning. This was one of the areas of twisting streets and dark
bridges where scores could be settled and unwary citizens
helped to another life. In earlier centuries one might well have
paused before crossing by night a bridge that had earned the
name Ponte degli Assassini.

On the left-hand side, the Rio Terrà della Mandola takes us
to the Fortuny Museum, once the home of Mariano Fortuny,
the Spanish painter and designer whose exotic gowns, 'faithfully antique but markedly original', evoked for Proust all that
was most gorgeous about the ancient city of the Doges. 'The
Fortuny gown which Albertine was wearing that evening,'
remarks Marcel in *La Prisonnière*, 'seemed to me the tempting
phantom of that invisible Venice.'[34]

Behind the palace, an alleyway off the Calle Pesaro leads
down to the Grand Canal beside the Palazzo Benzon. Like
most of the palaces on the Grand Canal, this needs to be seen
from the water. In its day it was a place of rendezvous for all
that was most fashionable in Venetian society. Under the sway
of the Countess Marina Querini-Benzon the salon which was
held here welcomed among others Manzoni, Stendhal, and
Byron. Byron, in particular. At a time when the Countess was
already sixty, she is said to have excited enough interest in the
poet for him to sustain a brief affair with her. Admittedly,
Byron conferred the same distinction on a number of other
women during his Venetian period – well over two hundred
by his own reckoning – but it was a game gesture on the part of
the Countess. She seems to have been an engaging figure –
talented, witty, kind-hearted. Ten years later, when Longfellow visited her salon, she was still receiving company every
evening from ten or eleven o'clock until three in the morning.

'The Venetian ladies are not handsome,' commented the poet,
'but they have a great deal of vivacity.'[35]


SAN LUCA

From the Calle Pesaro a tortuous couple of minutes' walk will
bring us round to the front of the unlovely cinema which now
stands on the site of the old Teatro di San Benedetto, once the
most important theatre in Venice. The iron bridge in front of
the cinema leads straight across to the church of San Luca. It
was here in 1556 that Pietro Aretino was buried. His tomb was
visited in the mid-seventeenth century by Sir John Reresby, a
young Royalist who was keeping a comfortable distance
between himself and the rigours of the Commonwealth by
means of a well-timed Continental tour:

> In the church of St Luke lies interred Peter Aretin, that
> obscene profane poet, with this epitaph, till the inquisi-
> tors took it away, '*Qui jace Aretin, poeta Tusco, qui dice mal
> d'ogni uno fuora di Dio; scusandosi dicendo, Io no'l cognosco*'
> ('Here Aretin, the Tuscan poet, lies, who all the world
> abused but God, and why? he said he knew him not.')[36]

It is slightly surprising to find Aretino in a church at all. Not
a man of devout life, he was said to have died from an apoplexy
brought on by laughing at an obscene joke about his sister.
After receiving extreme unction, he remarked with scant
piety: 'Now that I'm well greased, you'd better keep the rats
away.'

Of Italian writers associated with Venice Aretino is probably the most colourful. A native of Arezzo, he had been
driven from Rome after some unguarded sonnets had found
their way to a high Vatican official, who responded by trying
to have the poet assassinated. At Mantua his savage pen again
made life precarious, and in 1527 he turned to Venice. In its
more liberal atmosphere his writings could offend with relative impunity. By flattering some and wounding others he
managed to finance a life of prosperous debauchery, earning

the friendship of Titian and Sansovino along the way. His final years were spent on the nearby Riva del Carbon.

## CAMPO MANIN

For those who wish to pay homage to a rather different hero of Venice, we are now only a few yards from the Campo Manin, a pleasant square spoiled by the ugly façade of the Cassa di Risparmio, on which even the statue of Manin seems to have turned its back. (Banks have a lot to answer for in Venice, as anyone who has stumbled into the Campo San Gallo will know.) It seems hard that the man who fought to restore the Republic should have been saddled with this monstrosity.

In the years before the Revolution of 1848 Daniele Manin lived with his wife and daughter in a house overlooking this square, which was then called San Paternian. Only moderately successful as a lawyer, Manin was brought to prominence by his part in the struggle against Austrian domination. It was he who on 22 March 1848 jumped on to a café table in the Piazza to proclaim the restored Republic. For the seventeen desperate months that followed he led the city's fight to remain independent. In the end, the Austrian blockade was too effective. By the summer of 1849 food was so scarce that one observer could note women among the crowd in the Campo San Giovanni e Paolo tearing off earrings and wedding rings in a frantic attempt to buy bread. To starvation was added cholera. As the summer wore on, the collapse of the Republic became inevitable. Starved, diseased, bombarded, it survived until the end of August. Finally, on 28 August, Manin sailed into exile aboard the French ship which was to carry him and his wife to Marseilles. By the time they made port, his wife was dead. Manin was left to eke out the last eight years of his life in Paris, making a modest living as a teacher of Italian.

## TEATRO GOLDONI

The other side of the Cassa di Risparmio presents an altogether more acceptable face to the lively Campo San Luca. As we walk round into the square, we notice at once the change in tempo that marks the start of Venice's main commercial district. From the middle of the square a left turn beside another bank, followed by a right turn into the Calle del Teatro – opposite yet another bank – will take us to the steps of the Teatro Goldoni. In spite of the unattractive façade with which various changes and restorations have left it, the theatre has a venerable past. Built by the Vendramin family in the seventeenth century, it enjoyed the great age of Venetian theatre and is now one of the oldest surviving playhouses in the city. On 10 October 1786 it was visited by Goethe. The entry in his Journal shows how well he understood the basis of Goldoni's popularity:

> At last I have seen a real comedy! At the Teatro San Luca today they played *Le Baruffe Chiozzotte*, one of the few plays by Goldoni which is still performed. The title might be roughly translated as *The Scuffles and Brawls in Chioggia*. The characters are all natives of that town, fishermen and their wives, sisters and daughters. The habitual to-do made by these people, their quarrels, their outbursts of temper, their good nature, superficiality, wit, humour and natural behaviour – all these were excellently imitated. I was in Chioggia only yesterday, so their faces were still vivid in my mind's eye and their voices still ringing in my ears. . . .
> I have never in my life witnessed such an ecstasy of joy as that shown by the audience when they saw themselves and their families so realistically portrayed on the stage. They shouted with laughter and approval from beginning to end. [37]

## CAMPO SAN SALVADOR

From the Calle del Teatro it is only a step to the bustling Campo San Salvador, a favourite meeting-place in the evenings for Venetian teenagers. The church, which contains the tomb of Caterina Cornaro, Queen of Cyprus, is now as staid a place of worship as any in Venice – more so than most perhaps, since even Titian's superb *Annunciation* attracts only a modest flow of tourists – but like many such places it had a rather different reputation in the eighteenth century. Maurice Andrieux quotes one of the Inquisition spies, whose report is dated 28 June 1771: 'the church of San Salvatore is being defiled by the mixed crowds of women who go there, not to hear Mass, but to be seen and accosted. God-fearing persons frequently remark that this church has turned into a brothel.'[38]

A more conscientious tourist than most, L. P. Hartley's Eustace decides to make San Salvatore the subject of an experiment:

> Hitherto Eustace had been a systematic sight-seer, choosing his quarry beforehand and going straight to it. But privately he felt that this method was touristy and crude: as the book said, one should be a wanderer in Venice, one should drift, one should take the object of one's search by surprise, not antagonise it by a vulgar frontal attack. Left alone, not hunted and cornered, the church would just 'occur'; against shock-tactics it would surely erect all its defences and withhold its message. Eustace determined that his discovery of the church of San Salvatore, which housed two important Titians, should be utterly unpremeditated. He would just look round and find himself there, and the picture, surprised out of a day-dream, would tell him something it would never have told in answer to a direct question.[39]

Unfortunately, Eustace's knowledge of the streets of Venice is not up to taking churches by surprise and San Salvatore continues to guard its secret.

## Campo San Bartolomeo

Past the side-entrance of the church the crowded Merceria San Salvador leads up towards the Piazza. It is one of the group of streets which used to be the preserve of the haberdashers' shops, or *mercerie*. Their starting-point is a short way beyond

San Salvador at the Campo San Bartolomeo, which for the
past hundred years has been dominated by the bronze statue of
Carlo Goldoni. Erected in 1883, it was the occasion of an
unmemorable poem by Browning – one of the few that bears
directly on the city in which he passed his final days. It was to
this vivid, noisy square that W. D. Howells moved in March
1862, towards the end of his first winter in Venice.
Surrounded by the cages of screaming finches, canaries,
blackbirds, and parrots which hung from the neighbouring
balconies, he was well placed to observe the more raucous side
of Venetian life. Looking down from his window, he could
also turn his attention to the assorted figures gathered in the
square below,

> to the placid dandies about the door of the caffè; to the
> tide of passers from the Merceria; the smooth-shaven
> Venetians of other days, and the bearded Venetians of
> these; the dark-eyed, white-faced Venetian girls, hooped
> in cruel disproportion to the narrow streets, but richly
> clad, and moving with southern grace; the files of heavily
> burdened soldiers; the little policemen loitering lazily
> about with their swords at their sides, and in their spotless
> Austrian uniforms.[40]

The scene described by Howells barely hints at the under-
current of tension that pervaded Venetian social life during the
years of his residence there. In 1797 Venice had been handed
over to Austria by Napoleon. Apart from the events of 1848–9
and a ten year interval from 1805 to 1815, she had remained
under Austrian domination ever since. The result was an
abiding hostility that expressed itself in continual acts of petty
tyranny by the Austrians and an unrelenting show of resent-
ment by the Italians. This incident, recalled by George Sand, is
perhaps not entirely typical either in the nature of the offence
or in its comparatively happy ending, but it conveys the bitter
tone of relations between the two communities:

> One evening when I was in the gondola moored at a jetty,
> waiting while my old boatman brought back something
> or other that I had told him to go and fetch, I heard the

sound of the *felze*, that is to say the cabin of the gondola, being sprinkled by a passer-by whom I supposed to be either drunk or distracted.

Since the shutters were closed, I had nothing to fear from this unseemly aspersion. Then I heard the hoarse voice of Catulle calling out:

'*Porco di Tedesco!* so you think you can pollute my gondola! Do you take it for a lamppost?'

'Know,' replied the other in bad Italian, 'that I am an officer in the service of His Austrian Majesty, and that I have a perfect right to piss on your gondola if I so choose.'

'But there is a lady in my gondola!' cried the gondolier.

Then the Austrian officer, who was not drunk at all, came to open the door of the *felze*, and, looking at me, said:

'The signora has had the *gentilezza e la prudenza* to keep quiet: she has done well. As for you, tomorrow you will go to prison, and you are very lucky that I don't run my sword through your body.'

And poor Catulle really would have been in prison if I had not interceded for him, saying that he was tipsy and seeming to take as an honour what the Austrian had deigned to let fall on my gondola.[41]

As it happens, the Campo San Bartolomeo was itself the scene of one of the last despairing acts of revolt against the surrender of the Republic to Napoleon. On the night of 12/13 May 1797 outraged Venetians rampaged through the streets intent on sacking the houses of those who were felt to have betrayed the Republic. The riot gained strength, and a local commander moved up artillery to the top of the Rialto bridge. As the crowd surged past the church of San Bartolomeo, a blast from the guns reduced the last Republicans to a bloody scattering of limbs along the Salizzada. As Giuseppe Tassini puts it, in a pardonable flight of rhetoric: 'Fatal destiny that the cannon of St Mark should loose their thunder for the last time not against the enemies of Venice but against her sons.'[42]

## MERCERIE

The streets which lead from the Campo San Bartolomeo back to San Marco are among the busiest in Venice, and have been for centuries. In 1645 John Evelyn was entranced by the luxury and colour of their display. He had reached Venice in high summer, just half way through the long continental tour that was to keep him out of England for most of the decade. He could not have timed it more adroitly. From the savageries of a country laid waste by Civil War he had escaped to something infinitely more congenial:

> Hence I pass'd through the *Merceria*, which I take to be the most delicious streete in the World for the sweetnesse of it, being all the way on both sides, continualy tapissry'd as it were, with Cloth of Gold, rich Damasks & other silks, which the shops expose & hang before their houses from the first floore, & with that variety, that for neere half the yeare, which I spent chiefly in this citty, I hardly remember to have seene the same piece twice exposd, to this add the perfumers & Apothecaries shops, and the innumerable cages of Nightingals, which they keepe, that entertaines you with their melody from shop to shop, so as shutting your Eyes, you would imagine your selfe in the Country, when indeede you are in the middle of the Sea. [43]

Thirty years after Evelyn's visit the Mercerie acquired even greater prestige when they became the first streets in the city to be paved in stone. Looking back to the Venice of his youth, Goldoni writes nostalgically in his memoirs of the flags outside the haberdashers' shops, chiselled to prevent customers slipping in the wet.

At a busy intersection just short of St Mark's stands the sixteenth-century church of San Giuliano, notable as the only church in Venice which can be walked all the way round. It was rebuilt at the expense of a scholar and physician called Tommaso Rangone, partly to the glory of God, partly to the glory of himself. He seems to have had little sympathy with the Venetian ethic of anonymity; above the main door, in much the place where one might expect an image of the

Redeemer, sits a handsome statue of him by Sansovino, surrounded by symbols of his scientific and literary achievements. The church was later the scene of his funeral, an elaborate affair in which a train of precious items was borne in the wake of his coffin, including all the books he had written, open at pages specified by him in advance. To ensure the right tone, he also stipulated what clothes his librarian should wear for the occasion. He had a long life, but not, perhaps, as long as he expected; his main professional claim was to teach people to live to the age of 120.

Just before reaching the arch of the clock tower, we pass on the right the Sottoportico del Cappello, now the entrance to a glass factory. Above it is a relief of the old woman who was credited with frustrating the revolt of Baiamonte Tiepolo in 1310. Coryate politely calls her a maid and explains that she happened to be using a pestle and mortar at the time when the rebel forces reached the edge of the Piazza. As she looked out of the window to see what was happening,

> her pestell which she then held in her hand, not intending any hurt with it, fell casually much against her will upon the head of the Ring-leader of this company, which strooke out his braines, and so by that dismall chance hee died in the place, being defeated of the effect of his project, for the execution whereof he assembled so many armed men . . .[44]

At the time of Coryate's visit tourists were still being shown the window from which the pestle fell; but the story had already drifted clear of reality. It was not Baiamonte whom the old woman killed but his standard-bearer, and she herself, according to other versions, was less undesigning than Coryate suggests. Certainly, she was treated as a heroine by the Republic. In recompense she asked that her rent should never be raised and that on feast days she should be granted permission to hang from her window the standard of St Mark. In his history of Venice John Julius Norwich notes that a century and a half later one of the old woman's descendants was still able to make a successful appeal against any increase in the rent.

## CAMPO SAN GALLO

Before retiring to a café, there is one more place to visit – a penance, this time, rather than a pleasure. The easiest way to reach it, tucked away behind the Procuratie Vecchie, is to enter the Piazza, walk along the arcade, then leave again by the sottoportico beside the Olivetti showroom. The street this takes us down is named after the *cavalletto* where horses were stabled in the fourteenth century for hire by visitors to the city. At the end of it is what remains of the Campo San Gallo. This charmless little spot is one of Venice's disaster stories. The shabby cinema, now being renovated, is of minor importance. What destroyed the square was the absurd pair of banks, heavy, humourless and quite alien to the spirit of Venetian architecture. The house where Canova died was an incidental casualty of this sad fiasco.

For an image of the life and colour that have been lost we can turn to Théophile Gautier. It was here that on a summer evening in 1850 he and his Italian mistress came to dine at a small German restaurant:

> We had our meal in the open air, under an awning of white and saffron stripes, side by side with French painters, German artists and Austrian officers. . . .
>
> In the middle of the campo was a well-head where the women of the neighbourhood and the water-carriers came at certain hours to draw water. At the far end stood a small church emblazoned with the arms of the Patriarch of Venice, and from its doorway, closed off by a red curtain, came a vague odour of incense and the sound of prayers and organ music – the one mingling with the kitchen smells of the restaurant, the other with the discussions of art and philosophy. . . .
>
> Bare-headed girls with strikingly coloured shawls went by, a fan in their hand and a smile on their lips, pushing back the flounces of their dresses with a delicate foot. Instead of going into the church, they took the little alley which leads from the Campo San Gallo to the Piazza. They will go into the church later, when there is

no one else for them to love but God – that final object of a woman's passion.[45]

Before we return to the Piazza, a last, short detour will take us to the Ponte dei Fuseri, where a plaque indicates the palace in which Goethe stayed from 28 September to 14 October 1786. He had come to Venice at the start of the great Italian journey which was to change both his life and his thought. His arrival is marked in the journal by a sigh of relief: 'So now, thank God, Venice is no longer a mere word to me, an empty name . . .'[46] It is, in its way, a striking tribute. How many other famous cities can match the fantasies their names evoke?

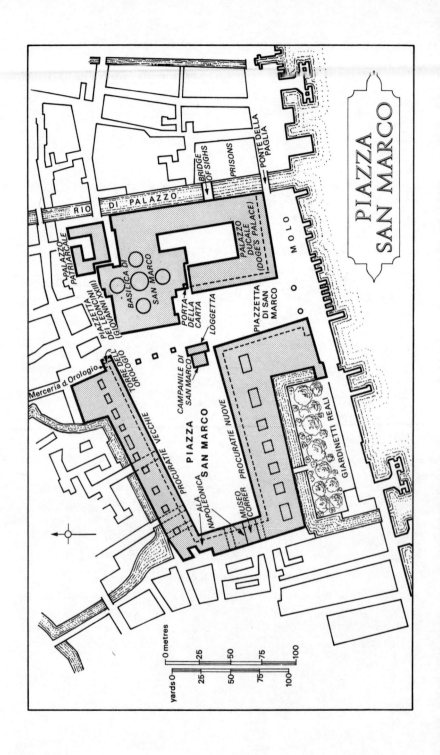

PIAZZA SAN MARCO

PALAZZO PATRIARCALE

RIO DI PALAZZO

BRIDGE OF SIGHS

PRISONS

PONTE DELLA PAGLIA

BASILICA DI SAN MARCO

PIAZZETTA DEI LEONCINI (GIOVANNI XXIII)

PORTA DELLA CARTA

LOGGETTA

PALAZZO DUCALE (DOGE'S PALACE)

MOLO

PIAZZETTA DI SAN MARCO

Merceria d. Orologio

TORRE DELL' OROLOGIO

CAMPANILE DI SAN MARCO

PROCURATIE VECCHIE

PIAZZA SAN MARCO

PROCURATIE NUOVE

ALA NAPOLEONICA

MUSEO CORRER

GIARDINETTI REALI

0 metres    25    50    75    100

yards 0    25    50    75    100

# 4

# PIAZZA SAN MARCO

*Piazza—Florian's—St Mark's—The Clock*
*Tower—Campanile—Piazzetta—The Doge's*
*Palace—The Bridge of Sighs—The Piombi—*
*The Pozzi—Broglio*

## PIAZZA

The more celebrated the place, the less interesting is likely to
be the traveller's description of it. Tedious accounts of the
wonders of St Mark's Square would comfortably fill a volume
of their own. Even the most evocative writing dwindles to
banality beside the fabulous images with which the reader's
mind is already stocked. And in turn the fabulous images pale
before the reality. 'Indeed,' writes Max Beerbohm, 'I should
not envy the soul of one who at first sight of such strange
loveliness found anything to say.' But in a sceptical world, he
adds, some evidence of love is demanded:

> Well, then, for me the church has hardly the effect of a
> building; of a garden, rather; an Eastern garden that had
> been by some Christian miracle petrified just when the
> flowers were fading, so that its beauty should last forever
> to the glory of Christ, and of S. Mark. But Mohammed
> had walked there, and his spirit haunts it yet, ranging
> from dome to dome, from cornice to cornice, unafraid of
> the Saint's own lion which, haloed, mounts golden guard
> in the midst, against a starred blue background; and one

almost wonders that among those stars no crescent is
gleaming.[1]

For upwards of three centuries it has been impossible to
write of the Piazza without a consciousness of all that has been
written of it before. It is one of the attractions of Coryate's
*Crudities* that he writes with a vivid conviction of telling things
for the first time. The Piazza is 'the fairest place of all the
citie':

> Truely such is the stupendious (to use a strange Epitheton
> for so strange and rare a place as this) glory of it, that at
> my first entrance thereof it did even amaze or rather
> ravish my senses. For here is the greatest magnificence of
> architecture to be seene, that any place under the sunne
> doth yeelde. Here you may both see all manner of
> fashions of attire, and heare all the languages of Christen-
> dome, besides those that are spoken by the barbarous
> Ethnickes; the frequencie of people being so great twise a
> day, betwixt sixe of the clocke in the afternoone and eight,
> that (as an elegant writer saith of it) a man may very
> properly call it rather Orbis than Urbis forum, that is a
> market place of the world, not of the citie.[2]

The exciting confusion of races was something later
travellers continued to remark upon. When Effie Ruskin,
newly married, reached Venice in 1849, it was still a noticeable
feature of the Piazza. Her wide-eyed delight in the scene
provides an appealing link with Coryate across the centuries of
more self-conscious observers. She wrote to her mother on 13
November, a few days after she and Ruskin had arrived:

> The place is like a vast drawing room lighted enough by
> the gas from the arcades all round the square under which
> sit all the Ladies & gentlemen at their coffee, iced water
> and cigars with a dense crowd in the centre of men,
> women, children, soldiers, Turks, magnificent Greek
> costumes and sky above studded with innumerable
> twinkling stars. I was walking there with John last night
> till past eight without any bonnet but my hair dressed –
> walking about like all the rest amongst the crowd, taking

our coffee under the Arcade and enjoying ourselves extremely.[3]

Her enthusiasm was perhaps a little unguarded. Before the end of the month an anxious letter had arrived from Ruskin's father warning against the possible impropriety of walking in public without a bonnet. Effie's first impressions had been anticipated by Napoleon, who called the Piazza 'the finest drawing room in Europe'. The same image reappears as a passing reference in Henry James's novel *The Princess Casamassima*, but for a more detailed picture we can turn to one of his slightly later books. The complacent narrator of *The Aspern Papers* makes a habit of repairing to the Piazza in the early evening:

> I sat in front of Florian's *café*, eating ices, listening to music, talking with acquaintances: the traveller will remember how the immense cluster of tables and little chairs stretches like a promontory into the smooth lake of the Piazza. The whole place, of a summer's evening, under the stars and with all the lamps, all the voices and light footsteps on the marble (the only sounds of the arcades that enclose it), is like an open-air saloon dedicated to cooling drinks and to a still finer degustation – that of the exquisite impressions received during the day. When I did not prefer to keep mine to myself there was always a stray tourist, disencumbered of his Bädeker, to discuss them with, or some domesticated painter rejoicing in the return of the season of strong effects. The wonderful church, with its low domes and bristling embroideries, the mystery of its mosaic and sculpture, looked ghostly in the tempered gloom, and the sea-breeze passed between the twin columns of the Piazzetta, the lintels of a door no longer guarded, as gently as if a rich curtain were swaying there.[4]

## FLORIAN'S

In books it is always Florian's that people choose – reasonably enough. E. V. Lucas quotes an advertisement for the café in

the Piazza musical programme just before the First World
War: 'the oldest and most aristocratic establishment of its kind
in Venice, it can count among its clients, since 1720, Byron,
Goethe, Rousseau, Canova, Dumas, and Moor', the last of
these apparently referring to the Moore who was Byron's
friend and biographer.

Coffee had first been brought to the attention of the
Venetians in 1585 when Gianfrancesco Morosini, who was
*bailo* in Constantinople, reported to the Senate that the Turks
were accustomed to drink 'a black water, boiled up as hot as
they can bear it, which is distilled from a seed they call *kahvé*
and which they say has the property of making a man stay
awake'. By the middle of the next century coffee was on sale in
Venice as a medicine. Its popularity increased, imports rose,
and in 1683 the first coffee shop opened under the Procuratie
Nuove, where Florian's still sets out its tables. 'The arcade
outside Florian's,' remarks Murray in 1877, 'is the rendezvous
of the Venetian *beau monde* in the warm summer evenings,
when the military band plays'. Even during the period of
Austrian occupation the café retained its dignity. While
Quadri's, patronized by the Austrians, was shunned by good
Venetians, Florian's managed to establish itself as neutral
ground where it was acceptable for either nationality to be
seen.

In 1850, sixteen years before the end of the Austrian occupation, Théophile Gautier describes how the upper-class
Venetian women are occasionally tempted as far as Florian's
on days of unusual mildness. In general, he says, they are
reluctant to risk themselves out of doors:

If there is one thing in the world that is unashamedly
indolent and lazy, it is the Venetian women of the upper
classes. The use of the gondola has made them un-
accustomed to walking. They scarcely know how to put
one foot in front of the other. For them to risk themselves
out of doors requires a rare conjunction of atmospheric
circumstances, even in this mild and gentle climate. The
sirocco, the sun, a cloud that threatens rain, too cool a
breeze from the sea – any of these is reason enough for

them to stay at home. The most trifling thing prostrates them, the most trifling thing fatigues them, and their greatest exercise is to go to the couch on their balcony and inhale the scent of one of the large flowers which bloom so well in the warm, humid air of Venice. This untroubled and secluded life gives them an immaculate and unvarnished pallor, an incredible delicacy of complexion.

When, by chance, there is the sort of exceptional weather we call in France *temps de demoiselle*, some of them take two or three turns round the Piazza at the time when the military band is playing its evening symphony, then settle down for a long rest outside Florian's with a glass of water turned opal in colour by a drop of aniseed, accompanied by their husbands, brothers or *cavalieri serventi*.[5]

For us, too, Florian's is a convenient place from which to survey the Piazza. Rhapsodies about churches, even about a church as fantastic as St Mark's, tend to be peculiarly indigestible. More appealing than Ruskin's description of the magnificence of the basilica's exterior is his mordant paragraph on the indifference to it of the local populace:

And what effect has this splendour on those who pass beneath it? You may walk from sunrise to sunset, to and fro, before the gateway of St Mark's, and you will not see an eye lifted to it, not a countenance brightened by it. Priest and layman, soldier and civilian, rich and poor, pass by it alike regardlessly. Up to the very recesses of the porches, the meanest tradesmen of the city push their counters; nay, the foundations of its pillars are themselves the seats – not 'of them that sell doves' for sacrifice, but of the vendors of toys and caricatures. Round the whole square in front of the church there is almost a continuous line of cafés, where the idle Venetians of the middle classes lounge, and read empty journals; in its centre the Austrian bands play during the time of vespers, their martial music jarring with the organ notes, – the march drowning the miserere, and the sullen crowd thickening round them, – a crowd, which, if it had its will, would

stiletto every soldier that pipes to it. And in the recesses of
the porches, all day long, knots of men of the lowest
classes, unemployed and listless, lie basking in the sun like
lizards; and unregarded children – every heavy glance of
their young eyes full of desperation and stony depravity,
and their throats hoarse with cursing, – gamble, and
fight, and snarl, and sleep, hour after hour, clashing their
bruised centesimi upon the marble ledges of the church
porch. And the images of Christ and His angels look
down upon it continually.[6]

Popular indifference could pose a threat that was physical as
well as moral. E. V. Lucas describes how in 1889 his guide
casually chipped off a few pieces of mosaic with his knife to sell
to tourists.

They do things differently today. Nonetheless, Ruskin's
diatribe would only need up-dating. Many years later he
himself added a tart footnote about the way his writings had
been received. It provides a sardonic cameo of Victorian
travellers in Venice, who have paid no attention to what he
said but have admired his manner of saying it:

and, as far as they found the things I spoke of amusing to
themselves, they have deigned for a couple of days or so
to look at them, – helped always through the tedium of
the business by due quantity of ices at Florian's, music by
moonlight on the Grand Canal, paper lamps and the
English papers and magazines at M. Ongania's, with such
illumination as those New Lamps contain – Lunar or
Gaseous, enabling pursy Britannia to compare, at her
ease, her own culminating and co-operate Prosperity and
Virtue with the past wickedness and present out-of-
pocketness of the umquhile Queen of the Sea.[7]

And yet if we try to think of the basilica on a summer
afternoon without its milling tourists and local hucksters, does
it gain or lose? To have the Parthenon to ourselves or Chartres
cathedral or the Taj Mahal would be an imaginative luxury;
but St Mark's is different. The French novelist Michel Butor
has pointed out that while many ancient monuments seem

profaned by the rout of tourists who fall upon them, these same tourists are as necessary to the façade of St Mark's as water is to the façades of the city's palaces:

> The basilica, like the city around it, has nothing to fear from this fauna or from our own frivolity; it was born under the perpetual gaze of the visitor, and so it has continued. Its artists have worked amid the chatter of sailors and merchants. Since the beginning of the 13th century, this façade has been a shop window, a show case for antiques. The shops under the arcades are in reality a continuation of it.[8]

## St Mark's

By a happy chance the one original mosaic that has survived in the five arches over the doorways of St Mark's is a thirteenth-century portrayal of the translation of the body of the saint himself to the basilica. In the early days of Venice the city's patron saint was St Theodore. His displacement by St Mark was the result of an enterprising piece of theft in the ninth century. Augustus Hare tells the traditional story:

> The translation of the body of S. Mark to Venice is said to have been caused by the rapacity of the King of Alexandria, who plundered the church where he was enshrined in that city to adorn his own palace. Two Venetian sea-captains who were then at Alexandria implored to be allowed to remove the relics of the saint to a place of safety, and at last the priests, fearful of further desecration, consented. 'They placed the corpse in a large basket covered with herbs and swine's flesh which the Mussulmans hold in horror, and the bearers were directed to cry Khwazir (pork), to all who should ask questions or approach to search. In this manner they reached the vessel. The body was enveloped in the sails, and suspended to the mainmast till the moment of departure, for it was necessary to conceal this precious booty from those who might come to clear the vessel in the roads. At last

the Venetians quitted the shore full of joy. They were hardly in the open sea when a great storm arose. We are assured that S. Mark then appeared to the captain and warned him to strike all his sails immediately, lest the ship, driven before the wind, should be wrecked upon hidden rocks. They owed their safety to this miracle.'⁹

It seems unlikely that the two sea-captains were as disinterested as this makes them sound. Legend had long ago given Venice a stake in St Mark, since the Evangelist had stopped at the site of the unborn city on his way back from Aquileia to Rome and been visited at the time by an angel who greeted him with the words, *Pax tibi, Marce evangelista meus. Hic requiescet corpus tuum.*' This was not the sort of prediction that the predatory Venetians were inclined to leave unfulfilled. St Theodore, for all his virtues – and he can still be seen with his crocodile on one of the columns of the Piazzetta – was scarcely a first-class saint, and Venice deserved nothing less.

In the vestibule of the church Thomas Mowbray, Duke of Norfolk, was buried after he had died in Venice in 1399. This is the same Mowbray whose quarrel with Bolingbroke and subsequent banishment by Richard II were dramatized in Shakespeare's play:

> The sly slow hours shall not determinate
> The dateless limit of thy dear exile;
> The hopeless words of 'never to return'
> Breathe I against thee, upon pain of life.

Bolingbroke later returned to depose Richard and become Henry IV. Mowbray lived less than a year in exile before he died of the plague here in Venice at the end of a pilgrimage to the Holy Land. In the sixteenth century his descendants retrieved his ashes and brought them back to rest in England.

The shadowy interior of the church, over-arched by gold mosaics, is a haunting place, especially in winter, when the crowd of tourists thins and the smoking candles light obscure corners with a flickering glow. But the connoisseur of such things might try to catch St Mark's on an afternoon in late summer at the moment suggested by Théophile Gautier:

At certain hours, when the shadows thicken and the sun only casts one ray of light obliquely under the vaults of the cupolas, strange effects rise for the eye of the poet and visionary. Brazen lightnings flash suddenly from the golden backgrounds. Little cubes of crystal gleam here and there like the sunlit sea: the outlines of the figures tremble in their golden field; the silhouettes which were just before so clearly marked become troubled and mingled to the eye. The harsh folds on the dalmatics seem to soften and take movement; mysterious life glides into these motionless Byzantine figures; fixed eyes turn, arms with Egyptian hieratic gestures move, sealed feet begin to walk; the eight wings of cherubim revolve like wheels; the angels unfold the long wings of azure and purple which an implacable mosaic holds to the wall . . .[10]

A strange sight to see the youthful saints smiling with their porphyry lips. The effect, says Gautier, is of a cathedral that 'seems as if it belonged to a pre-Christian Christianity, to a Church founded before religion existed'.

Before we begin, in Beckford's words, to pry about the great church of St Mark, it is worth pausing at the door to look back at the mosaic of the Apocalypse above the main entrance. It seems that while working on this mosaic in 1563 the Zuccato brothers had in places simplified their task by using paint. The enmity of a fellow mosaic worker revealed this to the Procurators and an inspection was held in which Titian, Tintoretto, and Veronese all took part. In spite of the committee's praise for the quality of the mosaic, the charge was proved. Francesco Zuccato was temporarily deprived of his salary and ordered to rework the painted areas at his own expense. It was on this episode that George Sand based her novel *Les maîtres mosaïstes*.

On the right-hand side of the church, as one looks towards the altar, is the baptistery, containing the tomb of Andrea Dandolo (1354), which E. V. Lucas thought 'one of the most beautiful things in Venice'. It is, writes Ruskin, 'like a narrow couch set beside the window, low-roofed and curtained, so that it might seem, but that it is some height above the pavement, to have been drawn towards the window, that the sleeper might be wakened early.'[11] Dandolo was the last of the Doges to be buried in St Mark's, and it is to him that we owe an early history of Venice in Latin, the *Chronicon Venetum*.

Readers of Proust will already have turned their attention to the baptistery floor. It was the precise sensation of standing on two of its uneven stones that held the key to all the images of Venice which his narrator, Marcel, had tried vainly to recapture. Years later, in a moment of deep depression, Marcel stumbles one afternoon in the entrance-way to the Hôtel de Guermantes. The sensation of the uneven paving-stones, suddenly repeated, unlocks this fragment of his past, and the whole of Venice comes back to him. It brings a rush of happiness more vivid than any effort of memory, restoring his faith in the literary task that was to become *À la recherche du temps perdu*.

Just beyond the baptistery is the basilica's Treasury, which at the end of the sixteenth century contained three unicorn horns, now lost. Visiting the Treasury some fifty years later, John Evelyn mentions only two, but his attitude to the relics was casual. He seems little moved by the 'divers heads of Saints, inchas'd in Gold' that were shown him by favour of the French ambassador, and his list of subordinate relics is unceremonious:

> Also a small Ampulla or glasse of B: Saviou[r]s blood, as they fancy: A greate morcell of the real Crosse, one of the nailes, a Thorne, a fragment of the Column to which our Lord was bound, when Scourged: The Labbarum or Ensigne of victorious *Constantine*, a piece of St *Lukes* arme, a rib of St *Stephen*, a finger of Mary Magdalene & a world of Reliques I could not remember.[12]

In a sceptical age, when lesser churches are sometimes diffident about their relics, St Mark's until recently displayed a satisfying range of venerable objects. This is no longer the case, and when the Sanctuary reopens after its renovation, it will probably be purged of even more of its riches.

The sacristy is difficult to get into, but we can at least, by paying to have a look at the Pala d'Oro, see Sansovino's door to it in the left-hand niche of the apse. Around the frame are bronze reliefs of Sansovino himself, Titian, and Aretino. Aretino is at the top right with prominent nose and flowing beard, Titian opposite and Sansovino below him.

The most exciting view of the interior of the church, and certainly of its mosaics, is to be had from the gallery, which also gives access to the Loggia. The prospect is splendid, but the bronze horses, replaced by replicas, have now been withdrawn to a display room inside. Those who touched the originals – 'so set,' Moryson tells us, 'as if at the first step they would leape into the market place' – will be conscious of a pang of disappointment.

Looking out across the Piazza, we share the view with a fair number of pigeons as well as with other tourists. In recent years few people have had much to say for these well-fed birds. Oscar Wilde's Dorian Gray was an exception. Stretched on his sofa, he reads some lines of Gautier and thinks back to his stay in Venice: 'The sudden flashes of colour reminded him of the gleam of the opal-and-iris-throated birds that flutter round the tall honeycombed Campanile, or stalk, with such stately grace, through the dim, dust-stained arcades.'[13]

According to tradition, it was from the gallery where we are standing that the original pigeons were released on Palm Sunday, weighted by pieces of paper tied to their legs. Most of them ended up on the dinner table as part of the Doge's Easter largesse to the populace, but the rugged survivors were felt to have earned St Mark's protection. So year by year a few more pigeons found refuge among the domes of the basilica. They have since grown numerous, and the enthusiasm of most tourists for the birds is short-lived, but as the average visitor now spends less than twenty-four hours in the city they still have plenty of friends. James Morris quotes an early Baedeker which makes little effort to conceal its distaste for the pigeon-fanciers: 'those whose ambitions lean in that direction,' it remarks, 'may have themselves photographed covered with the birds.' Even before the age of photographs, the pigeons were a popular diversion. In 1851 Elizabeth Barrett Browning, in Venice with Robert, describes their son in a letter to her sister: 'He has made friends with the "holy pigeons", & they were surrounding him like a cloud today for the sake of his piece of bread . . . he stamping & crying out for rapture in the grand piazza.'[14]


## THE CLOCK TOWER

The northern end of the Loggia offers an excellent view of the clock tower, which was built at the end of the fifteenth century. By the time Thomas Coryate came to Venice in 1608, the dangers of its spectacular system of striking the hours should have been better appreciated than they were. After a brief description of the clock, Coryate goes on:

At which clocke there fell out a very tragicall and rufull accident on the twenty fifth day of July being munday about nine of the clocke in the morning, which was this. A certaine fellow that had the charge to looke to the clocke, was very busie about the bell, according to his usual custome every day, to the end to amend something in it that was amisse. But in the meane time one of those wilde men that at the quarters of the howers doe use to strike the bell, strooke the man in the head with his brazen hammer, giving him such a violent blow, that therewith he fel down dead presently in the place, and never spake more. Surely I will not justifie this for an undoubted truth, because I saw it not. For I was at that time in the Dukes Palace observing of matters: but as soone as I came forth some of my country-men that tolde me they saw the matter with there owne eies, reported it unto me, and advised me to mention it in my journall for a most lamentable chance.[15]

True or not, the incident found its way into popular legend. Forty years later Evelyn reports talking to 'an honest merchant' who also claimed to have witnessed the event.

Along the south side of the piazza run the Procuratie Nuove. Once the residence of the procurators of St Mark, later a palace for Napoleon, they now house the rooms of the Correr Museum. (Those who have shivered round this intriguing museum in winter-time should note that its attractions now include a modern central heating system.) To give an idea of the museum's range, it is enough to say that it exhibits items as diverse as Jacopo de Barbari's map of Venice, Canova's *Daedalus and Icarus*, Giuliana di Collalto's sarcophagus (see p. 210), a brocaded ducal cap dating from the fifteenth century, a wide range of coins, including a zecchino with the portrait of Marin Falier, sundry lions of St Mark, and a signboard of the Barbers' Guild. All this without entering the fine picture gallery, where among the madonnas and saints Carpaccio's two Venetian women sit staring with terrible weariness from their balcony. It is a museum that well repays a visit.

## CAMPANILE

Rising beside the windows at the far end of the museum is the massive structure of the campanile. For as long as tourists have visited Venice, they have been recommending what Coryate called 'the fairest and goodliest prospect that is (I thinke) in all the world'. It was here that Galileo demonstrated his telescope to the Doge and Goethe first saw the sea. Convinced, like William Beckford, that the campanile would outlast every other monument in the Piazza, the tourists continued to climb its ramps and wonder at the view – until one summer's morning in 1902. A brief dispatch from Reuters, dated VENICE, 14 July (10.40 AM) carried the news:

> The Campanile of St. Mark's Cathedral, 98 metres high (about 318 feet), has just fallen down on to the Piazza.
>
> It collapsed where it stood, and is now a heap of ruins.
>
> The cathedral and the Doge's Palace are quite safe. Only a corner of the royal palace is damaged.
>
> It is believed, but it is not certain, that there has been no loss of life.
>
> A cordon of troops is keeping the Piazza clear.

The circumstances of the collapse were described in *The Times* a few days later when a reader sent in the account

received by him from an American architect who had been
there at the time:

> Workmen had been repointing the Campanile, and had
> discovered a bad crack starting from the crown of the
> second arched window on the corner towards St Mark's,
> and extending through the sixth window. This crack had
> shown signs of opening further, and they feared small
> fragments falling on the crowded Piazza; so the music was
> quietly stopped in the hope that the crowd would natu-
> rally disperse. The effect was exactly the opposite of that
> desired. Every one rushed to the Piazza. At eleven I was
> under the tower which rose in the dim moonlight. The
> crack was distinctly visible even in this half light, but
> apparently menaced only a corner of the tower. On
> Monday, early, the Campanile was resplendent in the
> sunshine. At nine my little girl Katharine went off with
> her horns of corn to feed the pigeons. Mrs – was at St
> Laccana, and I was near the Rialto sketching. The golden
> Angel on the tower was shining far away. Suddenly I saw
> it slowly sink directly downward behind a line of roofs,
> and a dense grey dust rose in clouds. At once a crowd of
> people began running across the Rialto towards the
> Piazza, and I ordered my gondolier to the Piazzetta. On
> arrival the sight was pitiful. Of that splendid shaft all that
> remained was a mound of white dust, spreading to the
> walls of St Mark's.[16]

The campanile is not the sort of thing that can be knocked
down to suit an architectural fancy, but when it had fallen of its
own accord it is questionable whether the Venetians need have
been quite so keen to rebuild it. Osbert Sitwell was one of
many who had reservations. Writing of a winter visit to
Venice, he remarks:

> The blue sky seemed very pale and far off. Above, the sun
> flashed its wings on the golden triangular edgings of the
> Campanile, but only succeeded in emphasizing the dis-
> crepancy between the magnificence of the top of it and the
> square, brick-built tower itself. It was impossible, I

found, not to regret this one piece of common sense in an otherwise magical world: especially since I could remember the square in a much rarer condition, when, as I now know, it was more beautiful than it is at present or had been during a thousand years. For at the time of my first visit to Venice, the Campanile was then in process of being rebuilt, and stood no higher than St Mark's Library.[17]

The bells of the reconstructed campanile play little part in the daily life of the city, but this was not always the case. There were five in all, each with a distinct function described by Horatio Brown:

The *Marangona* was the great bell of the city marking the main moments of the day; it rang at sunrise, at *Ave Maria* for the cessation of work, and at midnight. The *Trottiera* summoned the senate to its sittings; the *Ringhiera* tolled for those about to die by the hand of justice. The *Mezza Terza* and the *Nona* announced other important hours; the *Nona*, for example, rang midday. All these bells were rung either by hammer in the bell-chamber or by rope from the base of the Campanile. The holes through which the bell-ropes passed were coated with thick bottle-glass to diminish the wear and tear. In the fall of the tower the *Marangona* [which still survives] was but little injured; the rest were broken.[18]

Apart from the campanile itself, the only other building of importance to suffer in the disaster was Sansovino's Loggetta at the base of the campanile, and this too was reconstructed. Sansovino was not always lucky with his buildings in Venice. While the Library of St Mark was under construction in 1545, the vault of the great Hall suddenly collapsed, weakened by the hard December frost. The Republic did not expect errors from its City Architect. Sansovino was consigned to prison, where he remained until the intercession of Aretino and Titian secured his release. In the event, he seems to have weathered the experience pretty well, living on in Venice for another twenty-five years. Vasari tells us that his digestion was so remarkable that he could cope with more or less anything often eating as many as three cucumbers at a time with half a lemon in his extreme old age'.

The National Library that finally came into being is a monument to his genius. Among other treasures in its possession are the books which Petrarch gave to Venice. At the time no one seems to have been much impressed by this handsome prize and the books were left to moulder for a century and a half.


PIAZZETTA

The Piazzetta acquired its most distinctive characteristic towards the end of the twelfth century when the two monolithic columns were brought here from the east and set in place, one surmounted by St Theodore and his crocodile, the other by the winged lion of St Mark. The engineer who erected them claimed as his reward the right to set up gambling booths between them, but, according to the story, the Council immediately tried to neutralize the privilege by appointing this as the place of public execution, thereby making it ill-omened. If this was the intention, it failed; Coryate reports that dicing between the pillars was 'continually performed'.

In the natural course of things the public executions were a tourist attraction in themselves. From this point of view, few visitors can have had a more satisfactory introduction to the city than William Lithgow, who arrived in 1609. Originally from Lanark and known in his youth as 'cut-lugg'd Willie' after his ears had been cropped by the brothers of an early mistress, Lithgow spent much of his life in travels that were made even more perilous than necessary by his feverish antipapism. This incident in Venice seems to be one of very few episodes that did something to stir his rather grim sense of humour:

> Mine Associate and I were no sooner landed, and perceiving a great throng of people, and in the midst of them a great smoak; but we began to demand of a *Venetian* what

the matter was? who replied there was a gray Friar burning quick at S. *Mark's* Pillar, of the reformed order of St. *Francis*, for begetting fifteen young noble Nunns with Child, and all within one year; he being also their Father Confessor. Whereat I sprung forward through the throng, and my Friend followed me, and came just to the Pillar as the half of his Body and right Arm fell flatlings in the fire: The Friar was forty six years old, and had been Confessor of that Nunnery of *Sancta Lucia* five years: Most of these young Nuns were Senators Daughters; and two of them were only come in to learn vertue, and yet fell in the midst of vice.

These fifteen with Child were all re-called home to their Fathers Palaces; the Lady Prioress, and the rest of her voluptuous Crew, were banished for ever from the Precincts of *Venice*. The Monastery was razed to the ground, their Rents were allowed to be bestowed upon poor Families, and distressed Age, and their Church to be converted to an Hospital.[19]

Unfortunately, as Lithgow explains, he and his companion had had nothing to eat, and 'being inhungred, and also overjoyed' by all this, they stumbled into an extravagantly expensive inn without checking the prices. Next morning the reckoning came:

> Mr *Arthur* look'd upon me, and I laugh'd upon him: In a word, our dinner and supper cost us forty Julets, twenty shillings *English*, being four Crowns, whereat my Companion being discontented, bad the Devil be in the Friars Ballocks, for we had paid soundly for his Leachery.[20]

## The Doge's Palace

Lithgow's friar, like others who went the same way, had the doubtful consolation of breathing his last within sight of one of the most extraordinary buildings in the world. Extraordinary, at least, to modern eyes, but not to the average eighteenth-century traveller. 'There are but two squares in

Venice worth notice,' writes Major Ayscough robustly in his *Letters from an Officer in the Guards*, 'and they are the great and little square of Saint Mark . . . The little one fronts the great canal, and has in it part of the Doge's palace, which is a large old pile, gloomy, and not very beautiful.'[21]

Other verdicts have been more generous. For Henry James the whole experience is permeated by images of light. Every sentence offers a variation on the same theme:

> This deeply original building is of course the loveliest thing in Venice, and a morning's stroll there is a wonderful illumination. Cunningly select your hour – half the enjoyment of Venice is a question of dodging – and enter at about one o'clock, when the tourists have flocked off to lunch and the echoes of the charming chambers have gone to sleep among the sunbeams. There is no brighter place in Venice – by which I mean that on the whole there is none half so bright. The reflected sunshine plays up through the great windows from the glittering lagoon and shimmers and twinkles over gilded walls and ceilings. All the history of Venice, all its splendid stately past, glows around you in a strong sea-light.[22]

By the measured standards of James's prose this sounds almost frolicsome. Only an optimist would today imagine that fellow-tourists were so easy to avoid. The long march through the rooms of the Ducal Palace is not for the faint-hearted: in summer the crowds, in winter a succession of rooms that have been shut up or cordoned off. The effort is worth making, but perhaps tomorrow.[23]

## The Bridge of Sighs

Byron's line in *Childe Harold*, 'I stood in Venice, on the "Bridge of Sighs"', reads strangely when one sees that the bridge is in fact a covered passageway leading across the Rio di Palazzo to the prisons. It was Byron, nonetheless, who did most to invest it with the romantic appeal it still enjoys. He was perhaps helped in this by William Beckford who had

passed across the bridge a couple of decades earlier, in the final
years of the Republic. It was the sort of experience precisely
calculated to appeal to Beckford's Gothic romanticism. In this
account his imagination has already been overheated by a visit
to the old prisons under the Leads:

> Abandoning therefore the sad tenants of the Piombi to
> their fate, I left the courts, and stepping into my bark, was
> rowed down a canal over which the lofty vaults of the
> palace cast a tremendous shade. Beneath these fatal waters
> the dungeons I have also been speaking of are situated.
> There the wretches lie marking the sound of the oars, and
> counting the free passage of every gondola. Above, a
> marble bridge, of bold majestic architecture, joins the
> highest part of the prisons to the secret galleries of the
> palace; from whence criminals are conducted over the
> arch to a cruel and mysterious death. I shuddered whilst
> passing below; and believe it is not without cause, this
> structure is named PONTE DEI SOSPIRI.[24]

This was too much of a good thing to last. In the next
century W. D. Howells dismissed the bridge as a 'pathetic
swindle' – a rough equivalent of Ruskin's uncompromising
note in the *Venetian Index*:

> The well-known 'Bridge of Sighs', a work of no merit,
> and of a late period . . . owing the interest it possesses
> chiefly to its pretty name, and to the ignorant senti-
> mentalism of Byron.[25]

## THE PIOMBI

The prisons have fared rather better than the bridge. No one
since has quite matched Coryate's relish for them – 'a very fair
prison, the fairest absolutely that ever I saw . . . I thinke there
is not a fairer prison in all Christendome' – but they remained a
focus of romantic attention throughout the nineteenth century. Although the *piombi* have now been demolished, they
retain their hold on the imagination largely through their link

with Casanova. They seem in reality to have been a good deal less terrible than popular tradition suggests. According to Casanova himself,

> What are called 'the leads' are not gaols but small furnished lock-ups, with barred windows, at the top of the ducal palace, and the inmate is said to be 'under the leads' because the roof is covered with sheets of lead over the larch-wood beams. These leaden sheets make the rooms cold in winter and very hot in summertime. But the air is good, you get enough to eat, a decent bed and everything else you need, clothes, and clean laundry when you want it. The Doge's servants look after the rooms and a doctor, a surgeon, an apothecary and a confessor are always on hand.[26]

As Balzac put it, 'there are ten thousand zinc-covered garrets in Paris which are worse, and people pay up to two hundred francs a year for them – men of talent, as well.'[27] But realities of this kind make little headway against myth. A recent airline magazine was still declaring that Casanova 'was locked up in the dark and dismal prison beside the Doge's Palace', and assuring its readers that they could 'visit the very same dungeons today'.

Perhaps it is pedantic to trouble about these things. Casanova would have been the first to agree that the *piombi* were not the place for a protracted stay. He had gone home one morning in the early hours to find that his casino had been ransacked by officers of the State Inquisitors on the pretext of looking for contraband salt. Signor Bragadin, his friend and patron, urged him to post to Florence and stay there till the danger had passed. Casanova rejected the advice and went back to his home, where at dawn on 26 July 1755 he was arrested. The same day he crossed the Bridge of Sighs and spent the next fifteen months under the Leads. (He was in fact condemned on 12 September to five years' imprisonment for atheism, but he himself was unaware of this.)

In arresting Casanova, the Inquisitors had acted with their usual speed; the report on him furnished by their pious spy, Giovanni Battista Manuzzi, is dated 17 July. It gives an interesting glimpse of his daily life: dinner at the houses of the nobility, relaxation at a wine-shop in the Frezzeria, business at the gaming-houses where he casually hazards vast sums of money, pleasure in the company of women of whatever rank or condition Venice has to offer. All too much for a Christian spy: 'Conversing with and becoming intimate with the said Casanova, one sees truly united in him misbelief, imposture, lasciviousness and voluptuousness in a manner to inspire horror.'[28]

On the night of 31 October 1756 Casanova, in company with a timorous monk who was also trying to escape, first got on to the roof by forcing a hole through the Leads and from there managed to break into another part of the Doge's Palace through a window overlooking the canal. After penetrating as far as possible, he found himself, scratched and bleeding, trapped in the hall next to the Sala delle Quattro Porte. Here he put on some decent clothes, which left him looking, he says, like a man of quality who had been beaten up in a brothel, and then sat down to wait for something to happen. Finally, he was noticed at the window by some idlers in the palace courtyard. They informed the watchman, who assumed that this must be someone he had inadvertently shut in the previous evening. When the door of the Hall was unlocked, Casanova strode past the startled man without a word, walked coolly down the Giants' Staircase, out through the Porta della Carta, across the Piazzetta, and into the first gondola he came to.

As the gondoliers struck out for Mestre, and the lights of the Giudecca fell away to the left, Casanova must have thought he was looking on the shadowy outlines of Venice for the last time. But changes in circumstance were the stuff of his life. In 1780 he was back again, acting as a spy for the Inquisitors, until a libel he published against a patrician forced him once more to flee the city, this time for good.

## THE POZZI

The *pozzi*, or wells, were the palace dungeons, which can still be visited. Though a rather grimmer proposition than the

Leads, even they were probably a good deal above average for
contemporary Europe. Not that this deterred later visitors
from following Beckford's lead. Dickens went round the
prisons in November 1844 and obviously made the most of the
occasion:

> One cell I saw, in which no man remained for more than
> four-and-twenty hours; being marked for dead before he
> entered it. Hard by, another, and a dismal one, whereto,
> at midnight, the confessor came – a monk, brown-robed,
> and hooded – ghastly in the day, and free bright air, but in
> the midnight of that murky prison, Hope's extinguisher,
> and Murder's herald. I had my foot upon the spot, where,
> at the same dread hour, the shriven prisoner was
> strangled; and struck my hand upon the guilty door – low
> browed and stealthy – through which the lumpish sack
> was carried out into a boat, and rowed away, and
> drowned where it was death to cast a net.[29]

A quarter of a century later Mark Twain was still getting
some mileage out of the instruments of torture shown to
tourists, among them

> a devilish contrivance of steel, which enclosed a prisoner's
> head like a shell, and crushed it slowly by means of a
> screw. It bore the stains of blood that had trickled through
> its joints long ago, and on one side it had a projection
> whereon the torturer rested his elbow comfortably and
> bent down his ear to catch the moanings of the sufferer
> perishing within.[30]

No doubt there is a residue of truth behind these frightening
tales. The scars and scratchings on the walls were not all put
there by holiday-makers and Romantic poets – though in 1833
Bulwer Lytton's wife wrote home that 'the guide told us they
were nearly effaced till Lord Byron had spent two days
re-cutting them into the walls.'[31] Perhaps Byron was right. It
would have been a pity to lose them. Even refurbished, they
carry forward a tenuous memory of the hands that originally
carved them. Molmenti tells us that in the Torreselle, above

the name *Luchinus de Cremona 1458 31 Jan.*, were scratched
merely the words '*Disce pati*' ('Learn to endure').

## BROGLIO

The strange and grand exterior of the palace, begun in the
fourteenth century and partially reconstructed in the fifteenth
and sixteenth in the wake of a couple of devastating fires, has
been described in too many guide-books to warrant attention
here. For a brief and knowledgeable account the reader can do
no better than turn to J. G. Links's *Venice for Pleasure*.

Looking up at the lovely capitals today, we might sometimes get nudged aside by an impatient photographer, but on
the whole we have a pleasant time of it compared with our
eighteenth-century ancestor. The area round the Ducal Palace,
known formerly as the *broglio* or meadow, was a public
meeting-place, but also, it seems, an unofficial public lava-
tory. Alfonso Lowe quotes the remarks of an eighteenth-
century traveller on the 'nasty fellows' who 'let down their
breeches wherever and before whomsoever they please, so
that many open parts, including the Piazza and outside the
ducal palace, are dedicated to *Cloacina*, and you may see the
votaries at their devotions every hour of the day.'[32]

At about the same time Hester Piozzi, who during her first
marriage, as Mrs Thrale, had been the friend of Dr Johnson,
also found her enjoyment of the palace seriously overshadowed by the state of its surroundings:

> The truth is, our dear Venetians are nothing less than
> cleanly. St Mark's Place is all covered over in a morning
> with chicken-coops, which stink one to death, as nobody,
> I believe, thinks of changing their baskets; and all about
> the ducal palace is made so very offensive by the resort of
> human creatures for every purpose most unworthy of so
> charming a place, that all enjoyment of its beauties is
> rendered difficult to a person of any delicacy, and
> poisoned so provokingly, that I do never cease to wonder
> that so little police and proper regulation are established in

a city so particularly lovely to render her sweet and wholesome.[33]

The sensitive Beckford was accustomed to escape from the 'noxious atmosphere' of St Mark's by running up the campanile to 'breathe the fresh gales which blow from the Adriatic'. To judge from Ruskin's comments in this letter to his father, any improvement by the middle of the nineteenth century had been strictly partial. Set beside that of Mrs Piozzi, his reaction offers a compact image of how closely the aesthetic had become linked to the moral in Victorian England:

It is of no use, as far as I see – trying to protestantize these Italians. They are totally incapable of understanding the beauty of Christ's own character. The first thing to be done is to teach them common Decency – Manliness and Truth. They are at present a curious Hybrid between the Fox and the Pig. I may give you one most striking instance of their character – though it is one you cannot well read out to my mother. The four last arches of the Ducal palace next the bridge of sighs having been partially filled up in the Renaissance times, afford a series of corners which – ever since I have known Venice – have been used by the Italians as those portions of our railroad stations are which are externally described as being set apart for 'Gentlemen.' It is nearly impossible to approach the capitals, though among the most beautiful of the series; and this is on the broad front of the Palace – and in the place where the Venetian senators used to have their own separate walk – the most honourable and restricted piece of ground in Venice.[34]

Ruskin may have been overstating the former purity of the spot. When Gilbert Burnet came here in the 1680s, he found the gilded youth of Venice strolling to and fro under the arcade, taking the air as though it were the finest in the world, but 'honourable' is not a word that suggests itself to him:

It seemed to me a strange thing to see the Broglio so full of graceful young Senators and Nobles, when there was so glorious a War on foot with the *Turks*, but instead of

being heated in Point of Honour to hazard their Lives,
they rather think it an extravagant piece of folly for them
to go and hazard it when a little Money can hire strangers
that do it on such easie terms, and thus their Arms are in
the hands of strangers, while they stay at home managing
their intrigues in the Broglio, and dissolving their spirits
among their Courtisans.[35]

Burnet clearly found this lack of enthusiasm for being killed
by the Turks hard to fathom. One can only speculate what his
response would be to the sellers of T-shirts, trinkets, and
guide-books who have replaced the young nobles and their
imbroglios.

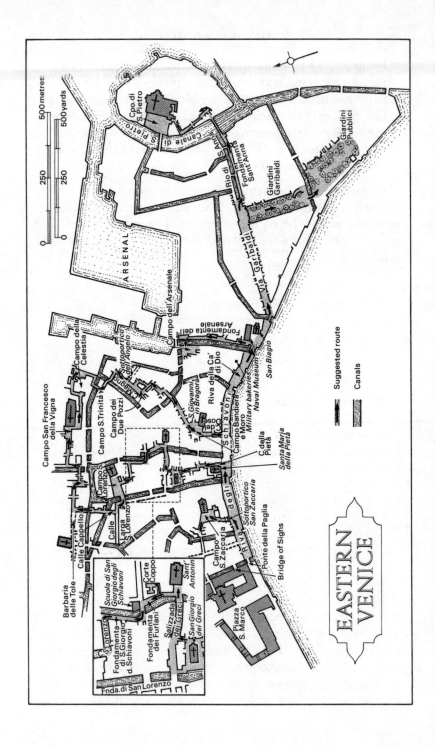

EASTERN VENICE

500 metres
500 yards
0   250
0   250

Suggested route
Canals

Cpo. di S.Pietro
Canale di S. Pietro
ARSENAL
Rio di S.Anna
Fondamenta Sant'Anna
Giardini Garibaldi
Giardini Pubblici
Via Garibaldi
Campo San Francesco della Vigna
Campo della Celestia
Sottoportico dell'Angelo
Rio di S.Magno
Campo dell'Arsenale
Campo dei Due Pozzi
Campo S.Trinità
Fondamenta dell'Arsenale
S.Giovanni in Bragora
Riva della Ca' di Dio
Fondamenta dei Schiavoni
Military bakeries
Naval Museum
San Biagio
Campo S.Lorenzo
C. dello Proso del
Campo Bandiera e Moro
C. della Pietà
Santa Maria della Pietà
Barbaria delle Tole
Calle Cappello
Calle Larga S.Lorenzo
Calle
Riva degli Schiavoni
Sottoportico San Zaccaria
Campo S.Zaccaria
Riva della Paglia
Ponte della Pietà
Bridge of Sighs
Piazza S.Marco
Sant' Antonin
Sottoportico Coppo
Corte Coppo
Scuola di San Giorgio degli Schiavoni
Fnda. di San Lorenzo
Fondamenta di S.Giorgio d.Schiavoni
Fondamenta dei Furlani
Salizzada dei Greci
San Giorgio dei Greci

# 5

# EASTERN VENICE

*Ponte della Paglia—Hotel Danieli—San Zaccaria—Riva degli Schiavoni—Santa Maria della Pietà—San Giorgio dei Greci and San Antonin—San Giorgio degli Schiavoni—San Lorenzo—Palazzo Dolfin—San Francesco della Vigna—Calli and Campi—Calle Magno—Arsenal—Castello—Public Gardens*

## PONTE DELLA PAGLIA

The Ponte della Paglia can usually be identified by the press of holiday-makers taking pictures of the Bridge of Sighs. Earlier tourists had the more arduous alternative of the sketch-book. In 1828 the American poet Longfellow, author of 'Hiawatha', was sketching here 'when a wench of a chambermaid emptied a pitcher of water from a window of the palace directly upon my head. I came very near slipping into the canal.'[1] Since this was in the middle of December, the experience must have been memorably uncomfortable.

Casanova had no cause to look with any fondness at the Bridge of Sighs, but the Ponte della Paglia makes a less sombre appearance in his memoirs. One afternoon, as he returned from Padua along the road which runs beside the Brenta, he had witnessed the upset of a coach containing a pretty woman and an officer in German uniform. The accident had lifted the woman's skirts and very nearly tipped her into the river. Only Casanova's prompt action had saved her from this last

indignity. The next day he is back in Venice. It happens to
be Ascension Day, when the Doge celebrates Venice's annual
wedding with the sea. There is nothing exceptional about the
episode, but it offers an attractive vignette of the endless party
that seems to have been Venetian life in the eighteenth century.
(Anyone who has visited the Ca' Rezzonico and seen Pietro
Longhi's picture of the rhinoceros on public display will have
no difficulty in imagining the scene advertised by the poster at
which Casanova's masked seductress is looking):

> I was drinking coffee unmasked under the Procuratie in
> the Piazza San Marco when a beautiful female masker
> who was passing by gave me a playful blow on the
> shoulder with her fan. Not knowing the masker, I pay no
> attention. After drinking my coffee I put on my mask and
> make my way to the Riva del Sepolcro, where Signor
> Bragadin's gondola was waiting for me. Near the Ponte
> della Paglia I see the same masker who had struck me with
> her fan staring at the picture of a caged monster which
> was shown to anyone curious enough to give ten soldi to
> go in. I approach the masked lady and ask her what right
> she had had to strike me.
> 'To punish you for not recognizing me after you saved
> my life yesterday beside the Brenta.'
> I compliment her, I ask her if she intends to follow the
> *Bucentaur*, and she answers that she would go if she had a
> perfectly safe gondola; I offer her mine, which is of the
> largest; she consults with the officer whom, though he is
> masked, I recognize by his uniform, and she accepts. . . .
> We followed the *Bucentaur*. As I am sitting on the bench
> beside the lady, I take a few liberties under cover of her
> cloak; but she discourages me by changing her position.
> After the ceremony we return to Venice, we disembark at
> the Colonne, and the officer says that they would be
> happy if I would dine with them at the 'Wild Man'. I
> accept. I had become greatly interested in the woman,
> who was pretty and of whom I had seen something more
> than her face. The officer left me alone with her, going on
> to order dinner for three.

I at once told her that I loved her, that I had a box at the
opera, that I offered it to her, and that I would attend her
throughout the fair if she would assure me that my time
should not be lost.[2]

So they head for the Wild Man, an inn whose name is still
borne by the Calle Selvadego just off the Piazza, and the whole
process of seduction and intrigue is set in motion once again.

In earlier times Casanova's purposes could have been served
nearer to hand. At the Ponte della Paglia in the fourteenth
century there was an inn called The Dragon, which was kept
by an Englishman. It was here that in March 1365, while Sir
Henry Stromin was waiting in Venice to make the spring
voyage to the Holy Land, two of his grooms, whose names are
given in the State papers as John and Robin, became embroiled
with a local artisan. George Parks summarizes the details to be
found in the city's archives:

> It seems that a Venetian named Mioranza, a cap-maker,
> made use of the inn to urinate in the straw behind one of
> the Englishman's horses. The two grooms rushed him
> out; he returned with a stone which he had picked up,
> threw it at Robin's head, but missed. John thereupon took
> him by the beard; he stabbed John with a bread knife,
> killing him, and ran away. Robin ran after him up the
> street inland; the fugitive jumped into the canal beyond
> the bridge to San Zaccaria, and was pulled into the
> basement windows of a house on the canal by two
> women who appeared there. The police at once made
> enquiry. Presumably justice was done, but we know no
> more of what may well have been a characteristic travel
> incident.[3]

## Hotel Danieli

Ahead of us stretches the Riva degli Schiavoni. The second
street on the left is the Calle delle Rasse, on the corner of which
Doge Vitale Michiel II was murdered in 1172. Venice had a
violent way with early Doges who failed to give satisfaction.

Vitale Michiel had just returned from an unlucky expedition to treat with the Emperor of Byzantium and was wisely removing himself from the attentions of the mob when he turned down the Calle delle Rasse. The assassin had anticipated him. It was later discovered that the man had sheltered in one of the houses at the top of the calle, and these were accordingly razed to the ground. For almost eight centuries nothing was built there but the humble wooden structures we can see in paintings by Canaletto and others. Only in 1948 did the Hotel Danieli at last get permission to use the space for the construction of its new wing. The result does little credit to Venice's most distinguished hotel.

'The beginning of everything was in seeing the Gondola-beak come actually inside the door at Danieli's, when the tide was up, and the water two feet deep at the foot of the stairs.'[4] So Ruskin described in *Praeterita* the start of his obsession with Venice. Previously known as the Palazzo Dandolo, the Danieli had been partly converted to a hotel in 1822 by a Swiss, Joseph dal Niel,[5] and it was here that the newly married Ruskins stayed while John was writing the first volume of *The Stones of Venice*. On 13 November 1849 Effie writes to her mother: 'We are living in Danieli's Hotel, formerly a splendid Palace with marble staircase and doors and Balconies looking out on the sea covered with ships and churches and the Doge's Palace, the finest building in the world, with St Mark's Place & Church 100 yards off.'[6] Their first-floor sitting-room, no. 32 in the Danieli today, was in front, at the far end on the Piazzetta side.

Fifteen years earlier the hotel had witnessed the end of the tempestuous affair between George Sand and Alfred de Musset. The relationship was already precarious when they arrived, and de Musset's illness finished it off. While he sweated in the bedroom, Sand took stock of the young Dr Pagello who had been called in to treat him. Soon they were lovers – less spectacularly than Sand and de Musset, but perhaps more happily. Years afterwards Pagello described finding the feverish de Musset 'in a large room with windows overlooking the Riva degli Schiavoni, where there was a couch, a fireplace protected by a screen, a large table and, adjoining, a darkened room with two beds'.[7] Such was the setting for the violent, wearisome scenes that were to ensure Sand and de Mussett their place in the Pantheon of romantic lovers.

A later guest, in every way more discreet, was Marcel Proust: 'When I went to Venice I found that my dream had become – incredibly but quite simply – *my address.*'[8]

## SAN ZACCARIA

Fifty yards beyond the Danieli, a sottoportico leads down to the campo and church of San Zaccaria. Adjoining the campanile, behind a small garden, can be seen parts of the old Benedictine convent, patronized by the nobility and famed for its licentiousness. Max Beerbohm wrote evocatively of the campo as it appeared to him in the early years of the century:

Nowhere in Venice is a more Venetian thing than this little, melancholy shabby Campo; this work of so many periods; this garment woven by so many cunning weavers, and worn threadbare, and patched and patched again, and at length discarded. Few people, and they poorest among the poor, live here now. One can hardly imagine that the well-head was ever open, ever gossiped around. Shutters interpolated in delicate Gothic windows are mouldering on their hinges; shutters that seem hardly incongruous now that they have been blistered by so many summers, and are so faded and so crazy. Piteous is the expression of gaunt misery on the façade of the church. The old low building that straggles away from beneath the tōwer and is railed off from the pavement, was once a nunnery, the richest of all the nunneries in Venice. A sentinel stands at its door; and now and again a soldier passes in or out, looking depressed. No children play here. A cat or two may be seen lying about when the sun shines. And the brightlier shines the sun the sadder seems the Campo San Zaccaria, seeming, indeed, to shrink away from the sun's rays, like a woman who has been beautiful, or like a woman who is ill.[9]

Today this seems rather harsh. The campo is often empty, and a little bare after the activity of the Riva, but it is a respectable spot, well-kept even, compared with much of Venice. In the middle is the well-head which figures in the pretty legend Beerbohm tells about the square:

> And it was here, . . . on Michaelmas morning, that a devil, in the guise of a very beautiful youth, came and, smiling, plucked by the sleeve the bride of Sebastiano Morosini, and whispered in such sweet wise that she let go the arm of her bridegroom and gave her hand to the stranger. Sebastiano would have drawn his sword, but, under a spell that the devil had cast, it stayed in its scabbard. By a frantic inspiration of the moment, he went down on his hands and knees, and, crawling, roared, insomuch that the devil (having, like all the devils of that day, a share of simplicity) mistook him for the lion of S. Mark, and instantly vanished. Nor, so far as we know, did he ever reappear. But Sebastiano's stratagem, S. Mark's miracle, had laid such hold on the hearts of the Venetians that every man who was soon to be married would come on Michaelmas morning to the Campo San Zaccaria, and crawl once around the well-head, roaring. Thereby, it was thought, he assured for himself happiness of wedlock: his wife would never be inconstant to him, even in thought. She, the intended wife, accompanied him, with her parents, and with his parents, to see the pious little ceremony performed. All through Michaelmas morning the Campo San Zaccaria was crowded. Carpaccio painted a picture of the scene: a scene after his own heart . . .[10]

Some four centuries later, on Michaelmas morning 1906, Beerbohm posts himself in the shadow of the sottoportico and waits. He is on the point of giving up when a small party of peasants appears, dressed in their Sunday clothes:

> There were six of them – two middle-aged men, two middle-aged women, and a young man, and a girl. For a minute or so they stood talking. Then the young man detached himself from the group, tossing his sombrero to an elder, and came across to the well-head. There, having

crossed himself, he went down on his hands and knees, and did as Sebastiano had done before him; and, little though the roaring may have been like a lion's, I did not once smile on my way home along the Riva Schiavoni.[11]

The Carpaccio painting was stolen from the church and lost for ever, but Giovanni Bellini's *Madonna and Saints* has had better luck. In 1845 Ruskin wrote to his father, 'There is a glorious John Bellini which the priests are burning to pieces with their candles.'[12] He had thoughts at the time of getting it back to England, but in San Zaccaria it has stayed, in the middle of the left aisle, looking better now after its restoration than it has done, perhaps, for most of its life.

At the far end of the square, beside the street leading towards the Campo San Provolo, is a tablet threatening the usual 'severe penalties' for gambling, swearing, and general misbehaviour in the campo. Given the pace at which the nuns were living, a casual blasphemer might reasonably have felt hard done by when faced with the prospect of prison, cord,[13] and galleys.

## Riva degli Schiavoni

Continuing along the Riva, we pass at no. 4161 the green shutters of what is now the Pensione Wildner. It was from the windows of this building that Henry James looked out across the lagoon while he worked on *The Portrait of a Lady*:

I had rooms on Riva Schiavoni, at the top of a house near the passage leading off to San Zaccaria; the waterside life, the wondrous lagoon spread before me, and the ceaseless human chatter came in at my windows, to which I seem to myself to have been constantly driven, in the fruitless fidget of composition, as if to see whether, out in the blue channel, the ship of some right suggestion, of some better phrase, of the next happy twist of my subject, the next true touch for my canvas, mightn't come into sight. . . .

There are pages of the book which, in the reading over,

have seemed to make me see again the bristling curve of
the wide Riva, the large colour-spots of the balconied
houses and the repeated undulation of the little hunch-
backed bridges, marked by the rise and drop again, with
the wave, of foreshortened clicking pedestrians. The
Venetian footfall and the Venetian cry – all talk there,
however uttered, having the pitch of a call across the
water – come in once more at the window, renewing
one's old impression of the delighted senses and the
divided, frustrated mind.[14]

A short way further along the Riva, close to the Ponte del
Sepolcro, a plaque between nos. 4144 and 4143 marks the site
of Petrarch's house. This was the Palazzo delle Due Torre,
whose twin towers can just be seen in the famous Bodleian
picture of the departure of Marco Polo. Petrarch came to
Venice in 1362, having arranged to bequeath his library to the
Republic in exchange for the use of this house. It was here in
the following spring that he entertained Boccaccio, and from
the upper windows of the palace that he looked out on the
cradle of Venice's maritime power.

In a letter which conveys something of the restless enterprise that inspired the city's commercial expansion through
the fourteenth century he describes the scene one squally
night, when the shouts of the sailors reach him through the
storm. Putting down his pen, he goes to the window and looks
out to sea at the ships which have been moored there for the
winter, their masts reaching above the towers of his house:

The larger of the two ships was at this moment – though
the stars were all hidden by the clouds, the winds shaking
the walls, and the roar of the sea filling the air – leaving the
quay and setting out upon its voyage. . . . If you had seen
it, you would have said it was no ship but a mountain
swimming upon the sea, although under the weight of its
immense wings a great part of it was hidden in the waves.
The end of the voyage was to be the Don, beyond which
nothing can navigate from our seas; but many of those
who were on board, when they had reached that point,
meant to prosecute their journey, never pausing till they

had reached the Ganges or the Caucusus, India and the Eastern Ocean.[15]

## SANTA MARIA DELLA PIETÀ

Between James's house and Petrarch's stands Santa Maria della Pietà, the church where Vivaldi was concert-master. It was originally attached to an orphanage, which had been moved here from San Francesco della Vigna in the early sixteenth century. If you walk down the Calle della Pietà, you can still see at the corner of the church a plaque, dated 12 November 1548, invoking God's anger against those who leave their children here without need. The macabre background to this hospital is explained by Pero Tafur, a well-to-do Spaniard who had visited Venice in 1436 as part of his European tour:

> In times past there were few weeks, or even days, when the fishermen did not take out dead babies from their nets, and this, they say, came from the fact that the merchants were so long separated from their wives. These, urged by their fleshly lusts, gave way to them and became pregnant, and with intent to save their reputations threw the offspring out of the window into the sea as soon as they were delivered, the place being aptly disposed therefor. The rulers, in view of such enormous crimes, took counsel together and founded a great and rich hospital, very finely built, and placed in it a hundred wet-nurses to suckle the babes, and now those who would hide their shame take their children there to be reared.[16]

Tafur goes on to mention a further humane provision, which has a pleasantly Venetian twist. The papal bull secured by the city granted various pardons to anyone who visited the children in hospital. Without giving themselves away, the parents could thus go to see their children under colour of religious exercise.

To the outsider charitable bequests often seem a trifle eccentric, but few can have been more so than that received by the Pietà in 1697. An austere member of the Erizzo family had been so disgusted by contemporary fashions in dress that he left a special clause in his will disinheriting in favour of the Pietà any of his sons who had worn a periwig or red socks. This fell heavily on his son Niccolò whose addiction to the periwig was what had excited the old man's rage. In the event, Niccolò contested the will and managed to reach a compromise by which he handed over six thousand ducats but kept his wig and the rest of his fortune.

## San Giorgio dei Greci and San Antonin

At the bottom of the Calle della Pietà a left turn quickly followed by a right will bring us into the street that leads past the back of San Giorgio dei Greci. (To get round to the front, turn left when you reach the Salizzada dei Greci.) This sixteenth-century Greek Orthodox church with its dangerous-looking campanile is not always easy to get into. The visitor must either beg admission from the custodian of the neighbouring museum or lie in wait for one of the unpredictable periods when the door is open.

Coryate had no such problems, happening upon the place during the morning service. He thought it 'a very faire little Church', but took exception to the congregation's practice of wagging their hands up and down. Their appearance, too, caused him some misgiving – 'Most of these Grecians are very blacke, and all of them both men and children doe weare long haire, much longer than any other mans besides that I could perceive in all Venice, a fashion unseemly and very ruffian-like.'[17]

It was only a few months before his death that Richard Wagner visited the church, on 11 October 1882. The markedly eastern flavour of the Greci seems to have disconcerted him; he was uneasy about it at the time and returned to the subject on the following day, as Cosima records in her diary: 'In the morning R. talks to me again about the Greci church, saying that it does not give any warm feelings of Christianity but, rather, an impression of stiffness and pomp, like a relic of ancient Assyria!'[18]

San Giorgio dei Greci today is still an oddity. The central cross is set in a screen of icons and the seats are ranged lengthwise along either side of the nave. Overhead, the dark cupola offers only the dim glow of the haloes of the saints depicted in its roof. Both style and atmosphere mark its difference from other Venetian churches.

The network of streets in this part of Venice is more than usually labyrinthine. It is an area into which tourists tend to stray only when they have lost their way to San Giorgio degli Schiavoni, so that chance rather than design takes most people to the church of San Antonin at the far end of the Salizzada dei Greci. Closed at the moment for restoration, it was once, according to W. D. Howells, a source of some displeasure to the local population. The trouble sprang from St Anthony's traditional association with the emblem of the pig:

> Among other privileges of the Church, abolished in Venice long ago, was that ancient right of the monks of S. Anthony, Abbot, by which their herds of swine were made free of the whole city. These animals, enveloped in an odour of sanctity, wandered here and there, and were piously fed by devout people, until the year 1409, when, being found dangerous to children and inconvenient to everybody, they were made the subject of a special decree, which deprived them of their freedom of movement.[19]

More recently, the church enjoyed brief notoriety in 1819 when a large male elephant took refuge there after escaping from its cage on the Riva degli Schiavoni. Small arms were used without effect on the maddened beast. After a period of chaos artillery was brought up and in the end the runaway elephant was, as Captain Douglas puts it rather unfeelingly, 'despatched by a shot from a piece of ordnance'. The episode left its mark on literature in the form of a pamphlet entitled *The Elephanticide in Venice in the year 1819 written by the noble signor Pietro Bonmartini of Padua* and a poem, recently reprinted, called 'Elefanteide'.

## SAN GIORGIO DEGLI SCHIAVONI

In spite of various arrows that claim to show one the way, San Giorgio degli Schiavoni can be difficult to find. Fortunately, San Antonin is the easiest direction from which to approach it. On the right, as we walk down the Fondamenta dei Furlani, a calle leads into the little Corte Coppo, which was the home of the first woman to be quartered in Venice by way of punishment. Marin Sanudo records that on 1 May 1521, after twenty-two years of marriage, a certain Bernardina battered her husband to death, forced her daughter and a cousin to bury him and then gave out that he had gone on a pilgrimage to Loreto. It was only when a relative made enquiries in Loreto and Bernardina herself tried to interest a house-guest in digging up the ex-husband and reburying him more securely that the crime came to light.

What brings people here now is the marvellous group of paintings which line the ground-floor walls of the Scuola di San Giorgio degli Schiavoni. They are the work of Vittore Carpaccio, a painter whose most outlandish subjects are stamped with something quintessentially Venetian. Whatever their ostensible setting, the gorgeous architecture of Venice will usually find its way into the background. Equally constant, and perhaps equally Venetian, is an element of time-worn melancholy in the pictures; Carpaccio's characters have a languid elegance that makes them seem half-disengaged from the scene of which they are a part. Always his processions and regattas and receptions are witnessed by at least one youthful figure whose thoughts are caught in a dream. Not everyone feels quite the enthusiasm they express for Tintoretto, but it would be a strange and unsatisfactory person who could not love Carpaccio.

The room itself is not immediately prepossessing. It is, says Ruskin, 'a little room about the size of the commercial parlour of an old-fashioned English inn; perhaps an inch or two higher in the ceiling. . . .'[20] For Henry James the setting is still less acceptable, but as he looks at the painting of St Augustine in his study, he finds that even the sharpest criticism loses its edge:

It unites the most masterly finish with a kind of universal
largeness of feeling, and he who has it well in his memory
will never hear the name of Carpaccio without a throb of
almost personal affection. Such indeed is the feeling that
descends upon you in that wonderful little chapel of St
George of the Slaves, where this most personal and
sociable of artists has expressed all the sweetness of his
imagination. The place is small and incommodious, the
pictures are out of sight and ill-lighted, the custodian is
rapacious, the visitors are mutually intolerable, but the
shabby little chapel is a palace of art.[21]

In most respects things have improved since James's time;
one's fellow-visitors may still be intolerable, but the lighting
now is good, the charges are fixed, and, if you pick your time,
you can gaze at leisure from the relative comfort of a bench.

In Ruskin's view there is one particular detail that should
claim our attention. Writing, still hypnotically, in wayward
and obsessed old age, he directs us to the painting of the
*Triumph of St George*. We should for the moment disregard the
figures of St George himself and the conquered dragon and
instead focus our opera glass on the heads of the two princely
riders to the left – the Saracen king and his daughter – he in
high white turban, she beyond him in the crimson cap, high,
like a castle tower:

Look well and long. For truly, – and with hard-earned
and secure knowledge of such matters, I tell you, through
all this round world of ours, searching what the best life of
it has done of brightest in all its times and years, – you
shall not find another piece quite the like of that little piece
of work, for supreme, serene, unassuming, unfaltering
sweetness of painter's perfect art. Over every other
precious thing, of such things known to me, it rises, in the
compass of its simplicity; in being able to gather the
perfections of the joy of extreme childhood, and the joy of
a hermit's age, with the strength and sunshine of mid-life,
all in one.

Which is indeed more or less true of all Carpaccio's

work and mind; but in this piece you have it set in close
jewellery, radiant, inestimable.[22]


## SAN LORENZO

The bridge in front of the Scuola leads across to the Fondamenta di San Giorgio degli Schiavoni. A short way down
this a calle to the left takes us round to the church of San
Lorenzo, set in a plain and peaceful campo with five trees and
five benches. Today the church, closed for restoration, presents a façade of crazed brick ridges which in its decrepitude
can look oddly appealing. It was here, four and a half centuries
ago, that Marco Polo was buried.

In a city notorious for the laxity of its convents, San Lorenzo
already enjoyed a reputation more colourful than most. Since
upper-class women were frequently dispatched to a convent
for financial reasons rather than to answer any vocation, it is
unsurprising that chastity to many seemed tiresome. It was
often the case that younger sons who might have made
husbands for them were being firmly directed to the brothel
rather than the marriage bed, in order to avoid any dispersal of
the family's estate. As the sixteenth-century scholar Roger
Ascham noted in *The Scholemaster*: 'I learned, when I was at
*Venice* that there it is counted good pollicie, when there be
foure or five brethren of one familie, one onelie to marie: and
all the rest to waulter with as little shame in open lecherie, as
Swyne do here in the common myre.'[23] The result was
inevitable. By the fourteenth century the Council had already
started passing laws to discourage the fornications of libertine
nuns and their partners, pleasantly called *monachini*. Convent
chaplains had to be fifty years old or more, while confessors,
by a nice distinction, had to be at least sixty.

The effects of these measures seem to have been disappointing. For successive centuries Venetian convents remained a
byword for dissolute living. To get some idea of their atmosphere, we need only look at Francesco Guardi's painting in the
Ca' Rezzonico of a convent *parlatorio*. It catches precisely the

tone that delighted Charles de Brosses when he visited the city in the eighteenth century. Having briefly described the squabble that was going on between three convents as to which should provide a mistress for the Papal nuncio who was soon to arrive, he adds:

> In truth, it would be to the nuns that I should most readily turn if I had to make a long stay here. All those I have seen through the grate at mass, chatting and laughing together as long as the service lasted, have struck me as good-looking and habited in such a way as to highlight their beauty. They have a charming little *coiffure* and a simple dress, but one that is of course perfectly white, revealing their shoulders and breasts to just the same degree as the dresses in the Roman style worn by our actresses.[24]

Across something over four centuries the convent of San Lorenzo recurs in the Venetian archives in one disreputable context after another. Its most famous graduate was probably Maria Da Riva, a patrician nun whose passionate affair with the French ambassador, Froulay, caused a diplomatic incident. Disguised only by a mask, Maria would leave San Lorenzo at night, accompany Froulay to the casinos, and then return to her convent with the dawn. When the State Inquisitors took exception to this and forbade her to meet the ambassador, Froulay ignored the prohibition and indignantly complained to Paris about his treatment. In the end, it was only by transferring Maria from San Lorenzo to a convent in Ferrara that the Inquisitors managed to resolve the situation – temporarily. Before long the incorrigible nun fell in love with an Italian colonel, fled to Bologna, and there got married.

In spite of everything, there was one event in its history which San Lorenzo could look back on with some complacency.

The summer of 1360 had not been a happy time for the convent. In June three men were imprisoned and fined for sleeping with some of the nuns, and then a month later another group of nuns was caught receiving love letters smuggled in by five women who were publicly whipped. It is a measure of divine tolerance that in the same year one of Venice's most celebrated miracles should have been staged on the convent's doorstep.

If you stand on the bridge at the far end of the campo, you will still be able to recognize enough of the surrounding architecture to identify the site of the *Miracle of the Holy Cross* from Gentile Bellini's painting in the Accademia. (In particular, the tall building which rises behind the house at the end of the fondamenta is unmistakable.) The Cross in question had fallen into the canal and then miraculously floated to the surface again so that it could be recovered. Bellini depicts the episode at the moment when a swimming prelate triumphantly holds up the Cross to the watching crowds on the Fondamenta di San Lorenzo.

To readers of the modern thriller the fondamenta will be familiar for other reasons, for it is here, just behind Bellini's line of spectators, that we find the entrance to police headquarters. Among the weary heroes and frightened villains who have passed this way, there are few who leave much impression on the mind. With its twisting alleys and sunless courtyards Venice seems to offer a perfect setting for the business of the crime-writer, but it has on the whole produced a disappointing crop.

## PALAZZO DOLFIN

At the end of the fondamenta, a short way beyond the bridge, a left turn takes us into the Calle Larga San Lorenzo. Something less than a hundred yards down on the right a heavy door set into an archway gives access to the fifteenth-century Palazzo Dolfin at no. 5123. It was still relatively new when Pietro Casola saw it in 1494. The sixty-seven-year-old priest had just returned from a pilgrimage to the Holy Land and was preparing for the last stage of his journey back to Milan. His account of a visit to one of the Dolfin women who was in childbed gives a vivid image of the upper reaches of life in Venice at a time when England, less than ten years on from the Battle of Bosworth, was still hauling itself out of the Middle Ages:[25]

1. *Two Venetian Ladies on a Balcony*, by Vittore Carpaccio

PAX VAN
TIBI GELI
MAR STA
CE Æ MEVS

2. *(above)* *The Winged Lion of St Mark*, by Carpaccio
3. *(left)* Nobles dancing on the Giudecca
4. *(right)* *The Miracle of the Holy Cross*, by Gentile Bellini

5. Venice in the fourteenth century

6. Ponte dei Pugni

7. *Masked Revellers at the Ridotto*, by Pietro Longhi

8. *Campo Santa Maria Formosa*, by Canaletto

9. *Campo SS. Apostoli*, by Canaletto

10. *The Rhinoceros*, by Longhi

11. *The Stonemason's Yard* (detail), by Canaletto

12. John Ruskin

13. Browning
and son
outside the
Ca'Rezzonico,
1889

14. The
audience leaving
the Fenice
theatre, 1891

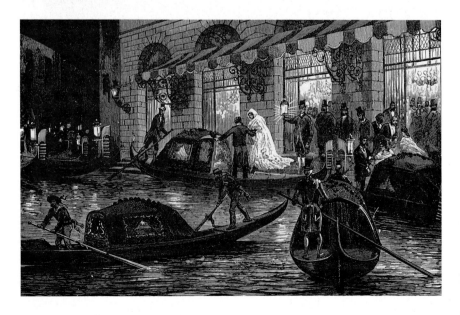

15. Frederick Rolfe, Baron Corvo

16. The fallen Campanile, 1902

17. Cannaregio, at about the time that Gautier visited it

18. Torcello, late nineteenth century

As the room was not capable of holding many persons the ducal Ambassador chose me specially to enter with him and he asked my opinion several times. I could only reply with a shrug of the shoulders for it was clear that the ornamentation of the room where we were with the invalid had cost two thousand ducats and more, although quite a small room. The fireplace was all of Carrara marble, shining like gold, and subtly carved with figures and foliage. The ceiling was so richly decorated with gold and ultramarine, and the walls so well adorned, that my pen cannot describe them. There was so much gold everywhere, such an abundance displayed in the ornaments of the bed and the lady, the coverings and the cushions, that I had better not try to describe them.

I must tell you one other thing. In the chamber there were twenty-five Venetian damsels, one more beautiful than the other, who had come to visit the invalid. They did not show less than four fingers' width of bare skin below their shoulders and had so many jewels on the head, neck and hands that these must have been worth a hundred thousand ducats.[26]

The lavishness of this kind of Venetian interior was not necessarily matched by its comfort, and as the domestic amenities in other parts of Europe improved, Venice came to be regarded less respectfully. Gilbert Burnet visited the city towards the end of the seventeenth century:

As for their houses they have nothing convenient at Venice, for the Architecture is almost all the same, one stair-case, a Hall that runs along the body of the house, and chambers on both hands, but there are no apartments, no Closets, no Back-stairs; so that in houses that are of an excessive wealth, they have yet no sort of convenience. Their bedsteads are of iron, because of the vermin that their moisture produces, the bottoms are of boards, upon which they lay so many quilts that it is a huge step to get up to them, their great chairs are . . . hard in the bottom, and the wood of the arms is not covered: they mix water with their wine in their Hogsheads, so that for above half

the year the wine is either dead or sour, they do not leaven
their bread, so that it is extream heavy, and the Oven is
too much heated, so that the crum is as dough, when the
crust is as hard as a stone . . .[27]

## SAN FRANCESCO DELLA VIGNA

It is by no means simple to get to San Francesco della Vigna,
but the church has some attractive paintings and is reckoned to
be the spot where St Mark put down on his way back from
Aquileia (see p. 114), so the serious tourist will persevere.
(Goethe managed it with a map and compass; he arrived to
find the Capuchin preacher competing in a loud voice with the
shouts of the vendors in front of the church.) The easiest route
from the Palazzo Dolfin is probably to go back a few yards to
the Calle Cappello, entered under a stone arch, continue down
it as far as possible and then turn right along the Barberia delle
Tole.

One of the church's curiosities is the tomb of Francesco
Barbaro in the last chapel along the right-hand aisle. On the
wall is a plaque surmounted by the family arms with above
them a lion's head. The device on the arms, a red circle on a
field argent, has an unusual history. Augustus Hare tells us
that it was granted in 1125 'to the Admiral Marco Barbaro, in
remembrance of his having, during the battle of Ascalon, cut
off the hand of a Moor who had seized the flag of his vessel,
slain him, and turned his turban into a banner, after having
traced a red circle with his bleeding arm.'[28] Here we do seem
closer to Bosworth Field.

## CALLI AND CAMPI

We are now almost at the edge of the lagoon and can start
heading back towards the Riva degli Schiavoni. The winding
streets and unexpected campi make this a particularly agreeable
area to wander through. It would have been to this part of the
unknown city that Proust first turned when he emerged from

the Danieli in search of adventure. He had come to Venice in the spring of 1900, accompanied by his mother. For the young writer it was pre-eminently the city of Ruskin; but it was also a place of subtle and ambiguous sexual suggestion. A few months later, in October of the same year, Proust returned to Venice alone, and it is this visit which furnished the yearning memories of exploration, discovery, and loss that found their way into *Albertine disparue*:

> After dinner, I went out by myself, into the heart of the enchanted city where I found myself wandering in strange regions like a character in the Arabian Nights. It was very seldom that I did not, in the course of my wanderings, hit upon some strange and spacious piazza of which no guide-book, no tourist had ever told me. . . .
>
> All of a sudden, at the end of one of those little streets, it seemed as though a bubble had occurred in the crystallised matter. A vast and splendid *campo* of which I could certainly never, in this network of little streets, have guessed the importance, or even found room for it, spread out before me flanked with charming palaces silvery in the moonlight. It was one of those architectural wholes towards which, in any other town, the streets converge, lead you and point the way. Here it seemed to be deliberately concealed in a labyrinth of alleys, like those palaces in oriental tales to which mysterious agents convey by night a person who, taken home again before daybreak, can never again find his way back to the magic dwelling which he ends by supposing that he visited only in a dream.
>
> On the following day I set out in quest of my beautiful nocturnal piazza, I followed *calli* which were exactly like one another and refused to give me any information, except such as would lead me farther astray. Sometimes a vague landmark which I seemed to recognise led me to suppose that I was about to see appear, in its seclusion, solitude and silence, the beautiful exiled piazza. At that moment, some evil genie which had assumed the form of a fresh *calle* made me turn unconsciously from my course,

and I found myself suddenly brought back to the Grand Canal. And as there is no great difference between the memory of a dream and the memory of a reality, I ended by asking myself whether it was not during my sleep that there had occurred in a dark patch of Venetian crystallisation that strange interruption which offered a vast piazza flanked by romantic palaces, to the meditative eye of the moon.[29]

These secret places that are found, enjoyed, then lost again as the city closes around them, offer a thrill of gratified possession. Venice is not only, like Paris, a context for romantic encounters, it is also a partner in them, becoming almost, for the solitary traveller, itself the object of desire. There is always an intriguing ambiguity about the place, born of its fluidity, its shifting light, the perpetual uncertainty of one's destination. Often the images used of it seem more appropriate to the exploration of unmapped territory than to rambles through the streets of a famous city. Tourists in Venice are explorers, with all that this implies of violation, penetration, conquest. The anatomy of the city – its dark alleys, liquid channels, and sudden clearings – is a maze of temptation. As James Morris remarked, it is a place that, unlike others, seems to excite an emotion close to lust. Venice is always female. The desire so often directed towards its inhabitants can be displaced with mysterious ease, so that lust for its creatures becomes lust for the hidden places and yielding textures of the city itself – the desire to know and to penetrate but also to be embraced, cradled, rocked, protected. No one has conveyed this sense of the city's sexual allure more powerfully than Thomas Mann in his description of Aschenbach's feverish gondola chase after Tadzio, the Polish boy with whom he has fallen in love:

> Leaning back among soft, black cushions he swayed gently in the wake of the other black-snouted bark, to which the strength of his passion chained him. Sometimes it passed from his view, and then he was assailed by an anguish of unrest. But his guide appeared to have long practice in affairs like these; always, by dint of short cuts or deft manoeuvres, he contrived to overtake the coveted

sight. The air was heavy and foul, the sun burnt down through a slate-coloured haze. Water slapped gurgling against wood and stone. The gondolier's cry, half warning, half salute, was answered with singular accord from far within the silence of the labyrinth. They passed little gardens high up the crumbling wall, hung with clustering white and purple flowers that sent down an odour of almonds. Moorish lattices showed shadowy in the gloom. The marble steps of a church descended into the canal, and on them a beggar squatted, displaying his misery to view, showing the whites of his eyes, holding out his hat for alms. Farther on a dealer in antiques cringed before his lair, inviting the passer-by to enter and be duped. Yes, this was Venice, this the fair frailty that fawned and that betrayed, half fairy-tale, half snare; the city in whose stagnating air the art of painting once put forth so lusty a growth, and where musicians were moved to accords so weirdly lulling and lascivious. Our adventurer felt his senses wooed by this voluptuousness of sight and sound, tasted his secret knowledge that the city sickened and hid its sickness for love of gain, and bent an ever more unbridled leer on the gondola that glided on before him.[30]

## CALLE MAGNO

If we go back towards the Riva by way of a couple of bare, largely unvisited squares, the Campo della Celestia and the Campo San Trinità, we shall shortly afterwards turn right into the Calle Magno. It is not often that one gets the chance to see a hedgehog carved in stone, so it is worth glancing at the entrance to the Sottoportico dell'Angelo, half-way along on the left. Over the low arch, on either side of a slightly battered angel, two of these amiable creatures are outlined in bas-relief, stepping forward with long legs. There is a touching intimacy in the way animals are depicted around the city. Images of them grace paintings and buildings with a friendly profusion that was noted by Jan Morris in *A Venetian Bestiary*:

The animal legends of Venice are seldom legends of hostility: sea-birds are helpful, cats are loyal, lions lie affectionately at the feet of saints, pigeons bring news of victory, cows and sheep give guidance to ecclesiastical surveyors and even monsters seem to bear no grudge. . . .

No doubt the loneliness of their circumstances made the Venetians more than usually tender towards their fellow-creatures, and gave the birds, beasts and fishes such prominence in their art.[31]

## Arsenal

From the Calle Magno we can wander back through the Campo dei Due Pozzi and then perhaps pause in the Campo Bandiera e Moro, a large, pleasant square, which contains the church of San Giovanni in Bragora, where Vivaldi was baptized. From here the Calle del Dose will take us back on to the Riva degli Schiavoni. Beyond the next bridge this becomes the Riva della Ca' di Dio, site of the ancient military bakeries and biscuit stores at nos. 2179–80. This is not exactly a tourist attraction, but the biscuits baked here deserve some sort of memorial. Not only were they reputed to defy attack by weevils, they were also exceptionally long-lived. The great historian of Venice, Pompeo Molmenti, tells us that a stack of them was left on Crete in 1669 when it was handed over to the Turks; the biscuits remained undisturbed until they came to light again in 1821, when they were still, after a century and a half, reported to be uncommonly wholesome.

The function of the bakeries was to supply the Arsenal, spread out behind them across a large part of eastern Venice. (Like 'ghetto', 'Arsenal' is a usage that the Venetians have given to the western world. It derives not from Italian but from the Arabic for workshop.) Beside the land entrance to the Arsenal there is on the right a bust of Dante and on the left a plaque inscribed with some less than inspiring verses from Canto XXI of his *Inferno*, comparing the gulf of boiling pitch in which barterers and venal public servants are confined to the scene in the Venetian Arsenal.

Dante himself might have noted a certain irony in this posthumous tribute. While he was actually there, the Venetians proved less cordial. He had gone to the city in the summer of 1321 as part of an embassy from Ravenna. Some Venetian sailors had been killed in a fracas with soldiers there and this was a diplomatic effort to patch things up. The poet got a dusty reception. According to one chronicler, the Venetians went so far as to refuse him a passage back to Ravenna by sea, and in the subsequent journey overland he caught the fever which killed him later in the year. It is possible that the description of the Arsenal was inserted into the *Inferno* at the last moment, but more likely, perhaps, that the poet had paid an unrecorded visit to the city during the earlier years of his exile from Florence.

In visiting the Arsenal Dante would have been taking in one of the standard tourist attractions of his time – and of several centuries to come. The basic system was observed by Pero Tafur on his visit in 1436:

> As one enters the gate there is a great street on either hand with the sea in the middle, and on one side are windows opening out of the houses of the arsenal, and the same on the other side, and out came a galley towed by a boat, and from the windows they handed out to them, from one the cordage, from another the bread, from another the arms, and from another the balistas and mortars, and so from all sides everything which was required, and when the galley had reached the end of the street all the men required were on board, together with the complement of oars, and she was equipped from end to end.[32]

The efficiency of this Venetian conveyor-belt was the theme of numerous later accounts. When the young Henri III of France visited Venice in 1574, he was taken to the Arsenal one morning to see the keel of a ship being laid. That evening he was invited back to see the launching of the same ship, fully equipped and ready for the open sea.[33] To achieve this sort of feat, the Arsenal could employ in its heyday over sixteen thousand men.

That was long ago. Today one of the many reasons for taking a trip on the vaporetto line no. 5, the *circolare*, is that it passes through the previously forbidden heart of the Arsenal, revealing to the privileged tourist a scene of sad abandonment. The buildings are derelict and the empty magazines a prey to invading weeds. Even the land entrance is little frequented; the imposing walls and the echoes of departed glory attract relatively few tourists. Nonetheless, it is worth a visit, if only to see the wonderful lions that guard the main gateway. The two principal ones were brought back from Athens in the seventeenth century by Francesco Morosini after his successful campaign against the Turks. (Morosini seems to have had a particular fondness for cats. The embalmed body of his domestic pet is still in the possession of the Correr Museum.) The sitting lion, which was originally stationed at Piraeus, has a singular feature that was explained in an article for the *Quarterly Review*, quoted by Augustus Hare:

> Close observers must from the first have noticed with surprise that the statue of the sitting lion [the one now on the left] bore around each of its shoulders, and in serpentine folds, the remains of barbaric inscriptions. These strange characters were after a time recognized as Norwegian Runes. . . . If reduced to straight lines the inscription on the lion's left shoulder is as follows:
>
> 'Hakon, combined with Ulf, with Asmund, and with Orn, conquered this port (the Piraeus). These men and Harold the Tall imposed large fines, on account of the revolt of the Greek people. Dalk has been detained in distant lands. Egil was waging war, together with Ragnar, in Roumania and Armenia.'[34]

According to the inscription on the right shoulder, it was Harold the Tall who ordered these runes to be engraved, against the wishes of the Greeks. It is curious to reflect that this same Harold, also known as Hardrad, the Severe, who was then apparently working as a mercenary for the Byzantine emperor, was later to be killed by an arrow at the Battle of

Stamford Bridge near York, fighting in 1066 against King Harold the Saxon. It was immediately after this battle that the Saxon Harold turned south to meet his death at Hastings.

## CASTELLO

From these teasing byways we can return, past the naval museum and the church, to the Fondamenta San Biagio. Just across the bridge, by a plaque which marks the house of the great navigators John and Sebastian Cabot, the wide Rio Terrà Garibaldi opens off to the left. If we follow this to the end and then continue along the fondamenta beside the Rio di S. Anna, we shall come to the long wooden bridge leading over to the Isola di San Pietro.

It is a restful, oddly nondescript part of Venice. At times one might almost fancy oneself in a small fishing village. Yet the church of San Pietro di Castello, with its white stone campanile, was for more than six centuries the cathedral of Venice, displaced by San Marco only in 1807. According to legend, it was one of the many churches founded in Venice by San Magno. Doge Andrea Dandolo tells in his *Chronicon Venetum* how St Peter appeared to the Bishop and told him to build a church in that part of the city of Rivoalto where he should find oxen and sheep grazing – 'And thus he did'.

It was in this district that the marriage market described by W. D. Howells took place:

At a comparatively late period Venetian fathers went with their daughters to a great annual matrimonial fair at San Pietro di Castello Olivolo, and the youth of the lagoons repaired thither to choose wives from the number of the maidens. These were all dressed in white, with hair loose about the neck, and each bore her dower in a little box, slung over her shoulder by a ribbon. It is to be supposed that there was commonly a previous understanding between each damsel and some youth in the crowd: as soon as all had paired off, the bishop gave them a sermon and his benediction, and the young men gathered up their

brides and boxes, and went away wedded. It was on one
of these occasions, in the year 944, that the Triestine
pirates stole the Brides of Venice with their dowers, and
gave occasion to the Festa delle Marie (see p. 116).[35]

This was a dramatic episode in an area of the city that has
otherwise been remote from the grander moments of Venetian
history. It was the home of the poor, and to some extent still is.
Its fishermen, in particular, gave it a reputation which
attracted the epicurean Théophile Gautier. In his *Voyage en
Italie* he gives a pleasant account of an evening here that
belongs unmistakably to a past century:

> Rounding the Public Gardens, we approached the house
> of Ser Zuane along the Canale di San Pietro. In front of his
> simple home were boats drawn out of the water and
> stranded picturesquely on the sand, nets stretched out in
> the sun, scattered beams and planks. All composed a
> rustic scene that would have made a lively subject for a
> sketch by Eugène Isabey.[36]

They have a table set out for them at the bottom of the
garden under an arbour shaded by vines and fig leaves. After a
princely meal the old hostess comes to chat with them, gives a
bouquet of flowers, picked on the spur of the moment, to one
of the women in the party, and then presents them with a
massive bill written on the back of a plate. Gautier, however,
knows the law by which foreigners pay an additional 30 per
cent 'translation costs' when restaurant bills are made out.
Without demur they pay what is asked and allow themselves
to be conducted back to their gondolas by Ser Zuane. 'We had
had an exquisite and unusual dinner . . . there was nothing
more to be said.'

## PUBLIC GARDENS

To reach the Public Gardens mentioned by Gautier we must
retrace our steps as far as the end of the Via Garibaldi and then
turn left through the Giardini Garibaldi. Laid out under

Napoleon, the gardens have never held much appeal for the English visitor – with the exception, perhaps, of Robert Browning. In his case it was the animals once confined here who were the main attraction, as Mrs Bronson records:

> In Venice, as elsewhere, Browning rose early, and after a light breakfast went with his sister to the Public Gardens. They never failed to carry with them a store of cakes and fruits for the prisoned elephant, whose lonely fate was often pityingly alluded to by the poet, in whom a love of animals amounted to a passion. A large baboon, confined in what had once been a greenhouse, was also an object of special interest to him. This beast fortunately excited no commiseration, being healthy and content, and taking equal pleasure with the givers in his daily present of dainty food. After saying 'Good morning' and 'Good appetite' to these animals, he gave a passing salutation to a pair of beautiful gazelles, presented to the gardens by one of his friends; then a word of greeting to two merry marmosets, the gift of another friend; then a glance at the pelicans, the ostriches, and the quaint kangaroos; he had a word and a look for each, seeming to study them and almost to guess their thoughts. After this he made the tour of the gardens, three times round the inclosure with great exactness, and then returned to his temporary home in the Palazzo Giustiniani-Recanati.[37]

Even the Venetians seem to leave these gardens less frequented than the average public park, and this has long been the case. It is an aspect of them that George Sand noted in her *Lettres d'un voyageur*. She had gone there one afternoon in the spring of 1834:

> I was in the park towards sunset. As usual there were very few people about. Venetian ladies dread the heat and would not think of going out during the day; but they also dread the cold and do not venture out at night. . . . Civilized males, on the other hand, prefer to frequent places where there is a chance of meeting the fair sex – such as the theatre, the *conversazioni*, the cafés or the

sheltered enclosure of the Piazzetta at seven in the evening; so that the only people one meets in the parks are a
handful of grumbling old men, some senseless smokers
or some bilious melancholics. (You can put me in which
category you please.)[38]

For Sand, as for the modern visitor, the lure of the gardens
was not the park itself but its sweeping view. On a final
evening in Venice there is no more beautiful place from which
to take a last, regretful look at the city:

> The sun had already set behind the hills of Vicenza. Great
> purple clouds were passing over the Venetian sky. The
> tower of San Marco, the dome of Santa Maria and the
> nursery-garden of spires and steeples rising from every
> corner of the city stood out as black needles against the
> sparkling horizon. The sky turned by subtle gradations
> from cherry red to cobalt blue while the water, smooth
> and clear as a mirror, faithfully reproduced its infinite
> iridescence; it lay like a vast sheen of copper below the
> city. Never have I seen Venice more beautiful and en-
> chanted. Its black silhouette, cast between the sky and the
> glowing waters as on to a sea of fire, seemed to be one of
> those sublime architectural aberrations the poet of the
> Apocalypse must have seen floating on the shores of
> Patmos as he dreamt of the New Jerusalem and likened it
> in its beauty to a newly wed bride.[39]

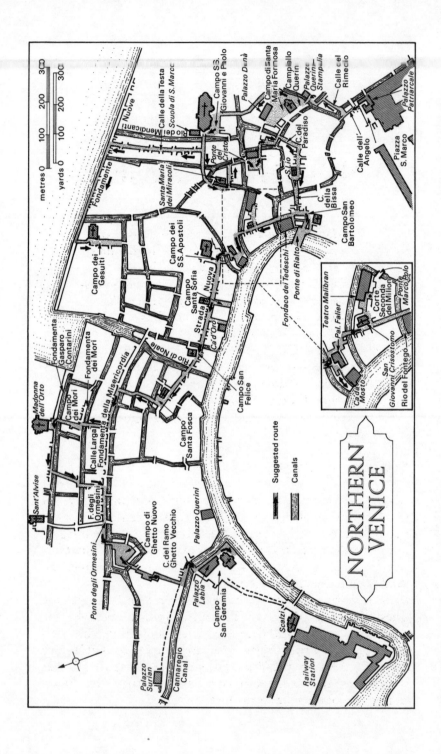

NORTHERN VENICE

Suggested route

Canals

metres 0    100    200    300
yards 0    100    200    300

Palazzo Surian
Cannaregio Canal
Ponte degli Ormesini
Sant'Alvise
Madonna dell'Orto
F. degli Ormesini
Campo dei Mori
Calle Larga
Fondamenta dei Misericordia
Fondamenta Gasparo Contarini
Fondamenta Nuove
Campo dei Gesuiti
Campo Santa Fosca
Campo di Ghetto Nuovo
C. del Ramo Ghetto Vecchio
Palazzo Querini
Palazzo Labia
Campo San Geremia
Scalzi
Railway Station
Campo San Felice
Ca'd'Oro
Rio di Noale
Campo Santa Sofia
Strada Nuova
Campo dei SS. Apostoli
Santa Maria dei Miracoli
Rio del Mendicanti
Calle della Testa
Scuola di S. Marco
Campo SS. Giovanni e Paolo
Palazzo Dona
Campo di Santa Maria Formosa
Palazzo Querini Stampalia
Campello Querini
Calle del Rimedio
Palazzo Patriarcale
Piazza S. Marco
Calle dell' Angelo
C. del Paradiso
S. Lio
C. della Bissa
Campo San Bartolomeo
Ponte del Cristo
Ponte di Rialto
Fondaco del Tedeschi
Campo San Felice

Teatro Malibran
Pal. Falier
Corte Seconda del Milion
Ponte Marco Polo
San Giovanni Crisostomo
Rio del Fontego
Ca'da Mosto

# 6

# NORTHERN VENICE

## ST MARK'S TO SANTA MARIA FORMOSA

Somewhere among the intricate patterns of stone and water
that lie between St Mark's and Santa Maria Formosa there is a
narrow street which makes a haunting appeal to the imagination. It is perhaps too late to identify it now: the fountains
have probably gone, there will be no flute music to guide us.
And yet the clues are teasing.

In the spring of 1911 the poet Rilke went to Venice as the
guest of Princess Marie von Thurn und Taxis-Hohenlohe. He
was still exhausted and depressed after completing *The Note-
books of Malte Laurids Brigge*. A leisurely exploration of Venice
was prescribed by the Princess to restore his spirits. In her
*Memoirs* she describes the mysterious street they came upon
during one of their walks through the city:

One fine morning we wanted to go to Santa Maria Formosa . . . and lost our way in a labyrinth of streets, passages, bridges and archways – most humiliating for a born Venetian like myself! Then suddenly we found ourselves in a strange, unknown place. . . . It was a long street, not exactly the kind we call *calle* in Venice, with a little fountain at either end, and very tall, large houses on either side – sad, severe houses bare of the grotesque ornamentation and the filigree windows one finds in the poorer quarters of Venice. All was silent with a silence that seemed to have survived from bygone times, made deeper still by the shrill notes of a flute incessantly playing an alien Eastern melody. We both stopped still, gazing with a feeling of weird oppression at the broken pavement from which grass sprouted (grass – in Venice!), the closed, dumb, wretched houses, the barred windows from which no face looked out, the deserted street. Far and wide no sound was to be heard except the monotonous lament of the flute. . . . We searched in vain for the name of the street; it was not marked in the usual place. I believe we shall never find that spot again, never again hear the little flute's long-drawn-out Eastern melody quavering through the empty streets.[1]

The streets where Rilke and Princess Marie wandered are an attractive jumble of intersecting alleys to the north of the Piazza. If we go through the Piazzetta dei Leoncini, past the two long-suffering lions, we can turn left opposite the Cardinal Patriarch's palace into what becomes the Calle dell'Angelo. The name of this calle is explained at the bottom of the street, where three canals come together. At the house on the corner, no. 4419, a carved angel, looking somewhat morose, is framed between two of the first floor windows. It was put there to prevent the return of a devil who had taken possession of the pet monkey belonging to the house's owner, a miserly advocate of the Ducal Courts. Exorcised from the palace, the demon had made his escape by forcing a hole through the wall at just this point, and is now for ever barred from re-entering.

Browning came across the story in Tassini's *Curiosità Veneziane* and made an excursion to the place, where he asked his gondolier, 'broad-backed Luigi', to recite the legend for him. Later he reworked it in his poem 'Ponte dell'Angelo', published in *Asolando*.

Rather than heading straight for Santa Maria Formosa, we might go back a few steps and turn down the Ramo dell'Angelo over the pretty Ponte del Rimedio, which gives us a less familiar view of the Bridge of Sighs. From here we can walk on to the next canal, where a left turn will take us into the Campiello Querini, site of the Palazzo Querini-Stampalia.

This sixteenth-century palace must be one of the most undervalued spots in Venice. Among the paintings in its gallery is a splendid collection of works by Pietro Longhi. His subjects were clearly ravished by their own reflection. For these doll-like figures the admiration of the onlooker will always be more important than whatever business is on hand, whether church service or geography lesson, dance or hunt. Longhi catches their vanity with wry precision.

Elsewhere in the gallery, at the end of the hall, there is a room filled with scenes of eighteenth-century life around the city – bear-baiting in the Campo Sant'Angelo, games in the Campo dei Gesuiti, fights at the Ponte dei Pugni, a patrician wedding at the Salute, the Doge's Easter visit to San Zaccaria. They are not the most celebrated pictures in Venice, but they offer some of the most engaging views of Venetian life. And where else is one's visit likely to be so untroubled by fellow-tourists?

## SANTA MARIA FORMOSA

A few yards from the Campiello Querini the calle runs up to the church of Santa Maria Formosa. At the southern end of a busy campo, this pleasing church has an appearance and setting faithfully recorded by Muriel Spark in *Territorial Rights*. Standing at the main door of the church, we can follow her glance around the square:

> From the outside, Santa Maria Formosa is a bulbous and comely church. Behind it laps one of the narrow lanes of

Venetian water which link streets to churches, squares to alleys. The church is wide and peaceful in its volume as if the front doors opened to show off the square before it, the square and all that stands around, the pharmacy, the funeral shop with its shiny coffins stacked one on top of another and carved with enthusiasm, the uneven roof-line, the Bar dell'Orologio wherein youth and age stand eyeing each other, and, on the far left, the Communist Party's ornate and ancient headquarters with its painted façade.[2]

Tradition has it that the church was another of those founded in the seventh century by Bishop San Magno, this time after the Virgin had appeared to him in the form of a buxom (*formosa*) matron commanding him to build a church in the place where a white cloud had come to rest. For over eight hundred years the church was notable for a ceremony which owed its origins to the marriage festival on Castello described by Howells (see p. 157). In his *Cities of Northern Italy* Augustus Hare gives this account:

On the 2nd February, 944, a number of Venetian maidens who had gone to be married at S. Pietro in Castello, taking with them the *arcelle* (coffers) containing their dowries, were carried off by a sudden inroad of pirates. They were pursued and vanquished by the Venetians under Doge Pietro Candiano III, and the brides were brought back; but the victory was owing to the bravery of the cabinet-makers of S. Maria Formosa, who asked as their sole reward that the Doge should visit their church on that anniversary every year. 'But if it rains?' said the Doge. 'We will give you hats to cover you.' 'But if I am thirsty?' 'We will give you to drink.' Hence dated the *Festa delle Marie*, which was always held in this church on February 2. First twelve and afterwards three poor maidens were always dowered here by the city on that day, when the Doge came in state to the church, and received from the priest two hats of gilt straw, two flasks of malvagia, and two oranges.[3]

It is worth taking a moment to look at the church's baroque campanile. Walk round to the side facing the canal and you will see above the doorway the grotesque head which excited one of Ruskin's more memorable outbursts:

A head – huge, inhuman, and monstrous, – leering in bestial degradation, too foul to be either pictured or described, or to be beheld for more than an instant: yet let it be endured for that instant; for in that head is embodied the type of the evil spirit to which Venice was abandoned in the fourth period of her decline; and it is as well that we should see and feel the full horror of it on this spot, and know what pestilence it was that came and breathed upon her beauty, until it melted away like the white cloud from the field of Santa Maria Formosa.

This head is one of many hundreds which disgrace the latest buildings of the city, all more or less agreeing in their expression of sneering mockery, in most cases enhanced by thrusting out the tongue. Most of them occur upon the bridges, which were among the very last works undertaken by the republic, several, for instance, upon the Bridge of Sighs; and they are evidences of delight in the contemplation of bestial vice, and the expression of low sarcasm, which is, I believe, the most hopeless state into which the human mind can fall.[4]

Among the private houses that overlook the square is the Palazzo Donà at nos. 6125–6, part of which now serves as the funeral shop mentioned by Muriel Spark. Recognizable by its pointed arches and the armorial shield carved above the door, this was once the home of the distinguished senator, Ermolao Donato. On the night of 5 November 1450, returning late from the Ducal Palace, Donato had almost reached the door when he was struck down by an assassin. On evidence collected after a denunciation had been slipped into one of the city's *bocche di leone*, the Doge's son, Jacopo Foscari, was arrested, tortured, and banished to Crete. It was a central chapter in the long tragedy that inspired Byron to write *The Two Foscari*.

## SAN GIOVANNI E PAOLO

If we leave the campo beside the Bar All'Orologio and follow
the appropriate signs, we shall come after a couple of minutes
to the Campo San Giovanni e Paolo. In a city that has not been
noted for religious fervour the many churches have often
proved useful sites for the conduct of intrigue. It may have
given a certain ironic satisfaction to Protestant England's
ambassador to select the great Dominican church of San
Giovanni e Paolo as a place of secret rendezvous. In the early
seventeenth century England was eager to profit from the
strained relations between Venice and Rome. The political
situation was delicate; foreigners, diplomats especially, were
closely watched. It was here that Sir Henry Wotton would
from time to time appoint meetings with his spies to collect
information and issue instructions. The huge, crowded spaces
of the church, the echoing stones and smoking candles must
have offered a congenial setting for such business.

Once inside a Venetian church most people give their time,
reasonably enough, to art rather than devotion and to the
paintings rather than the sculptures. This has not always been
easy. In 1826 William Hazlitt was reprimanded by a priest in
San Giovanni e Paolo for turning his back on the host while
attempting to get some light on Titian's *St Peter the Martyr*.[5] In
the end, he had to return in the afternoon. Even twenty years
ago one could often see the pictures only by catching a
convenient shaft of sunlight or illuminating the sacred limbs
piecemeal with the help of a torch. Floodlights have now for
the most part done away with the problem, enabling anyone
with enough coins to admire the paintings at leisure.

No doubt the tombs are usually of less artistic interest than
the pictures, but their presence makes its own contribution to
the murky atmosphere of many of the larger churches, and in
the case of the Frari and San Giovanni e Paolo these monuments are of some importance. Along the right aisle, between
the first and second altars, is the tomb of Marcantonio
Bragadin, the courageous defender of Famagusta. In 1571
Cyprus was the last remnant of Venice's Eastern empire, and it
was Bragadin who, as governor, was left to stand against the

victorious Turks. After a heroic but hopeless defence, honourable terms were granted to the garrison and Bragadin declared
that he would himself hand over the keys. The Turkish
commander replied in courteous words that he would be
honoured to receive him. What followed was described in
grim detail in a piece for the *Quarterly Review* of October
1874:

> Bragadino came, attended by the officers of his staff,
> dressed in his purple robes, and with a red umbrella, the
> sign of his rank, held over him. In the course of the
> ensuing interview the Pasha suddenly springing up,
> accused him of having put some Mussulman prisoners to
> death: the officers were dragged away and cut to pieces,
> whilst Bragadino was reserved for the worst outrages that
> vindictive cruelty could inflict. He was thrice made to
> bear his neck to the executioner, whose sword was
> thrice lifted as if about to strike: his ears were cut off:
> he was driven every morning for ten days, heavy laden
> with baskets of earth, to the batteries, and compelled to
> kiss the ground before the Pasha's pavilion as he passed.
> He was hoisted to the yard-arm of one of the ships and
> exposed to the derision of the sailors. Finally, he was
> carried to the square of Famagosta, stripped, chained to a
> stake on the public scaffold, and slowly flayed alive,
> whilst the Pasha looked on. His skin, stuffed with straw,
> was then mounted on a cow, paraded through the streets
> with the red umbrella over it, suspended at the bowsprit
> of the admiral's galley, and displayed as a trophy during
> the whole voyage to Constantinople. The skin was
> afterwards purchased of the Pasha by the family of
> Bragadino,[6] and deposited in an urn in the church of SS.
> Giovanni e Paolo.[7]

A fresco of Bragadin being flayed by the cruel Turks can
be seen above the monument, whose Latin epitaph moved
Coryate to tears: 'Truly I could not reade it with dry eyes,
neither do I thinke any Christian to be so hard hearted . . . that
can read the same without either effusion of teares, or at the

least some kinde of relenting, if he doth understand the Latin tongue.'[8]

It is impossible not to notice in the middle of the same aisle a vast baroque extravaganza over the entrance to the chapel of the Madonna della Pace. This is the pompous tomb of a couple of seventeenth-century Doges, Bertuccio and Silvestro Valier. Beside them is that of Silvestro's wife, a formidable woman who outraged her contemporaries by having medals struck, bearing her own effigy. (It seems that Silvestro died of a heart attack following an argument with her.) After reading Ruskin, it is hard to pass her tomb without a sympathetic glance, both for the Dogaressa herself and for the hapless lion at the base of the monument:

> The statues of the Doges, though mean and Polonius-like, are partly redeemed by the Ducal robes; but that of the Dogaressa is a consummation of grossness, vanity, and ugliness, – the figure of a large and wrinkled woman, with elaborate curls in stiff projection round her face, covered from her shoulders to her feet with ruffs, furs, lace, jewels, and embroidery. Beneath and around are scattered Virtues, Victories, Fames, genii, – the entire company of the monumental stage assembled, as before a drop scene, – executed by various sculptors, and deserving attentive study as exhibiting every condition of false taste and feeble conception. The Victory in the centre is peculiarly interesting; the lion by which she is accompanied, springing on a dragon, has been intended to look terrible, but the incapable sculptor could not conceive any form of dreadfulness, could not even make the lion look angry. It looks only lacrymose; and its lifted forepaws, there being no spring nor motion in its body, give it the appearance of a dog begging.[9]

## VERROCCHIO'S STATUE

The *condottiere* Bartolommeo Colleoni was luckier in his monument. Even if the church is closed, Verrocchio's equestrian statue is reward enough for your journey. To live as a *condottiere* in fifteenth-century Italy and die of old age shows talent of a kind, but Colleoni's career was perhaps as remarkable for his financial acumen as for any feats of arms. The troubled history of his statue, which was completed by Alessandro Leopardi, is told in Vasari's *Lives of the Artists*. Verrocchio had already finished modelling the horse when the Venetian Senate decided to hand over the figure of Colleoni himself to another artist:

> On hearing this, Andrea smashed the legs and head of his model and returned in a rage to Florence without saying a word. And when the Signoria heard what had happened they gave him to understand that he had better not return to Venice or they would cut off his head. To this Andrea wrote in reply that he would take good care not to, since once they had cut off a man's head they had no way of replacing it, certainly not one like his; whereas he would have been able to replace the head of the horse, and with something more beautiful at that.[10]

With remarkable urbanity the senate thereupon reversed its decision and brought Verrocchio back at double his previous salary. Before he could finish the work, however, he was carried off by a chill.

Coryate, who saw the statue in the early seventeenth century, offers a description which is surprising for more than its confident etymology of the *condottiere*'s name:

> In a greene yard adjoyning hard to this Church, there is erected a goodly Colossus all of alabaster, supported with six faire pillars of the same, on the toppe whereof the statue of Barthelmew Coleon (who had his name from having three stones, for the Italian word Coglione doth signifie a testicle) is advanced in his complet armour on horse-backe.[11]

Looking back from the end of the twentieth century, it is not easy to imagine a Venice in which many of the campi were still green fields. It was outside San Giovanni e Paolo that Coryate

came across the one horse he saw in Venice, 'a little bay nagge
feeding in this Church-yard of St John and Paul'.

Whatever Colleoni might have thought of his statue, he
would have been less than happy with its site – opposite the
Scuola di San Marco. He had left a huge and much needed
legacy to the Venetian State on condition that the monument
should be erected in the *Piazza* San Marco. The Council was
keen on the money, less so on the *condottiere*'s posthumous
self-aggrandisement. The scuola seemed an excellent compromise. So the State took the legacy, and Colleoni ended up
with the Dominicans in the Campo San Giovanni e Paolo.

After all, he has not fared badly. Five centuries later Verrocchio's statue remains one of the great equestrian monuments
of the world. At the climax of *The Aspern Papers* Henry
James's narrator finds himself gazing up at the statue in the
evening light. His attempt to secure the Aspern papers has
ended in humiliation; he is left with much to repent and repair:

> I forget what I did, where I went after leaving the Lido
> and at what hour or with what recovery of composure I
> made my way back to my boat. I only know that in the
> afternoon, when the air was aglow with the sunset, I was
> standing before the church of Saints John and Paul and
> looking up at the small square-jawed face of Bartolom-
> meo Colleoni, the terrible *condottiere* who sits so sturdily
> astride of his huge bronze horse, on the high pedestal on
> which Venetian gratitude maintains him. The statue is
> incomparable, the finest of all mounted figures, unless
> that of Marcus Aurelius, who rides benignant before the
> Roman Capitol, be finer: but I was not thinking of that; I
> only found myself staring at the triumphant captain as if
> he had an oracle on his lips. The western light shines into
> all his grimness at that hour and makes it wonderfully
> personal. But he continued to look far over my head, at
> the red immersion of another day – he had seen so many
> go down into the lagoon through the centuries – and if he
> were thinking of battles and stratagems they were of a
> different quality from any I had to tell him of. He could
> not direct me what to do, gaze up at him as I might.[12]

## Scuola Grande di San Marco

Visitors to this corner of Venice tend to move briskly from church to statue to one of the nearby cafés. There is little time to spare for the attractive building with coloured marble façade and pillared hall which occupies the north side of the square. This is the Scuola Grande di San Marco mentioned above. Designed by the Lombardi, the scuola later became the site of what is now the main civic hospital of Venice. To judge from Count Zorzi's recollections, it has done well to keep so much of its original appearance:

> I do not exactly remember when, but I know that one day some passers-by rescued Mr Ruskin at San Giovanni e Paolo from the 'Canaglia', whose ire he had excited because he had launched into just invective against the urchins who, with sharp instruments, were amusing themselves by damaging the façade of the Scuola di San Marco as far as it was in their reach.[13]

Revulsion from the doings of the Italian lower classes was probably one of the few sentiments that Ruskin shared with the Goncourt brothers, who visited the hospital late in 1855. They were already beginning the investigations into the underside of French social life which were later to result in novels like *Soeur Philomène* and *Germinie Lacerteux*. A holiday in Italy merely changed the scene of their interests. True to form, they headed for the venereal ward:

> Under the vaults of a magnificent coffered ceiling, wonderfully carved, beds are lined up with their heads to the wall . . . I am with Dr Callegari at the Scuola di San Marco, in the hospital at which the sick arrive and from which the dead are taken away by gondola.
> We are here in the venereal ward. Some of the women are sleeping, others are searching for fleas . . . six or seven of them with shining faces, like newly scoured saucepans, are crowded round a table, talking, shouting, making a racket. They are bizarrely tricked out in showy rags, sleeveless red smocks over white petticoats. In front of each of them, set out like the mosaic floor in Murano

Cathedral, is a collection of fake stones and jewels, and one of them is shaking a bag in which you can hear the rattle of pieces of wood. The hussies are playing tombola.

The doctor pinches the nurse's cheek in fun and passes through the ward to the sound of laughter, crude sallies, ironic cheers and lewd remarks from the table.[14]

Alongside the Scuola, the Rio dei Mendicanti leads straight out to the lagoon, towards the tall cypresses which rise behind the walls of San Michele. This easy access to the open water was another feature that made San Giovanni e Paolo a convenient place of rendezvous. On one of the many occasions when Casanova had made a discreet assignation with an amorous nun, it was here that he waited for her to arrive from the convent on Murano:

At the first hour of the night I took up my post by the statue of the heroic Colleoni. She had told me to be there at the second hour, but I wanted to have the sweet pleasure of waiting for her. The night was cold, but magnificent, and without the least wind.

Exactly at the second hour I saw a gondola with two rowers arrive and disembark a masker, who, after speaking to the gondolier at the prow, came toward the statue. Seeing a male masker, I am alarmed, I slip away, and I regret not having pistols. The masker walks around the statue, comes up to me, and offers me a peaceable hand which leaves me in no more doubt. I recognize my angel dressed as a man. She laughs at my surprise, clings to my arm, and without a word between us we make our way to the Piazza San Marco, cross it, and go to the casino [see p. 18], which was only a hundred paces from the Teatro San Moisè.[15]

## GESUITI

A few yards beyond the canal our path meets the Calle della Testa, which takes its name from the head carved above the door of no. 6216. From here, if time allows and the sky is clear, we can make an excursion to the Fondamente Nuove – which turn out to be rather less new than their name implies, having been built in the 1580s. At the time this was a fashionable part of Venice, because the air was believed to be particularly healthy and free from pestilence. It was here that Titian lived in the years immediately before the construction of the fondamenta.

Set beside the meadows which then stretched down to the edge of the lagoon, the painter's house was close to the spot where the extraordinary church of the Gesuiti now stands. Built in the early eighteenth century, the church offers a fine example of the sort of decorative effects which, in Gautier's view, 'make the chapel of the Holy Virgin look like a chorus girl's boudoir.' W. D. Howells reckoned it to be the coldest church in Venice:

> The workmanship is marvellously skillful, and the material costly, but it only gives the church the effect of being draped in damask linen; and even where the marble is carven in vast and heavy folds over a pulpit to simulate a curtain, or wrought in figures on the steps of the high-altar to represent a carpet, it has no richness of effect, but a poverty, a coldness, a harshness indescribably table-clothy. I think all of this has tended to chill the soul of the sacristan, who is the feeblest and thinnest sacristan conceivable, with a frost of white hair on his temples quite incapable of thawing. In this dreary sanctuary is one of Titian's great paintings, the Martyrdom of St. Lawrence, to which (though it is so cunningly disposed as to light that no one ever yet saw the whole picture at once) you turn involuntarily, envious of the Saint roasting so comfortably on his gridiron amid all that frigidity.[16]

The harsh judgements of one century inevitably invite a more tolerant response from the next. Today we are likely to take a kinder view of some of the Gesuiti's marble extravagances. It is, in any case, perhaps appropriate that this should have proved a somewhat controversial church. The Jesuits themselves had an uneasy relationship with Venice, never marked by great affection on either side. 'Venetians first, then Christians' was a popular motto unlikely to recommend itself to them. At the time of the Papal Interdict In 1606, their primary allegiance to Rome was clear, and they were accordingly banished. Work on the Gesuiti began shortly after their return, but it had not been long completed when they were again sent on their way.


## SANTA MARIA DEI MIRACOLI

Today the Fondamente Nuove, lined for the most part with undistinguished buildings, look a little drab, and it can be something of a relief to turn back towards the centre of the city. Our point of departure, beside the large primary school on the corner of the Calle della Testa, is only a moment away from the concealed beauty of one of Venice's loveliest churches. Islanded on a patch of the city that is cut into a rough triangle by the course of three canals, Santa Maria dei Miracoli yields itself unexpectedly to view. In describing it, almost every guide-book turns sooner or later to metaphors of caskets and jewels, and for once the reader cannot complain. Built by Pietro Lombardo in the late fifteenth century, the Miracoli seems to have been set down in a small patch of Venice perfectly fashioned for it.

Inside the church, with its vaulted roof and starry dome, we may indeed have the impression of sitting within a beautifully marbled casket. The sculptures are reluctantly allowed by Ruskin to be 'the best possible example of a bad style'. Particularly good, and bad, is the child's head on the right of the altar. In the middle of a mixed company of cherubs and mermaids, it looks out from among the vine-leaves at the base of the pilaster. What upsets Ruskin is the way the sculptor has chosen to tie it up by the hair:

> A rude workman, who could hardly have carved the head at all, might have been allowed this or any other mode of expressing discontent with his own doings; but the man who could carve a child's head so perfectly must have been wanting in all human feeling, to cut it off, and tie it by the hair to a vine leaf.[17]

Outside the Miracoli on 27 January 1516 an event of casual, unexplained violence took place. It was the sort of thing which happens and is forgotten. That the scene and its wretched actors might drift through our mind as we stand beside the little canal today is just a freak of chance. Marin Sanudo recorded it, and so the memory survives:

> This morning something happened to a most beautiful woman, called Samaritana Zon, wife of Zuan Francesco Benedeto, just after she had left the church of Santa Maria dei Miracoli. While she waited to get into her boat and go home, there was a masked man sitting at the canal-side. Having seen her, he stabbed at her with a dagger and slashed her face from the eye down to the mouth, so that her woman's looks will be ruined. Such was the outrage this caused that the incident was brought to the attention of the Council of Ten.[18]

We are told that the guilty man was found and banished, but why he did it or what happened to the luckless woman is beyond our knowledge.

## PONTE DEL CRISTO

From the church of the Miracoli the Calle Castelli leads off towards the Ponte del Cristo and beside it the Palazzo Marcello-Papadopoli. There is nothing especially notable about either the palace or the bridge, but the prospect as we cross over to the Campo Santa Marina has a particular charm. Glance to the left – on one side a flaking pink wall, on the other the windows of the palace; further down, the trailing branches of a garden, and behind it a high, blank wall somehow hung with colourful washing. The canal is a shade too wide; in other respects it is just the setting that Henry James evokes in one of his most enticing visions of the city. The name of Venice, he tells us, does not make him think of the Piazza or the Grand Canal or St Mark's:

> I simply see a narrow canal in the heart of the city – a patch of green water and a surface of pink wall. The gondola

moves slowly; it gives a great smooth swerve, passes under a bridge, and the gondolier's cry, carried over the quiet water, makes a kind of splash in the stillness. A girl crosses the little bridge, which has an arch like a camel's back, with an old shawl on her head, which makes her characteristic and charming; you see her against the sky as you float beneath. The pink of the old wall seems to fill the whole place; it sinks even into the opaque water. Behind the wall is a garden, out of which the long arm of a white June rose – the roses of Venice are splendid – has flung itself by way of spontaneous ornament. On the other side of this small water-way is a great shabby façade of Gothic windows and balconies – balconies on which dirty clothes are hung and under which a cavernous-looking doorway opens from a low flight of slimy water-steps. It is very hot and still, the canal has a queer smell, and the whole place is enchanting.[19]

## CALLE DEL PARADISO

From the Campo Santa Marina we can turn left along the Calle Marcello and across the bridge. This circuitous route has brought us back to the edge of Santa Maria Formosa. If we turn down the Calle del Dose and then skirt the canal for a few yards, we shall come to a street distinguished by the Gothic arch at its entrance – 'one of the most exquisite little pieces of detail in the whole city', according to the architect G. E. Street. This is the Calle del Paradiso, notable also for its fine wooden eaves.

It was here that a certain musician called Leonardo da Conegliano was living in 1369. Tassini relates in his *Curiosità Veneziane* how Leonardo arranged one winter's morning to go to the parish of San Gregorio with some friends, among them Lorenzo di Bonifazio, who had proposed the outing:

At the appropriate time all of them repair to the house of the musician, who comes downstairs and goes off with them. Lorenzo, meanwhile, first hides himself in the house and then makes an attempt on the musician's wife,

Armellina. She screams to the neighbours through an open window, puts the seducer to flight, and, on her husband's return, tells him the whole story. Leonardo flies into a rage and wants to swear out a complaint before a magistrate, but his friends try to calm him, pointing out that in the event things went no further than a simple attempt. However, the good man refuses to believe this and will only accept it when Lorenzo goes into the church of San Giovanni Crisostomo, lights a two-branched candlestick and swears on the holy ciborium that he has had no criminal intercourse with Armellina and that he repents of the attempt he made. Leonardo thereupon allows him once again to frequent his house. But alas! the musician returns one fine day from Treviso to hear from the neighbours that the rogue has committed adultery with his wife, and indeed the woman confesses through her tears that she has been unable to resist the seductions of Lorenzo and that she has lain with him four times, thrice at home and once at a shoe-maker's in SS. Apostoli. The records of the trial do not say what became of the unfortunate husband, they record only that Lorenzo was sentenced on the 28th February 1369 to two years in prison and a fine of five hundred lire, Armellina to two months in prison and the loss of her dowry, and Lorenzo's companions to six months in prison and a fine of a hundred lire.[20]

## CALLE DELLA BISSA

Another right turn at the bottom of the Calle del Paradiso will take us into the Salizzada di San Lio, past the church and on towards the Rialto. The busy commercial aspect of the streets in this area does nothing to suggest that we are entering what was once among the most fearful regions of the city.

Now one of the main shopping centres, it could hardly be less threatening. But beyond the church of San Lio is the Calle della Bissa. It starts genially enough with a row of shops and bars, but in the last section, after we have passed under the

dilapidated sottoportico, its character changes. Quite suddenly we are among the serpentine twists that give the calle its
name – *biscia* meaning snake. Openings to the side lead off into
rank little alleys, and courtyards out of reach of the sun. Here,
in the narrow spaces, among high, crumbling walls, the
atmosphere is quite different. It is surprising how quickly one
slips out of the comforting bustle. The eighteenth-century
chronicler G. B. Gallicciolli notes that under Doge Domenico
Michiel (1118–30) special laws were passed to check the activities of cut-throats in the Calle della Bissa and other such
streets.

> It had become common to wear false beards in the style of
> the Greeks, with the consequence that great evil was done
> by night, and especially in cramped passageways, like the
> Calle Bissa and the Ponte degli Assassini. Many were
> found murdered and no one knew who was responsible,
> because no one could recognize the malefactors. So
> throughout the territories of Venice these beards were
> banned by day and night, on pain of the gallows.[21]

The measure did little to secure the streets at home or to
salvage Venice's reputation abroad. At the beginning of the
seventeenth century Thomas Coryate gave a thumb-nail
sketch of the sort of figure tourists hope to avoid:

> There are certaine desperate and resolute villains in
> Venice, called Braves, who at some unlawful times do
> commit great villainy. They wander abroad very late in
> the night to and fro for their prey, like hungry Lyons,
> being armed with a privy coate of maile, a gauntlet upon
> their right hand, and a little sharpe dagger called a stiletto.
> They lurke commonly by the water side, and if at their
> time of night, which is betwixt eleven of the clocke and
> two, they happen to meete any man that is worth the
> rifling, they will presently stabbe him, take away all about
> him that is of any worth, and when they have throughly
> pulled his plumes, they will throw him into one of the
> channels: but they buy this booty very deare if they are
> after apprehended. For they are presently executed.[22]

By the time Otway was writing *Venice Preserved* later in the century, the *bravo* was firmly entrenched in the city's mythology:

Can thy great heart descend so vilely low,
Mix with hired slaves, bravoes, and common stabbers,
Nose-slitters, alley-lurking villains! join
With such a crew, and take a ruffian's wages,
To cut the throats of wretches as they sleep?[23]

The alley-lurking villains were not always intent on private enterprise. For most of its history the Republic was as anxious to employ such people as in other moods it was to suppress them. The archives of the Council of Ten reveal details of State-sponsored attempts on the lives of political figures ranging from the Emperor Sigismund to Pope Pius VI. For the most part, these schemes involved the sort of cut-throats for whom murder was the business of every day; but there were exceptions. On 13 September 1419 the Ten were dealing with an offer from the Archbishop of Trebizond to arrange the poisoning of Marsilio Da Carrara. By way of encouragement he was voted 50 ducats for out-of-pocket expenses.

Perhaps the most ambitious project was proposed by a doctor called Michiel Angelo Salomon, who had it in mind to wipe out the Turkish army. In 1649 the Provveditore Generale of Dalmatia wrote to the State Inquisitors with details of the project. Salomon, he explained, had

availed himself of the presence here of the plague to distil a liquid expressed from the spleen, the buboes, and carbuncles of the plague-stricken; and this, when mixed with other ingredients, will have the power wherever it is scattered to slay any number of persons, for it is the quintessence of plague. . . . I believe, however, that some ruse must be adopted to entice the Turks into the trap, and would suggest that we should make use of the Albanian fez, or some other cloth goods, which the Turks are accustomed to buy, so that the poison may pass through as many hands in as short a time as possible. The cloth should be made up in parcels as if for sale, after

having been painted over with the quintessence, and then
placed in separate boxes destined for the various places
where we desire to sow the poison.[24]

The Provveditore goes on to suggest that pedlars might
hawk the cloth about the country 'so that the enemy, hoping
to make booty, may gain the plague and find death'. Sensitive
to the possibility that this could be unhealthy work for the
pedlars, he adds that 'while handling the quintessence, it will
be of use to the operator to stuff his nose and mouth with
sponges soaked in vinegar'. And presumably hope that intending purchasers will notice nothing out of the way.

The Ten were delighted with the scheme, but when they
insisted that Salomon himself must take the plague jar to their
Commander-in-Chief, the doctor's enthusiasm waned. He
was, in the end, persuaded, but the story has no dramatic
conclusion. Salomon perhaps thought better of journeying
with the plague and substituted some less unpredictable
potion.


## RIO DEL FONTEGO

For the cut-throats of the Middle Ages there was good money
to be made around the Rialto. Beside the bridge, on the corner
of the Grand Canal and the Rio del Fontego, stand the square
walls of the Fondaco dei Tedeschi, which now houses the
Central Post Office. Originally decorated with frescos by
Giorgione and Titian, this was once the trading centre for
German merchants in Venice. Unlike most post offices, it has
its service counters ranged under the arcades of a fine courtyard with a well-head in the centre and a main gate opening on
to the Grand Canal. In spite of over-zealous restoration, the
setting is recognizably the same as in old prints, where
the activity depicted was among stocky German traders rather
than the chequered crowd of tourists to be seen in the
courtyard today.

Throughout the Middle Ages, pilgrims who intended to
take ship for the Holy Land were obliged to spend several

weeks in the city making their arrangements. For pilgrims from Germany this was the most popular area, and the Inn of St George, owned by a Frankfurt businessman and run by his manager, Master John, was the most popular hotel. The map of Venice by Jacopo de' Barbari in the Correr Museum shows the inn standing immediately beside the Fondaco dei Tedeschi.

In the spring of 1483 a middle-aged Dominican friar called Felix Fabri, who had journeyed down from Ulm and across the Brenner pass, arrived in Venice to undertake his second pilgrimage:

Presently we sailed into the city and went along the Grand Canal as far as the Rialto, where on each side of us we saw buildings of wonderful height and beauty. Below the Rialto we turned out of the Grand Canal into another canal, on the right bank of which stands the Fondaco de' Tedeschi, by which we proceeded among the houses right up to the door of our inn, which was called the Inn of St George, and in German commonly known as 'Zu der Fleuten'. Here we disembarked, walked up about sixty stone steps from the sea to the rooms which were prepared for us, and carried all our things into them. Here Master John, the landlord, and Mistress Margaret, the landlady, received us with great good humour, and greeted me with especial friendliness because I was the only one of us they knew, through my former pilgrimage during which I had been a guest in their house for many days. The rest of the household also met us, greeting us and showing their eagerness to wait on us.[25]

Inn-keepers like Master John were carefully vetted by a committee of the Venetian Senate. The pilgrims were an important source of revenue, and it was a matter of concern that they should not come to harm. To this end the same committee supervised the activities of a dozen guides, *tholomarii*, who were stationed in the Piazza San Marco and whose job it was to look after the pilgrims' welfare. The account of these guides given by Rosamund Mitchell might make one regret that their office was ever discontinued:

The *tholomarii* existed for the benefit of the pilgrims, they were not expected to line their own pockets. In particular, they were forbidden to accept commission from trades-men whose shops they visited. Because the guides were paid a decent salary, tips from clients were considered unnecessary; indeed, from time to time their acceptance was forbidden. In actual fact it was not possible to prevent rich pilgrims from trying to buy preferential treatment, but the practice was certainly frowned upon. The number of *tholomarii* had been raised from eight to twelve by the mid-fifteenth century; they served in shifts, two always being on duty from dawn till dusk, while a rota was formed to deal with any emergency during the night. Although they were allowed (singly) to take an hour off for their mid-day meal, any attempt to institute a 'tea-break' (or its equivalent) was immediately disallowed. From the pilgrims' point of view the system of 'piazza guides' was highly satisfactory, for it saved them from all worry as well as from exploitation. It was the pride of the Venetian Senate to give such good service: it was also excellent business.[26]

The fifty or so ducats required by pilgrims for basic pay-ments were only the beginning of their expenses. Writing in 1480, Santo Brasca, a Milanese who had himself made the voyage, advised the pilgrim to take at least 150 ducats, along with an equal store of patience:

Further, let him take a supply of good Lombard cheese and sausages and other salt meats, white biscuits, some loaves of sugar and several kinds of preserved sweet-meats, but not a great quantity of these last because they go bad. Above all he should have with him a great deal of fruit syrup because that is what keeps a man alive in the great heat; and also syrup of ginger to settle his stomach if it should be upset by excessive vomiting, but the ginger should be used sparingly, because it is very heating. Likewise he should take some quince without spice, some aromatics flavoured with rose and carnation and some good milk products. When he goes ashore in any place he should furnish himself with eggs, fowls, bread, sweet-meats and fruit, and not count what he has paid the captain because this is a voyage on which the purse must not be kept shut.[27]

## CORTE SECONDA DEL MILION

From the Fondaco dei Tedeschi a busy salizzada leads towards the Campo dei SS. Apostoli. Midway along it, beside the church of San Giovanni Crisostomo, a passageway opens into the Corte Prima del Milion and then, via another passage and a low sottoportico, into the Corte Seconda del Milion.

This pleasant courtyard was once the site of Marco Polo's house, and a plaque has been set just beyond it on the side-wall of the Teatro Malibran. From the time of the Ca' Polo there remains a splendid Byzantine arch, immediately on your left as you enter, decorated with carvings of animals and flowers. This same arch must have met the traveller's glance as he looked round the courtyard for the last time before setting off with his father and uncle in 1271. He was then only sixteen years old. By the time he saw Venice again he was forty. The account of his return has passed into legend. No doubt the details have been embellished in the process, but the story was first set down as early as the sixteenth century by Marco Polo's biographer, Giambattista Ramusio. The travellers entered the city in Tartar dress, having all but forgotten the Venetian dialect. They made their way to this courtyard only to find that the relatives who now occupied the house flatly refused to believe that these three shabby figures were the same members of the Polo family they had long assumed to be dead. The Polos therefore devised a scheme to ensure their recognition:

> They invited a number of their kindred to an entertainment, which they took care to have prepared with great state and splendour in that house of theirs; and when the hour arrived for sitting down to table they came forth from their chamber all three clothed in crimson satin, fashioned in long robes reaching to the ground such as people in those days wore within doors. And when water

for the hands had been served, and the guests were set, they took off those robes and put on others of crimson damask, whilst the first suits were cut up and divided among the servants. Then after partaking of some of the dishes they went out again and came back in robes of crimson velvet, and when they had again taken their seats, the second suits were divided as before. When dinner was over they did the like with the robes of velvet, after they had put on dresses of the ordinary fashion worn by the rest of the company. These proceedings caused much wonder and amazement among the guests. But when the cloth had been drawn, and all the servants had been ordered to retire from the dining hall, Messer Marco, as the youngest of the three, rose from the table, and, going into another chamber, brought forth the three shabby dresses of coarse stuff which they had worn when they first arrived. Straightway they took sharp knives and began to rip up some of the seams and welts, and to take out of them jewels of the greatest value in vast quantities, such as rubies, sapphires, carbuncles, diamonds and emeralds, which had all been stitched up in those dresses in so artful a fashion that nobody could have suspected the fact.[28]

Ramusio goes on to explain how, in attempting to convey an impression of the great wealth of the East, Marco would continually make use of the word *millions*, 'so they gave him the nickname of Messer Marco Millioni: a thing which I have noted also in the public Books of this Republic where mention is made of him. The court of his house, too, at S. Giovanni Crisostomo, has always from that time been known to the common people as the Court of the Millioni.'[29]

The elements of popular myth are clear. And yet we might note, however sceptically, the claim by Sir Henry Yule, Marco Polo's nineteenth-century editor, that Polo's name does in fact appear in the records of the Great Council as Marco Millioni. Even the fairy-tale business with the clothes, Yule suggests, is not without parallels in Mongol customs of the time.

## Teatro Malibran

Passing under the Byzantine arch, we come to the early Venetian playhouse that rose on the foundations of the old Ca' Polo. An attractive theatre, which has lately been reopened for ballets and concerts, it was renamed for the opera singer Maria Malibran after she gave two benefit performances in aid of its reconstruction in 1834. Almost a hundred years earlier Jean-Jacques Rousseau had spent an evening here, recalled in his *Confessions*:

> One day, at the Teatro di San Crisostomo, I fell asleep, and far more soundly than if I had been in bed. The loud and brilliant arias did not wake me. But who could describe the delicious sensation produced in me by the delicate harmony and angelic singing of that song which finally did! What an awakening, what bliss, what ecstasy when I opened my ears and my eyes together! My first thought was that I was in paradise.[30]

To the nicer sensibilities of the visiting English, the productions of the eighteenth-century stage were sometimes less acceptable. 'The Comedies that I saw at *Venice*,' remarks Addison, 'or indeed in any other part of *Italy*, are very indifferent, and more lewd than those of other countries. Their poets have no notion of genteel Comedy, and fall into the most filthy double-meanings imaginable, when they have a mind to make their audience merry.'[31]

It was not only the plays that excited misgiving; some of the other arrangements were casual enough to disconcert at least one English traveller. Arthur Young reached Italy in the autumn of 1789. Though his main business was to study methods of agriculture, he was ready to take note of whatever came his way:

> There is nothing more striking in the manners of different nations than in the idea of shame annexed to certain necessities of nature. In England a man makes water (if I may use such an expression) with a degree of privacy, and a woman never in sight of our sex. In France and Italy

there is no such feeling, so that Sterne's Madame Ram-
bouillet was no exaggeration. . . . There is between the
front row of chairs in the pit and the orchestra, in the
Venetian theatre, a space five or six feet without floor: a
well-dressed man, sitting almost under a row of ladies in
the side-boxes, stepped into this place, and made water
with as much indifference as if he had been in the street;
and nobody regarded him with any degree of wonder but
myself. It is, however, a beastly trick: – shame may be
ideal, but not cleanliness; for the want of it is a solid and
undoubted evil. For a city of not more than 150,000
people, Venice is wonderfully provided with theatres;
there are seven; and all of them are said to be full in the
carnival.[32]

## SAN GIOVANNI CRISOSTOMO

Before moving on, we might look into the church of San
Giovanni Crisostomo, contructed on the Byzantine model in
the shape of a Greek cross. Above the high altar is a painting by
Sebastiano del Piombo for which Henry James felt a curious
fascination. His words draw one back to it, in particular to the
female figure in the foreground whose face is turned towards
the spectator:

This face and figure are almost unique among the beautiful things of Venice, and they leave the susceptible observer with the impression of having made, or rather
having missed, a strange, a dangerous, but a most
valuable acquaintance. The lady, who is superbly handsome, is the typical Venetian of the sixteenth century, and
she remains for the mind the perfect flower of that
society. Never was there a greater air of breeding, a
deeper expression of tranquil superiority. She walks a
goddess – as if she trod without sinking the waves of the
Adriatic. It is impossible to conceive a more perfect
expression of the aristocratic spirit either in its pride or in
its benignity. This magnificent creature is so strong and

secure that she is gentle, and so quiet that in comparison
all minor assumptions of calmness suggest only a vulgar
alarm. But for all this there are depths of possible disorder
in her light-coloured eye.[33]

Others before James had allowed their thoughts to take a
secular turn in San Giovanni Crisostomo. The city archives
note the case of six young patricians condemned to two years
exile and a fine of 500 lire for stealing the handkerchiefs of
several women who were at their devotions in the church.
Such incidents were not uncommon. Since a visit to church
was one of the few occasions when a Venetian woman of good
birth was likely to venture from home, the city's social life saw
a happy alliance between the sexual and the religious which
survived well into Casanova's time.

## CA' DA MOSTO

Just beyond the next bridge, but invisible from the street, is the
venerable Ca' da Mosto, best seen by standing under the
arcade of the Rialto markets and looking across from the other
side of the canal. This ancient palace was once the home of
Alvise da Mosto, discoverer of the Cape Verde islands. From
the fifteenth century it became a well-known inn called the
Albergo del Leon Bianco, and it was here that William Beckford took rooms when he arrived in Venice at the beginning of
August 1780. Young, good-looking and immensely rich, he
seemed an enviable figure. In other respects his life at the time
was less straightforward. His marriage to Lady Margaret
Gordon was not yet on the horizon, but he was already
entangled in an affair with his cousin's wife, and he was also
hopelessly in love with the twelve-year-old son of Lord and
Lady Courtenay. In this context his European journey, elo-
quently, if discreetly, recorded in *Dreams, Waking Thoughts,
and Incidents*, should have been a welcome escape. And for his
first night in the Ca' da Mosto Venice did everything possible
to meet the requirements of his imagination. His spacious
balcony, twined round with plants, looked out over the Grand
Canal:

Here I established myself, to enjoy the cool, and observe, as well as the dusk would permit, the variety of figures shooting by in their gondolas. As night approached, innumerable tapers glimmered through the awnings before the windows. Every boat had its lantern, and the gondolas moving rapidly along were followed by tracks of light, which gleamed and played on the waters. I was gazing at these dancing fires, when the sounds of music were wafted along the canals, and, as they grew louder and louder, an illuminated barge, filled with musicians, issued from the Rialto, and stopping under one of the palaces, began a serenade, which . . . suspended all conversation in the galleries and porticos; till, rowing slowly away, it was heard no more. The gondoliers, catching the air, imitated its cadences, and were answered by others at a distance, whose voices, echoed by the arch of the bridge, acquired a plaintive and interesting tone. I retired to rest, full of the sound; and long after I was asleep, the melody seemed to vibrate in my ear. [34]

The moment of tranquillity did not last. In a matter of days Beckford was at the centre of a grotesque affair with three children of the noble Vendramin family, loved by the daughters, in love with the son. (One of the daughters was so far lost to caution that she inadvertently plied herself with a dose of the poison intended for her obstructive husband.) Sixty years later Beckford looked back to an evening in the Palazzo Corner:

The Vendramin upbraided me with loving her sister. I told her I did not, but that my friendship for her brother was unbounded. She answered with a convulsive gasp, 'Respiro – I have nothing to do with friendship, but if you dare to return my sister's frantic passion, I will be revenged, and terribly.' [35]

By the end of the month he had made his escape, haunted not by La Vendramin but by the image of her brother. If, as his gondola slipped past the fields of flowers that lined the Brenta, Beckford had been allowed a glimpse of the future, he would have found little to answer his dreams. The exotic tale *Vathek* was to earn him a place in English literature, but by then he was more concerned about his place in English society. Within a few years his wretched mistress had died of tuberculosis, his relationship with the young Courtenay had been exposed as a public scandal, and his wife, who had stood by him throughout, was approaching the end of her short life. The possessor of one of the largest fortunes in England, Beckford was now a virtual pariah in his own country. The rest of his life was given over to travel, to the building of Fonthill Abbey, and to the sad, passionate enthusiasms of the collector.

## Sottoportico Falier to Ca' d'Oro

A short way further along, at the end of the Calle Dolfin, we turn left into the Sottoportico Falier. At the corner, on a large tablet looking something like a tombstone at the edge of the canal, the Serenissima makes it known that neither man nor woman should make bread or cause it to be made, sell it or cause it to be sold, unless they belong to the bakers' guild – this, as usual, on pain of cord, prison, galleys, a fine, and so forth.

On the bridge that leads into the Campo dei SS. Apostoli we can pause to look back at the Sottoportico Falier and the palace above it. Admired by Ruskin for its Byzantine windows, the palace was once the home of Marin Falier, the same ill-fated nobleman who became in turn Venice's Doge and her most notorious traitor (see p. 61). The square itself is a cheerful spot, but it rarely holds people for long. Bitten into by the canal on one side and the Strada Nuova on the other, it lacks a proper resting-place. One's impulse is to head further into Cannaregio.

The broad, busy Strada Nuova is a young street by Venetian standards, carved out of the huddle of surrounding buildings a hundred and twenty years ago. About half-way along, it slices clear through the Campo Santa Sofia, leaving the church on one side and what is left of the square on the other. It is an arrangement that would anyway impose a certain insignificance on the unfortunate pair, even if the church had not been almost entirely obscured by shop-fronts. 'It's a miserable old place,' writes Corvo of the church, 'though well enough formed, squarish, capable of extremely pompous functions in its nave: but it's piteously neglected and tawdry; and, being in a populous slum and overshadowed by its neighbours Santapostol and Sanfelice, no one seems to care a pajanca about it.'[36]

The next street to the left, parallel with the Campo Santa Sofia, leads down to the Ca' d'Oro, which now houses the modern Galleria Giorgio Franchetti. This may not be an ideal employment for such a setting, but it is a considerable improvement on the palace's fate in the middle of the last century, when it fell into the hands of Marie Taglioni, a ballet dancer to whom it had been given by Prince Trubetskoy. Ruskin looked on frantically as she set about improving it. On 23 September 1845 he wrote to his father:

> You cannot imagine what an unhappy day I spent yesterday before the Casa d'Oro, vainly attempting to draw it while the workmen were hammering it down before my face. It would have put me to my hardest possible shifts at any rate, for it is intolerably difficult, & the intricacy of it as a study of colour inconceivable . . . but fancy trying to work while one sees the cursed plasterers hauling up beams & dashing in the old walls & shattering the mouldings, & pulling barges across your gondola bows & driving you here & there, up & down & across, and all the while with the sense that *now* one's art is not enough to be of the slightest service, but that in ten years more one might have done some glorious things.[37]

## CAMPO SANTA FOSCA

Venice follows the usual law of tourist cities: the least frequented areas are among the most agreeable. The heart of Cannaregio, into which we are about to step, is still a somewhat isolated region with its own unmistakable atmosphere. As one moves further north, towards the Madonna dell'Orto, the canals and fondamente grow wider. There is more space, more light, and yet a general sense of diminished prosperity.

The rhythms of life here are slower and more communal than in the swirl of the city centre.

Théophile Gautier had come to Venice in August 1850. With his lover Marie Mattei, a turbulent Italian he had met in London the previous year, he enjoyed a four-week idyll which led them into parts of the city that were largely unvisited at the time, and to some extent remain so today:

> From alley to alley, by crossing bridges and mistaking the way, we had got deep into Cannaregio, into a Venice quite different from the pretty city of the watercolours. Crumbling houses with windows stopped up by planks of wood, deserted squares, empty spaces where clothes hung out to dry and a few ragged children played, desolate wharfs where caulkers were repairing boats in thick clouds of smoke, abandoned churches, battered by Austrian shells . . . green, sluggish canals in which floated vegetable refuse and the remnants of straw mattresses – all this combined to give a painful impression of wretchedness, solitude and neglect.[38]

Cannaregio had not always been so far from the centre of things. In the early seventeenth century it was the home of both Paolo Sarpi and the British ambassador Sir Henry Wotton. If we cross the Rio di Noale into the Campo Santa Fosca, we shall find a bronze statue of Sarpi looking somewhat sorrowfully down from a pedestal decorated with the usual graffiti. He was one of a handful of individuals who stand out from the largely anonymous flow of Venetian history.

In 1606 Venice was placed under an interdict by the Pope.[39] In effect, the entire city was excommunicated. It was Paolo Sarpi, a Servite monk, who was primarily responsible for presenting the Venetian case to the outside world. An unusual man both in his integrity and in the range and penetration of his intellect, Sarpi was content to live and work in a cell in the nearby convent. (Traces of its garden can be seen behind the wall opposite the Fondamenta della Misericordia.) His friend Wotton describes him there 'fenced with a castle of paper about his chair and over his head when he was either reading or writing alone, for he was of our Lord St. Albans' opinion that all air is predatory, and especially hurtful when the spirits are most employed.'[40]

From this monastic cell Sarpi masterminded Venice's strategy with brilliant success. Rome was obliged to yield. The interdict had failed, leaving papal power weakened for ever. But the Pope was a dangerous enemy, and the consequences to Sarpi himself were almost fatal. The blow fell one autumn evening as he was crossing the bridge just behind the spot where his statue now stands. Horatio Brown has woven together some of the details from contemporary accounts:

On October 5, 1607, Sarpi was returning home about five o'clock in the evening. With him was an old gentleman, Alessandro Malipiero, and a lay brother, Fra Marino; the people of the Santa Fosca quarter were mostly at the theatre, and the streets were deserted. As Sarpi was descending the steps of the bridge at Santa Fosca, he was set upon by five assassins. Fra Marino was seized and bound, while the chief assailant dealt repeated blows at Fra Paolo; only three took effect, two in the neck, of small consequence, and one in the head which was given with such violence that the dagger, entering the right ear, pierced through to the cheek-bone and remained fixed there. Sarpi fell as though dead, and the assassins, believing their work accomplished, and being disturbed by the cries of Malipiero and some women who had witnessed the assault from a window, fired their harquebuses to terrify the people, who were running up, and made off. Sarpi was carried into his monastery, where he lay for long in danger of his life. The Republic insisted upon calling in all the celebrated doctors and surgeons of Venice and Padua – though Sarpi himself desired to be left to the care of Aloise Ragozza, a very young man in whom he had confidence. The multitude of doctors nearly killed their patient. But at length the wound healed, and Sarpi resumed his ordinary course of life.[41]

No one had much doubt who was behind the attempt. Looking at the dagger which had wounded him, Sarpi observed punningly that he recognized the *style* of the Roman Curia.

Afterwards he hung the dagger as an ex voto offering in the church of his monastery. The hostility of Rome was not quickly allayed. It was the end of the nineteenth century before Venice was able to erect this statue in the Campo Santa Fosca.

## CAMPO DEI MORI

A short way beyond the square we reach the Fondamenta della Misericordia, where a left turn will take us along the edge of the canal, opposite the site of Sarpi's monastery. From here the Calle Larga leads up to the Campo dei Mori, past the stark injunction, 'BESTEMMIA NON PIU' ['Blaspheme no more'], which is inscribed on a plaque beside the door of no. 2554. It was to this quiet square – in reality a slightly dilapidated triangle – that Edmond and Jules de Goncourt made their way through the surrounding streets:

The *quartier Mouffetard* of Venice. – Grey plaster, several centuries old, brick façade on which the sun was shining in the year 1400, houses lived in by generation after generation, decorated lintels wearing away stone by stone, old ogival windows bricked up, funnel chimneys with their necks broken right off, balcony railings come adrift, hanging over the canal: a whole district in decay, like an antique sculpture eaten away by rain and sun. – Tottering bridges, shored up by a series of piles, and beneath them the stagnant water of the canals, leaving a green line on the houses, whose ancient shutters of rotten wood are the colour of mud.

. . . In these sullen streets there is the silence of towns that are dead, and everywhere the rusty brick backdrops that Tintoretto looked out on from his window in the Campo degli Mori.

It is a corner of Africa, full of the mournful atmosphere of the old moorish civilization, which has left in the angle of a wall the profile of one of its own, half-hidden under an enormous turban, and further along, on the old palazzo, blackened by modern industry . . . the worn silhouette of a camel loaded with spices.[42]

The turbanned figure noted by the Goncourts is in fact on
the Fondamenta dei Mori, set into the wall beside nos. 3398–9,
which a plaque now identifies as the house where Tintoretto
lived from 1574 until his death in 1594. For the best view of it,
we should stand on the bridge that leads into the Campo dei
Mori.

Opposite the bridge, at the corner of the square, is the first
of a curious trio of stone statues. Known as Sior Antonio
Rioba, he was given the role, according to Lorenzetti, of a
Venetian 'Pasquino', the figure in whose name satires and
lampoons – so-called pasquinades – were spread about the
city. The statues are thought to represent Levantine merchants
of the Mastelli family, whose palace facing the Fondamenta
Gasparo Contarini is decorated with the laden camel Goncourt
mentions. Now somewhat bruised by time, the various
sculpted figures in the area have long been a subject of
speculation to travellers. Some years ago they were noted by
Mary McCarthy in the attractive book she made of her stay in
Venice in 1955. She, like the Goncourts, was drawn by the
faded tones of this part of the city. Heading for the Madonna
dell'Orto, she passes first the monastery of Paolo Sarpi:

> I came upon the Servite monastery by accident, being
> attracted by the high walls and the garden, as I passed
> along the Rio della Misericordia, in that same northern,
> unfrequented quarter, with its grey, even, lifeless light,
> where the Ghetto lies . . . It is the section of Venice I like
> best to walk in and contains two lovely Gothic churches,
> the rosy Madonna dell'Orto, with a beamed wooden
> ceiling and tall ogival arcades, a wonderful Cima and the
> Tintoretto 'Presentation of the Virgin' (far surpassing, I
> think, Titian's in the Academy), and Sant'Alvise, with a
> painted ceiling in *trompe-l'oeil* architectural perspectives, a
> Tiepolo Crucifixion and the curious knightly pictures
> called baby-Carpaccios, after Ruskin's attribution. The
> two small, all-but deserted churches secrete a flowery
> essence of medieval Venice, still half-oriental and perme-
> ated with spice; . . . Nearby along a house front are those
> strange figures on camels called the Moors, thought to

represent Levantine merchants who inhabited the quarter. Tintoretto lived in this melancholy region and he is buried in the Madonna dell'Orto. Children are ready to point out his house to you.[43]

## MADONNA DELL'ORTO

Tintoretto's church has a noble brick façade and a graceful interior. It also preserves in the Cappella di San Mauro the hefty statue of a Madonna and child which fell unexpectedly from heaven one day into a nearby orchard, causing the recently built church to be renamed the Madonna of the Orchard (*orto*). But it is probably the church's paintings that draw most visitors out to this northern reach of the city – as they have done for over a hundred years. Even if nothing else had signalled danger for the newly married Ruskins, their visit to the Madonna dell'Orto must surely have caused a few tremors of uneasiness. This is Ruskin on *The Last Judgement*, one of the two huge Tintorettos beside the high altar:

. . . the river of the wrath of God, roaring down into the gulf where the world has melted with its fervent heat, choked with the ruin of nations, and the limbs of its corpses tossed out of its whirling, like water-wheels. Bat-like, out of the holes and caverns and shadows of the earth, the bones gather, and the clay heaps heave, rattling and adhering into half-kneaded anatomies, that crawl, and startle, and struggle up among the putrid weeds, with the clay clinging to their clotted hair, and their heavy eyes sealed by the earth-darkness . . .[44]

On Effie the place had a markedly different effect:

John took me to see two large Tintorets, but going in hot to a place like a well to see a death's head crowned with leaves gave me such a shiver that I ran out of the church and I do not intend to return again.[45]

PONTE DEGLI ORMESINI: PALAZZO SILVIA

The broad canals in this region of Venice partition it with
unusual regularity. To reach the Ghetto we can cross from
fondamenta to fondamenta fairly easily until we get to the
Fondamenta degli Ormesini. About half-way along, opposite
the Calle della Malvasia, is the Ponte degli Ormesini. It was
here that the old Palazzo Silvia once stood, where Sarpi's
friend, Sir Henry Wotton, lived during his first period as
British ambassador (1604–10). At first sight the young
Englishman seems an unlikely friend for the Servite monk. He
was not noted either for his asceticism or for his religious
piety. A friend of the London circle of wits which included the
poet John Donne, he came close to ruining his career for a
witticism of his own. The caustic remark that an ambassador is
an honest man sent to lie abroad for the good of his country
was not appreciated when it found its way back to James I. The
association with Sarpi, however, belonged to the early days,
when his career was still set fair. His home in the Palazzo Silvia
has been described by Logan Pearsall Smith:

> From an inventory in the Record Office, made when
> Wotton left Venice in 1610, we can get some idea of how
> this palace was furnished. The walls were hung with arras
> and gilded leather, and adorned with pictures and
> armour; there were green velvet armchairs, great and-
> irons and lanterns, tables with their 'carpets' (as table-
> covers were called); and a 'ground carpet' is mentioned in
> the dining-room. There was a billiard-table in the house,
> and in Wotton's study hung a portrait of the young Prince
> Henry. Many of the large pieces of furniture Wotton
> hired from the Jews, and apparently on exorbitant terms;
> for after his departure they boasted that they had had 'a
> fleece of him', and looked for his return as they hoped for
> the coming of the Messiah.[46]

Although Wotton's main business in Venice was to win
over Sarpi to the Protestant cause, he was charged with all the
normal diplomatic duties, including the care of distressed
British nationals. A letter to his minister, the Earl of Salisbury,

dated 31 December 1609, gives an idea of the sort of situation with which he had to cope. It records an incident that had occurred a few weeks earlier:

> . . . I was taking the air in my gondola, and being told of a galley newly come in, wherein was an English slave unjustly detained, I thought it both duty and charity in me to understand his case; so coming to the galley's side (which lay almost in my way home) and talking there with the poor fellow, a certain Greek bred in Spain (who was at that time the chief commander on board), being half drunk, and by nature unpityful, stroke down the Englishman with a great cudgel before my face; and besides, for my approaching so near, gives me very uncivil language, with some menacement, even after he had understood who I was; whereupon I sent my secretary to complain the next morning. To be short, the Greek was by present order from the College drawn out of the galley to prison through the common piazza, with a long chain at his heels, like a slave; and the Senate taking the cause into their own hands, did sentence him to perpetual close imprisonment, neither did he miss above four or five balls to be hanged. . . . As for his Majesty's subject, he was likewise by the Senate not only freed of the galley (where he had been held for lack of one to tell his case) but pardoned also some small debts, in which he was run for apparel and other things.[47]

It was no slight service that Wotton had done this unnamed Englishman. The rigours of life as a galley-slave were fierce. A sombre light is cast on them by a law passed in the sixteenth century for the suppression of *bravi*. Under this law, anyone caught exercising the profession of *bravo* would be led to the place between the columns of the Piazzetta and there have his nose and ears cut off, after which he would serve five years in a state galley. But the provision that gives one pause states that if some physical defect should render service in the galleys impossible, the criminal will instead have one hand chopped off and spend ten years in prison.[48] The equation makes a grim comment on life in the galleys.

## The Ghetto

The next bridge along from the Ponte degli Ormesini leads into the Campo di Ghetto Nuovo. Although the Ghetto was opened up by Napoleon, it remained for many years a largely Jewish quarter, and to that extent a somewhat suspect region of the city to the nineteenth-century traveller – even to one as cosmopolitan as Théophile Gautier:

> We had been walking for some time through a maze of little streets which often brought us back to our starting point. We noticed with surprise the absence of any religious images at the street-corners: no more shrines, no more madonnas adorned with ex-voto offerings, no more carved crosses in the squares, no more images of saints, none of the signs of outdoor devotion so frequent in other parts of the city. Everything had a look of strangeness, sullenness, mystery. Curious figures, furtive and silent, slipped by close to the high walls with a fearful air. . . .
>
> The alleyways got narrower and narrower; the houses rose like towers of Babel, hovels stacked one on top of another to reach for a little air and light above the darkness and filth through which crept misshapen beings. . . . All the forgotten diseases of the leproseries of the Orient seemed to gnaw these blistered walls; the damp stained them with black marks like gangrene; the efflorescence of the salts caused eruptions in the plaster that looked like boils and plague spots; the roughcast, flaking like diseased skin, peeled away in scaly pieces. Not a single line kept to the perpendicular . . .
>
> At length we emerged into quite a spacious square, reasonably well paved, in the middle of which yawned the stone mouth of a well. In one corner stood a building of more human proportions, the door of which was surmounted by an inscription carved in oriental letters which we recognized as Hebrew. The mystery was explained. This fetid and purulent district, this watery Cour des Miracles was quite simply the Ghetto, the Jewish

quarter of Venice, which had preserved the characteristic squalor of the Middle Ages.[49]

Gautier was not alone in viewing this part of the city with some distaste. The author of the *Cook's Handbook* of 1875 summed up the Ghetto in a single trenchant sentence: 'The houses are immensely tall, the streets ridiculously narrow, and a great deal of filth abounds.'

The decision to restrict Jews to a certain area of the city was taken in 1516. After dismissing the idea of the Giudecca and Murano as possible locations, the Council fixed on the site of the new foundry. (Hence the name ghetto, *gettare* meaning to cast in metal.) Once taken, the decision was acted on with the Republic's usual vigour. A proclamation was made from the Rialto and other bridges throughout the city on 1 April: the Jews had just ten days to uproot themselves and move into their first ghetto.

Irrepressibly curious, Thomas Coryate made a point of visiting it. He was unable to catch a circumcision, but he did attend one of the religious services and was struck by the handsome appearance of both men and women:

> To looke like a Jewe (whereby is meant sometimes a weather beaten warp-faced fellow, sometimes a phren-ticke and lunaticke person, sometimes one discontented) is not true. For indeed I noted some of them to be most elegant and sweet featured persons, which gave me occa-sion the more to lament their religion. . . . In the roome wherein they celebrate their divine service, no women sit, but have a loft or gallery proper to themselves only, where I saw many Jewish women, whereof some were as beautiful as ever I saw, and so gorgeous in their apparel, jewels, chaines of gold, and rings adorned with precious stones, that some of our English Countesses do scarce exceed them, having marvailous long traines like Princes-ses that are borne up by waiting women serving for the same purpose. An argument to prove that many of the Jewes are very rich.[50]

Unfortunately, Coryate was in combative mood and started taxing a local Rabbi with the shortcomings of his religion. The result might have been predicted by anyone but Coryate himself:

> But to shut up this narration of my conflict with the Jewish Rabbin, after there had passed many vehement speeches to and fro betwixt us, it happened that some forty or fifty Jewes more flocked about me, and some of them beganne very insolently to swagger with me, because I durst reprehend their religion: Whereupon fearing least they would have offered me some violence, I withdrew my selfe by little and little towards the bridge at the entrance into the Ghetto, with an intent to flie from them, but by good fortune our noble Ambassador Sir Henry Wotton passing under the bridge in his Gondola at that very time, espyed me somewhat earnestly bickering with them, and so incontinently sent unto me out of his boate one of his principall Gentlemen Master Belford his secretary, who conveighed mee safely from these unchristian miscreants, which perhaps would have given mee just occasion to forsweare any more comming to the Ghetto.[51]

It is perhaps lucky that William Lithgow steered clear of the Ghetto when he came to Venice in the following year. He was not a tolerant man:

> The *Jews* here, and in *Rome*, wear red and yellow Hats for notice sake, to distinguish them from others: which necessary custom (would to God) were enjoyned to all the Papists here in *England*, so should we easily discern them from the true Christians.[52]

As a glance at the map will show, the Campo di Ghetto Nuovo constituted a natural island. A high wall was built round it, pierced by three gates – corresponding to the modern bridges – which were closed at nightfall. The movements and activities of the inhabitants were circumscribed at every turn. Their business acumen was needed but it was also feared. The coloured hats to which Lithgow refers were a simple and humiliating means of keeping a check on their movements. (When Rome adopted a similar practice, these hats caused some consternation. The unfortunate Cardinal of Lyons, being short-sighted, one day mistook the significance of a red hat seen from his carriage window and saluted its wearer as a fellow-Cardinal. Thereafter it was decreed in Rome that the hats should be yellow.)

For Venice there was one obvious consequence of the conditions in which the Jews were forced to live. Since housing could not spread outward, it had to reach upward. The ramshackle skyscrapers which grew up around the Campo di Ghetto Nuovo were the result. Today the buildings are not much higher than elsewhere in Venice, but the campo still has a distinctive appearance, marked by the relative lack of balconies and the absence of church or palace. With its stone benches, three well-heads and scattering of trees the square is an attractive spot in which to linger.

A few yards before the sottoportico that leads out of the Ghetto to the Cannaregio Canal, you might notice on the right a tablet dated 20 September 1704, set into the wall of no. 1131 in the Calle del Ramo Ghetto Vecchio. It gives a bleak glimpse of life on the social and religious margins of the Republic. Its purpose is to lay down the penalties – as usual, cord, whip, galleys, prison, pillory – that will be suffered by any Jew or Jewess who has been converted to Christianity and who thereafter sets foot in the house of another Jew. So that transgressors may more easily be brought to justice, the Officers of the Republic will receive secret denunciations and reward informers with the sum of a hundred ducats from the property of the guilty party, if their information proves accurate – 'This proclamation to be carved in stone in the most frequented part of the Ghetto.'


## PALAZZO SURIAN AND PALAZZO LABIA

Founded on commerce, Venice does not lend itself well to the kind of social partitioning that is a feature of most cities. Machiavelli early noted that the absence of a traditional land-owning class was a significant factor in the creation of the Venetian Republic. A hundred years later Coryate observed that it was quite normal for a Venetian senator, 'worth perhaps two millions of duckats', to go into the market and buy fish or fruit for himself and his family, instead of employing his cook or cater 'about those inferior and sordid affaires'.

This mingling of social classes also has a geographical aspect. In whatever quarter of Venice one stands it is only a short distance to the Grand Canal, and beside it the dwellings of the rich and powerful. Elsewhere, too, palaces are sprinkled through the city with a fine disregard for the tone of the area. Shabby streets open on to unexpected squares ringed with splendid architecture, the same canal laps indifferently at the entrance-way to palace and tenement.

Running alongside the area of the Ghetto is the Cannaregio Canal, widest of the secondary canals, where private houses boasted luxuriant gardens that once stretched across acres of the cramped city. At a time when the Jews were still walled into their tiny enclave, Jean-Jacques Rousseau spent a year beside the same canal in the grand Palazzo Surian, which was then the French embassy. He had come to Venice in 1743 as secretary to the ambassador, but like most of his relationships this one proved difficult. By his account, the ambassador was incompetent and he himself much abused. Of Venice he has little to say beyond recording his occasional lapses from virtue: an episode with a Paduan woman that left him terrified of the pox, another with a beautiful courtesan which ended in humiliation, and finally a story that reveals a darker edge to the eighteenth-century world of pleasure. It starts with a proposal from the secretary to the Spanish ambassador:

Carrio, who was a lady's man, grew weary of always going to women who belonged to others and took it into his head to have one of his own; and as we were insepar-able he suggested to me an arrangement which is not rare in Venice, that we should keep one between us. I agreed. The next question was to find a safe one. He made such thorough investigations that he unearthed a little girl of eleven or twelve, whom her wretched mother wanted to sell. We went to see her together. My pity was stirred at the sight of this child. She was fair and as gentle as a lamb.

One would never have supposed she was an Italian.
Living is very cheap in Venice. We gave the mother some
money, and made arrangements for the daughter's keep.
She had a fine voice and, to provide her with a means of
livelihood, we gave her a spinet and paid for a singing
master. All this cost us barely two *sequins* a month each,
and saved us more in other expenses, but as we had to
wait until she was mature, we had to sow a great deal
before we could reap. However, we were content to go
and spend our evenings there and chatter and play most
innocently with the child, and perhaps we got more
agreeable amusement than if we had possessed her; so true
is it that what really attaches us to a woman is not so much
sensual enjoyment as a certain pleasure in living beside
her. . . . We were procuring for ourselves, unthinkingly,
pleasures no less charming but quite different from those
we had first contemplated; and I am certain that, however
beautiful that poor child might have become, far from
being the corrupters of her innocence we should have
been its guardians.[53]

In the event, Rousseau's stay in Venice comes to an abrupt end
and his resolutions remain untested.

Moralists in search of a lighter text for the delinquency of
the rich could do no better than cross the canal and walk down
towards San Geremia, where the proud Palazzo Labia,
adorned with its line of eagles, seems almost to be holding the
campanile of the church in place. It was here, Tassini tells us,
that a member of the family invited forty noblemen to a
banquet on plates of gold. Afterwards he tossed the plates out
of the window into the canal below, remarking airily, *Le abia o
non le abia, sarò sempre Labia.'* ('Whether I have them or not, I
shall always be Labia.') This extravagant pun may not have
been as costly as it looked; he was thought to have had a net
stretched across the canal below the surface, so that the plates
could be fished up for another day.

## PALAZZO QUERINI

There is little to detain us further west, where the railway
station, useful but dismaying, has carved a wedge from the
island. A taste for the Baroque might draw us that way to see
the church of the Scalzi, but it is perhaps pleasanter just to
stroll down beside San Geremia to the edge of the Grand Canal
and look across to the left towards the façade of the Palazzo
Querini. Outside the entrance today we shall see nothing more
notable than the battered blue *pali* with perhaps a motor launch
moored between them; but the palace dates from a more
violent age. At a time when only gondolas approached these
walls, they witnessed the last scene of one of the notorious
family feuds which periodically broke the city's peace. The
story is recounted by the young Thomas Hoby, who had
come to Venice in 1549 as an aspiring diplomat.

At Shrove-tide that year there was an incident in Padua.
One of the great della Torre family died in a brawl and
responsibility was laid at the door of the rival Soveragnani
family. Sentenced to exile, Giovanni Soveragnani came to
Venice with his wife and children and there waited for a ship to
Crete:

> As he thus tarried in Venice a season attending for
> passage, being lodged on the Canal grand over against
> San Geremia, he took boat many times to go up and down
> about sundrie his affairs. At his return upon a time he was
> watched, and by the walls side over against the house of
> Quirini there lingered a boat, such a one as commonly
> carry fruits up and down Venice, upon their fruits they
> use to lay mats to keep them fresh and to defend them
> from the heate of the sun. There were no more in sight but
> two within the boat. Under the mats there lay VII or VIII
> persons with each of them a hackbut in his hand. When
> the gondola that Count John Soveragnani was in came
> directly against them they shot all together levelling all at
> one mark. Count John was shot through in many places
> of his body. This enterprise thus achieved, as many as
> were in the boat fell to rowing and made so swiftly away

that none were able to follow them nor discern who they were nor yet whither they went. The dead body was brought into the house of Quirini, where it lay to be seen of all men. When the Signorie understood of this murther they caused immediately Francesco della Torre to be taken, who was then in Venice. But for all they put him to the torment of the cord, they could never make him confess that he was condescending of or counsel to this kind of murther. And the law is, except a man confess his trespass when he is put to this torment, he shall never suffer death for it. This chance happened in Lent.[54]

For the work of assassins the palace is well sited. Beside it the broad Cannaregio Canal leads out to the waters of the lagoon. Within a short distance Venice is left behind. Ahead are Mestre and Marghera and the cities of the mainland, places that belong to another world.

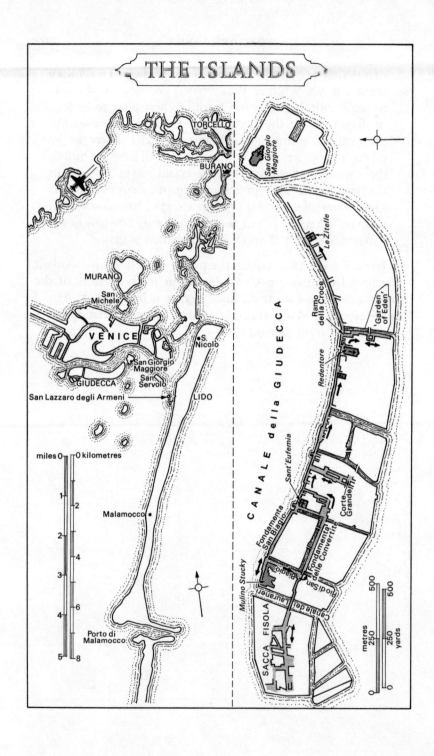

# 7

# THE ISLANDS

## Giudecca: San Biagio

The temptation is always to start with San Giorgio, but since this is to be an orderly tour, we must make our way first across the Accademia bridge and along the cheerful Rio Terrà Foscarini. From the vaporetto stop in the middle of the Zattere three lines plough across the wide canal to the Giudecca. On a crisp morning the short journey can leave one breathless with pleasure. '*Véritablement, on nage dans la lumière,*' wrote Hippolyte Taine. The island probably took its present name from a Jewish colony there in the Middle Ages, but before that its elongated shape had earned it the more evocative name of Spinalunga. 'There's only one street on the island of Spinalunga,' wrote Corvo, 'a quay half a mile long which runs from end to end with blind alleys running out of it like the teeth of a comb.'[1]

In earlier times the far side of the island was given over to the villas and pleasure gardens of the nobility. A few gardens still remain, most have been eaten away by the grim requirements of progress. Today the island is no longer the resort of favoured Venetians. Its landscape is dominated by commercial buildings and the ugly houses of the poor.

Nowhere is the change more striking than on the little island of San Biagio. To reach it we can disembark at Sant'Eufemia and wander to the right along the fondamenta and over the iron bridge. Where we are standing now was once the site of a hostel for pilgrims to the Holy Land, later turned into a Benedictine convent by Giuliana di Collalto, whose decorated wooden sarcophagus – one of the earliest examples of Venetian painting – can be seen in the Correr Museum. As usual in Venice, the nuns rubbed shoulders with the pleasure-seekers. When Casanova wants a retreat for himself and his latest *ingénue*, it is to this spot that he directs his gondola:

> We go to a garden I know in San Biagio, where a zecchino makes me lord and master of the place for the whole day. No one else was permitted to enter. We order what we want to eat, we go upstairs to the apartment, leave our disguises there, and go down to the garden for a walk. C.C. had on only a short taffeta bodice and a skirt of the same material; it was her entire costume. My amorous soul saw her naked, I sighed, I cursed duty and all feelings contrary to the nature which triumphed in the Golden Age.[2]

Echoes of the Golden Age recur in descriptions of San Biagio. In the next century it became the subject of a brief poem in which Alfred de Musset celebrated the last days of his happiness with George Sand:

> A Saint-Blaise, à la Zuecca,
> Vous étiez, vous étiez bien aise
> A Saint-Blaise.
> A Saint-Blaise, à la Zuecca,
> Nous étions bien là.
>
> Mais de vous en souvenir
> Prendrez-vous la peine?
> Mais de vous en souvenir
> Et d'y revenir,

A Saint-Blaise, à la Zuecca,
   Dans les prés fleuris cueillir la verveine,
A Saint-Blaise, à la Zuecca
   Vivre et mourir là!³

Some sixteen years later, Théophile Gautier found the poem threading his thoughts wherever he went in Venice. Its seductive refrain seemed to call him across the canal. He would have done better to resist the invitation. By the middle of the century the process of change had imbued Musset's words with irony:

We found no flowery meadow at St Blaise and, to our great regret, we could gather no verveine. Allotments are laid out round the church, market-gardens in which vegetables have taken over from flowers. . . . It may be that when the song was written the tip of the island was open ground, where in springtime the young grass was enamelled with flowers, and lovers walked hand in hand looking at the moon. An old guide to Venice describes the Giudecca as a place full of gardens, orchards and pleasure spots.
   Instead of a pretty flower with delicate colours and penetrating scent blooming on the grassy turf . . . instead of this, to find blowsy gourds growing yellow under their large leaves – well, it dampens the poetic fire, and from that moment we no longer sang:
                  A Saint-Blaise, à la Zuecca.⁴

If Gautier had visited the spot fifty years later, he might have sighed for even these remnants of vegetation. In their place had risen the massive walls of Stucky's flour mills, an industrial fortress set down like some grandiose monument to the Victorian age at the edge of the Giudecca canal. As with people, so with buildings: familiarity can breed an odd sort of affection for even the most ghastly. To the lover of Venice Stucky's flour mills have their place in the scheme of things. The narrator of L. P. Hartley's *The White Wand* surveys the canal-front under a stormy summer sky:

It was a heavy day threatening thunder, like so many June days in Venice; and in the thick, white sirocco sunlight the colours of the houses on the Giudecca – grey, yellow, terracotta, pink – seemed to merge and lose their proper qualities in a uniform lack of tone; and what stood out was the fenestration, the whitish oblongs and truncated ovals of the windows, monotonously repeated. Except for a dreadful travesty of Gothic, three enormous eyelets beyond the Redentore, scarcely a single pointed arch could I see.

'I suddenly felt a respect for the five factory chimneys, and I looked with indulgence, almost with affection, on the great bulk of Stucky's flour mill, battlemented, pinnacled, turreted, machicolated, a monument to the taste of 1870, that might have been built out of a child's box of bricks. A romantic intention had reared it, and left behind something that was solid and substantial and a benefit to mankind.[5]

## San Giorgio in Alga

For the few visitors who care to cross the Canale dei Lauraneri and walk to the edge of Sacca Fisola there is a sight of the desolate little island of San Giorgio in Alga. Tired of his work on Venice, tired of Venice itself, Ruskin wrote to a friend in 1859:

> There was only one place in Venice which I never lost the feeling of joy in – at least the pleasure which is better than joy; and that was just half way between the end of the Giudecca and St George of the Seaweed, at sunset. If you tie your boat to one of the posts there you can see the Euganeans where the sun goes down, and all the Alps and Venice behind you by the rosy sunlight: there is no other spot so beautiful.[6]

Too late, at the end of the twentieth century, to hope for the same display. It was already too late a hundred years ago. Before long, Ruskin was complaining that the view from the island had been 'spoiled by loathsome mud-castings and machines'. Much worse was to come; the prospect is now a battery of smoking chimneys. But in the western distance, beyond the filth of Mestre and Marghera, the evening light still silhouettes the lovely Euganean Hills, where Petrarch spent his final days. In 1595 Fynes Moryson made a literary pilgrimage to the poet's house at Arquà – but, as Moryson remarks, 'it is a needles worke to praise the Euganian hils, which so many Poets and Writers have magnified.'

Today the traffic past San Giorgio in Alga is mainly commercial, but at intervals during the week a tourist boat retraces the path of earlier pleasure-seekers who left Venice by this route to reach their villas along the banks of the Brenta.

## FONDAMENTA DELLE CONVERTITE

After recrossing the Canale dei Lauraneri and the Rio di San Biagio, we shall find ourselves walking along the Fondamenta delle Convertite beside a penal institute for women. This was once the notorious convent of the Maddalena. In a fascinating letter written in November 1551 the apostolic nunzio tells Cardinal Carlo Borromeo the details of a scandal that had shaken even the tolerant Venetians. The rector and confessor of the convent was called Giovan Pietro Leon, a priest so well respected by the Venetian authorities that he was consulted on the subject of pious undertakings by the Doge himself and other officers of State. They were serenely unaware of what went on when Leon got back to the seclusion of his convent on the Giudecca, where he reigned over some 400 nuns, 'the majority of them young and beautiful'. Pompeo Molmenti summarizes the nunzio's letter:

> Inside the convent walls he laid aside the mask of hypocrisy and showed himself in his true colours, as a lecherous tyrant. He made use of the confessional to seduce the nuns, and if he met with resistance, he had recourse to imprisonment and torture. In Summer he made the fairest of the sisters strip and bathe in the boat-house, while he

played the role of the Elders in the story of Susanna. If any of these hapless creatures became with child, he procured abortion, or drowned the fruits of his unholy loves. He stole the money bequeathed to the convent, and enriched himself by the embroidery and needlework which he exacted from the nuns. His table was loaded with pheasants, partridges, and exquisite wines, and his room was full of comfits and cordials. Some of the nuns, being able to stand it no longer, fled and denounced the enormities of the priest which he had carried on for nineteen years without the civil or ecclesiastical authorities ever having word of them.[7]

For these colourful misdeeds Leon suffered a rather messy beheading. The abbess, in spite of his attempt to exculpate her, ended her days in prison.

## Il Redentore

Anyone trying to walk across the middle of the Giudecca rather than along the fondamenta would do well to bear in mind Corvo's remark about blind alleys. It can be a slow and unrewarding business. In the centre of the island the Corte Grande, one side of which is now occupied by the monstrous Junghans building, is of some interest as the site of the old bull-fights on the Giudecca.

From here it is easy enough to return to the fondamenta and then stroll along the canal-front to the church of the Redentore – 'a passing sumptuous and gorgeous building', as Coryate termed it. Built at the end of the sixteenth century in thanksgiving for deliverance from plague, the church is the focus of the annual Feast of the Redeemer in July. A couple of short extracts will be enough to give a flavour of the festivities. The first is from L. P. Hartley's novel *Eustace and Hilda*. On the night of the festival Eustace's gondola is ideally positioned to see the bridge of boats stretching across the Giudecca canal in a slender 'V' whose apex is the church. The party has finished its traditional open-air meal of duck, mulberries, and mandarins

and is sitting with champagne, waiting for the first rocket to
go up:

Beyond the noise of voices, the snatches of music, the
swinging of paper lanterns, the tilting and dipping of
sterns and bows, the church in its grey immensity stood
motionless and silent. Now that Eustace was growing
accustomed to the light he saw that the façade was faintly
flood-lit by the lamps at its base, a wash of gold had crept
along the silver. Yet how stern were the uncompromising
straight lines, drawn like a diagram against the night; how
intimidating the shadows behind the buttresses which
supported roof and dome. The church drew his eyes to it
with a promise which was almost threatening, so powerfully did it affect his mind.[8]

In *Venice Observed* Mary McCarthy notes the pictorial
aspects of the scene:

For an hour, the sky is illuminated by bursts of coloured
stars; the *palazzi* rock with the explosions; greens and
golds, reds and violets are reflected in the water and in the
darkened windows of the houses. It is a picture, everyone
agrees, or rather a series of pictures; shades of Guardi, of
the Bassano night-scenes, even of Carpaccio, pass across
the Canal. Everyone seeks for a comparison, and all
comparisons seem true: I myself think of the Embarka-
tion of the Queen of Cyprus in a painting in the Correr
Museum. When the fireworks are over, nobody starts for
home; a second show (how typical of Venice) is about to
begin, the duplicate, the twin, of the first, at the other end
of the Canal, on the island of San Giorgio, where the
other Palladian church is lit up. All the boats move off in
procession, accompanied by music. Traditionally, after
the second fireworks display, you are supposed to be
rowed to the Lido to see the sunrise. As a gondolier
explained to me, gravely, the true colours of nature ('*i veri
colori della natura*') refresh the eye after the fires of artifice.

There spoke Venice, the eternal connoisseur, in the
voice of her eternal gondolier.[9]

Before walking on to take the vaporetto to San Giorgio, you might like to turn down the little Ramo della Croce, just beyond the Redentore. It leads to a quiet canal which for the first few yards borders the grounds of a Casa di Lavoro. Beyond this, it runs alongside a splendid private garden, known as the Garden of Eden after the Englishman, conveniently named Eden, who laid it out. Opposite the garden, at no. 149, stands the Palazzo Munster, its doorway surmounted by a small carving of a madonna and child. It was here that Lady Layard founded an English Hospital in 1903, where Baron Corvo, in expectation of a death that was still some years away, received the last sacrament. Lady Layard and her hospital had been treated with Corvo's usual venom in *The Desire and Pursuit of the Whole*, but it would be sentimental to imagine that this later episode would have made the slightest difference. There was a certain grandeur in the way Corvo's resentments could triumph over circumstance.

## SAN GIORGIO MAGGIORE

It must have been one of the drawbacks of Ruskin's sitting room in the Danieli that it had such an excellent view of San Giorgio. The Palladian church was one of Venice's many eyesores: 'It is impossible to conceive a design more gross, more barbarous, more childish in conception, more servile in plagiarism, more insipid in result, more contemptible under every point of rational regard.'[10] Applied to this restrained and graceful building, gross, barbarous and childish must be three of the least appropriate epithets ever to drop from Ruskin's erratic pen. Yet such was his influence that the judgement cast a marked shadow over the later years of the nineteenth cetury. Even Henry James found it hard to escape. From his lodgings at no. 4161 on the Riva degli Schiavoni he commanded a perfect view of the island, and in the essay of 1882 we can sense his response gradually taking flight from the tone of orthodox disapproval that Ruskin had established. It is easy, in this passage, to see why Venice so appealed to James's fastidious sensibility. Its subtleties of light and colour invite a process of discrimination as endlessly refined as even he could wish:

Straight across, before my windows, rose the great pink mass of San Giorgio Maggiore, which has for an ugly Palladian church a success beyond all reason. It is a success of position, of colour, of the immense detached Campanile, tipped with a tall gold angel. I know not whether it is because San Giorgio is so grandly conspicuous, with a great deal of worn, faded-looking brickwork; but for many persons the whole place has a kind of suffusion of rosiness. Asked what may be the leading colour in the Venetian concert, we should inveterately say Pink, and yet without remembering after all that this elegant hue occurs very often. It is a faint shimmering, airy, watery pink; the bright sea-light seems to flush with it and the pale whiteish-green of lagoon and canal to drink it in. There is indeed a great deal of very evident brickwork, which is never fresh or loud in colour, but always burnt out, as it were, always exquisitely mild.[11]

When Coryate reached Venice in the summer of 1608, the church was still being completed. The Benedictines were building lavishly, and their monastery on San Giorgio was 'the fairest and richest . . . without comparison in all Venice'. The easy circumstances of the Benedictines at this time were at least partly due to the adroit manner in which they had weathered the papal interdict of 1606–7 (see p. 193). In a report dated 26 May 1606 Henry Wotton explains how this was done:

The monks of St Benedict (which draw 200,000 crowns of yearly revenue out of the Venetian State) have found a notable way to delude the Pope's authority, not yet daring to deny it, which is this: they have caused a chest to be made without a lock, fast nailed on all sides, and in the top thereof a little hole, into which they throw all letters that are directed to their convent without exception, lest they might receive some prohibition from their General, and so mean to save their consciences by the way of ignorance: which point of subtle discretion is likely to be imitated by other orders.[12]

After visiting the church, Coryate was taken by the Scottish
monk who acted as his guide to see the refectory, 'where there
is a passing faire picture of an exceeding breadth and length,
containing the history of Christs sitting at the table at the
marriage at Cana in Galilie'. It was this same painting that
Hester Piozzi set out to inspect in 1785. The former Mrs Thrale
had left England a few weeks after her marriage to Gabriel
Piozzi in the summer of the previous year. The widow's
decision to marry an Italian Roman Catholic musician had not
gone down well with her family or with the rest of London
society, least of all with her old friend Dr Johnson; but she was
a resilient woman and in love with Piozzi. Her journal of their
continental tour is unshadowed by troubles at home. More
immediate vexations – like her unlucky visit to San Giorgio –
were less easy to ignore:

> It was to this church I was sent for the purpose of seeing a
> famous picture, painted by Paul Veronese of the marriage
> at Cana in Galilee. When we arrived, the picture was kept
> in a refectory belonging to friars (of what order I have
> forgotten), and no woman could be admitted. My dis-
> appointment was so great that I was deprived even of the
> powers of solicitation by the extreme ill-humour it
> occasioned, and my few entreaties for admission were
> completely disregarded by the good old monk, who
> remained outside with me, while the gentlemen visited
> the convent without molestation. At my return to Venice
> I met little comfort, as everybody told me it was my own
> fault, for I might put on men's cloths and see it whenever I
> pleased, as nobody then would stop, though perhaps all
> of them would know me.[13]

The modern visitor in search of Veronese's painting must
journey to the Louvre, where it has remained since it was
plundered by Napoleon. Its place in the refectory (itself now
transformed into the conference room of the Cini foundation)
has been taken by a less memorable picture of *The Marriage of
the Virgin*.

## The Lagoon

It is tempting to leave the lagoon to Venice's painters. According to Goethe, they will always see the world as a brighter and gayer place than the rest of us can:

> We northerners who spend our lives in a drab and, because of the dirt and the dust, an uglier country where even reflected light is subdued, and who have, most of us, to live in cramped rooms – we cannot instinctively develop an eye which looks with such delight at the world.
>
> As I glided over the lagoons in the brilliant sunshine and saw the gondoliers in their colourful costume, gracefully posed against the blue sky as they rowed with easy strokes across the light-green surface of the water, I felt I was looking at the latest and best painting of the Venetian school.[14]

The sea is not just the source of Venice's beauty, it is the source of the city itself. 'Like the water-fowl, / They built their nests above the ocean waves,' wrote Samuel Rogers in a poem once famous, now forgotten by all but enthusiasts. He was echoing the words of Cassiodorus, the Roman statesman and historian who gives us our first sketch of life around the lagoon in a letter of the sixth century requesting transport for wine and oil to Ravenna:

> For you live like sea birds, with your homes dispersed, like the Cyclades, across the surface of the water. The solidity of the earth on which they rest is secured only by osier and wattle; yet you do not hesitate to oppose so frail a bulwark to the wildness of the sea. Your people have one great wealth – the fish which suffices for them all. Among you there is no difference between rich and poor; your food is the same, your houses are all alike. Envy, which rules the rest of the world, is unknown to you. All your energies are spent on your salt-fields; in them indeed lies your prosperity, and your power to purchase those things which you have not. For though there be men who have little need of gold, yet none live who desire not salt.

Be diligent, therefore, to repair your boats – which,
like horses, you keep tied up at the doors of your dwellings – and make haste to depart . . .[15]

The splendour that grew from this early relationship with
the sea is celebrated in Wordsworth's dignified elegy for the
passing of the Republic:

> Once did She hold the gorgeous east in fee;
> And was the safeguard of the west: the worth
> Of Venice did not fall below her birth,
> Venice, the eldest Child of Liberty.
> She was a maiden City, bright and free;
> No guile seduced, no force could violate;
> And when she took unto herself a Mate,
> She must espouse the everlasting Sea.
> And what if she had seen those glories fade,
> Those titles vanish, and that strength decay;
> Yet shall some tribute of regret be paid
> When her long life hath reached its final day:
> Men are we, and must grieve when even the Shade
> Of that which once was great, is passed away.[16]

The Republic had been extinguished, but the long life of
Venice itself had still some way to go. Its attractions were not
calculated to appeal to Wordsworth either in his republican
youth or in more conservative old age, but another poet of the
time found them entirely to his taste. Byron's boastful enthusiasm for Venetian women was matched by the flattering
detail in which he recorded his swimming exploits. Gondolas
heading for the Lido one June afternoon in 1818 were able to
enjoy the unusual sight of an English *milord* going in the
opposite direction without a gondola:

> Since my last I have had another *Swim* against Mingaldo
> – whom both Scott & I beat hollow[17] – leaving him
> breathless & five hundred yards behind hand before we
> got from Lido to the entrance of the Grand Canal. – Scott
> went from Lido as far as the Rialto – & was then taken into
> his Gondola – I swam from Lido right to the end of the
> Grand Canal . . . I was in the sea from half past 4 – till a

quarter past *8* – without touching or resting. – I could not
be much fatigued having had a *piece* in the forenoon – &
taking another in the evening at ten of the Clock – The
Scott I mention is not the vice-Consul – but a traveller –
who lives much at Venice – like *Mysen*. – He got as far as
the Rialto swimming well – the Italian – miles behind and
knocked up – hallooing for the boat.[18]

## SAN SERVOLO

Among the few people in Venice who might not have thought
this sight rather odd were the inhabitants of the island of San
Servolo, which Byron passed on his left as he struck out from
the Lido. It is one of the group of islands in this part of the
lagoon of which Lorenzetti, in a poignant phrase, remarked,
'They are the islands of pain which human compassion has
turned into retreats for suffering people.'

In the early eighteenth century the monastery of San Servolo was set aside for mad people of noble family, and there,
until a few years ago, a church and a madhouse were all that the
visitor could find. That Byron himself had a certain interest in
this unhappy place is suggested by Shelley's poem 'Julian and
Maddalo', in which Byron is Count Maddalo to Shelley's
Julian. At this point the two friends are watching from a
gondola as earth and sky dissolve into a lake of fire in the
sunset. ('Only Shelley has given us an idea of this,' said
Browning.) Julian is the narrator, Maddalo his companion:

> . . . . 'Ere it fade,'
> Said my companion, 'I will show you soon
> A better station' – so, o'er the lagune
> We glided; and from that funereal bark
> I leaned, and saw the city, and could mark
> How from their many isles, in evening's gleam,
> Its temples and its palaces did seem
> Like fabrics of enchantment piled to Heaven.
> I was about to speak, when – 'We are even
> Now at the point I meant,' said Maddalo,
> And bade the gondolieri cease to row.

'Look, Julian, on the west, and listen well
'If you hear not a deep and heavy bell.'
I looked, and saw between us and the sun
A building on an island; such a one
As age to age might add, for uses vile,
A windowless, deformed and dreary pile;
And on the top an open tower, where hung
A bell, which in the radiance swayed and swung;
We could just hear its hoarse and iron tongue:
The broad sun sunk behind it, and it tolled
In strong and black relief. – 'What we behold
Shall be the madhouse and its belfry tower,'
Said Maddalo, 'and even at this hour
Those who may cross the water, hear that bell
Which calls the maniacs, each one from his cell,
To vespers.'[19]

While Maddalo draws out a gloomy analogy between the
lunatics at hopeless prayer and the conditions of our own
mortality, the sun drops out of sight:

                          The broad star
Of day meanwhile had sunk behind the hill,
And the black bell became invisible,
And the red tower looked gray, and all between
The churches, ships and palaces were seen
Huddled in gloom; – into the purple sea
The orange hues of heaven sunk silently.
We hardly spoke, and soon the gondola
Conveyed me to my lodging by the way.[20]

Some years later Théophile Gautier stopped at the island on
a wild afternoon in the late summer of 1850. The tossing
waves half hid the tiled roofs of its buildings and the reddish
stones of the campanile:

Close to us, like black swallows skimming the waves,
gondolas sped past in the opposite direction, heading
back to the city, flying before the storm and chased by the
wind which was against us.
    Finally, we reached the jetty of San Servolo, the sea

rocking our frail boat so violently that we had difficulty in landing.[21]

Once ashore he found a place well matched with the cheerless weather – long, white corridors opening on to rooms without warmth or character, the monastic cells of men for whom the world was nothing. 'It had been no great task to adapt their use from monks to madmen.'

## SAN LAZZARO DEGLI ARMENI

Almost due south of San Servolo, just off the Lido, is the little island of San Lazzaro degli Armeni whose associations are again with Lord Byron. It was here that he came in 1816 to beguile his ennui by studying Armenian, as he explained in the course of a long letter to Thomas Moore:

> By way of divertisement, I am studying daily, at an Armenian monastery, the Armenian language. I found that my mind wanted something craggy to break upon; and this – as the most difficult thing I could discover here for an amusement – I have chosen, to torture me into attention. . . . There are some very curious MSS. in the monastery, as well as books; translations also from Greek originals, now lost, and from Persian and Syriac, &c.; besides work of their own people.[22]

The community of Armenian monks was established on this peaceful island in the early eighteenth century and still survives. In a circular courtyard near the entrance a plaque commemorates Lord Byron, 'Amico Devoto dell'Armenia', and paintings of him hang in the room where he worked. In the visitors' book are recorded the names of Browning, Longfellow, and Proust, all of whom made the pilgrimage to San Lazzaro, where no doubt they, too, admired the ancient manuscripts, observed the portraits of the poet, and paused a moment in the tranquil cloister.

As we turn back towards the landing stage, we pass again the memorial tablet, inscribed at the bottom with Byron's words: 'The visitor will be convinced that there are other and better things even in this life.'

THE LIDO

Turning the pages of *Emaux et Camées*, Wilde's Dorian Gray comes to Gautier's poem 'Sur les Lagunes'. The words entrance him:

> *Sur une gamme chromatique,*
> *Le sein de perles ruisselant,*
> *La Vénus de l'Adriatique*
> *Sort de l'eau son corps rose et blanc. . . .*

How exquisite they were! As one read them, one seemed to be floating down the green water-ways of the pink and pearl city, seated in a black gondola with silver prow and trailing curtains. The mere lines looked to him like those straight lines of turquoise-blue that follow one as one pushes out to the Lido.[23]

By the time Wilde himself was pushing out to the Lido, the scene was rather less of an aesthete's dream than his highly-wrought sentences suggest. Having just returned to Venice in the summer of 1872, Ruskin declared on 23 June, in a passage choked with indignant punctuation marks, that he could not write that morning,

> because of the accursed whistling of the dirty steam-engine of the omnibus for Lido, waiting at the quay of the Ducal Palace for the dirty population of Venice, which is now neither fish nor flesh, neither noble nor fisherman; – cannot afford to be rowed, nor has strength nor sense enough to row itself; but smokes and spits up and down the piazzetta all day, and gets itself dragged by a screaming kettle to Lido next morning, to sea-bathe itself into capacity for more tobacco.[24]

The *vaporetto* service along the Grand Canal did not begin until 1881, but the screaming kettle to the Lido was a sign of things to come. As Ruskin implies, its establishment had much to do with the growing popularity of the Lido as a bathing resort. The practice had started here in 1857. Twenty years later, *Murray's Handbook* comments on it with obvious misgiving:

Venice is now much frequented on account of the bathing on the Lido . . . An omnibus conveys passengers in 5 min. across the narrow strip of land to the two large establishments there belonging to the owners of the Albergo Danieli, with good *restaurant* attached . . . The line of demarcation between the baths of the two sexes is not sufficiently observed to make bathing pleasant for English ladies, and the authorities ought to interfere.[25]

English ladies were in any case soon crowded out by Germans, and sea-bathers by sun-bathers. E. V. Lucas notes the change in his sketch of the Lido on the eve of the First World War:

German is the only language on the sea or on the sands, at any rate at the more costly establishments. The long stretch of sand between these establishments, with its myriad tents and boxes, belongs permanently to the Italians and is not to be invaded; but the public parts are Teutonic. Here from morning till evening paunchy men with shaven heads lie naked or almost naked in the sun. . . . The water concerns them but little: it is the sunburn on the sands that they value.[26]

Notable among these pre-war Germans, though hardly the sort of figure that Lucas had in mind, was Thomas Mann's Gustave von Aschenbach, respectably installed at the Grand Hotel des Bains – as Mann himself had been in the summer of 1911. Here, among the children and the sunbathers, the bearded men and the ripe indolent women, the family groups and the vendors of sea-shells, Aschenbach played out, in the windings of sexual obsession, the tragi-comedy of his death in Venice.

After the horrors of war, the search for pleasure in the twenties was more consuming than ever. D. H. Lawrence cast a puritanical eye on Venice in *Lady Chatterley's Lover*:

This was a holiday-place of all holiday-places. The Lido, with its acres of sun-pinked or pyjamaed bodies, was like a strand with an endless heap of seals come up for mating. Too many people in the piazza, too many limbs and

trunks of humanity on the Lido, too many gondolas, too
many motor-launches, too many steamers, too many
pigeons, too many ices, too many cocktails, too many
men-servants wanting tips, too many languages rattling,
too much, too much sun, too much smell of Venice, too
many cargoes of strawberries, too many silk shawls, too
many huge, raw-beef slices of water-melon on stalls: too
much enjoyment, altogether far too much enjoyment![27]

The popularity which the Lido has enjoyed for the last
century or so must have taken it by surprise. For most of
Venice's history it played little part in the affairs of the city. It
does, however, figure in an important episode at the beginning of the thirteenth century. At the time it was still called the
island of San Nicolò, and the monastery there was periodically
used as a residence for state visitors. Perhaps for this reason
Doge Enrico Dandolo chose the island as a suitable place to
lodge the motley hordes that had gathered in Venice for what
was planned as another crusade against the infidel. It was a
useful move. When the crusaders found themselves unable to
pay for the large fleet they had ordered from the Venetians,
Dandolo had merely to keep them boxed up until they agreed
to his terms. With a large private army at her disposal, Venice
went on to rake in the proceeds of what is charitably known as
the Fourth Crusade. The spoils of Constantinople made a large
contribution to her enormous wealth in the thirteenth and
fourteenth centuries. Doge Dandolo himself, a ninety-year-
old ruffian who was practically blind, retained both his energy
and his diplomatic genius to the last. He never returned to
Venice – his grave can still be seen in Aya Sophia – but the city
had reason to thank him.

After this doubtful enterprise, the Lido sinks into relative
obscurity – the site of a Jewish cemetery, the home of a few
fishermen, a barren stretch of land where noblemen could
exercise themselves and their horses. But for Goethe, on the
morning of 8 October 1786, it was a place of wonder:

Early this morning a gondola took me and my old
factotum to the Lido. We went ashore and walked across
the spit of land. I heard a loud noise: it was the sea, which

presently came into view. The surf was breaking on the
beach in high waves, although the water was receding,
for it was noon, the hour of low tide. Now, at last, I have
seen the sea with my own eyes and walked upon the
beautiful threshing floor of the sand which it leaves
behind when it ebbs. [28]

The whole island, as Goethe goes on to describe it, is little
more than a windswept dune. Certainly, the image of it that
Shelley gives at the start of *Julian and Maddalo*, only forty years
before the invasion of the bathing establishments, is desolate
indeed. It was here that he and Byron went riding:

> I rode one evening with Count Maddalo
> Upon the bank of land which breaks the flow
> Of Adria towards Venice: a bare strand
> Of hillocks, heaped from ever-shifting sand,
> Matted with thistles and amphibious weeds,
> Such as from earth's embrace the salt ooze breeds,
> Is this; an uninhabited sea-side,
> Which the lone fisher, when his nets are dried,
> Abandons; and no other object breaks
> The waste, but one dwarf tree and some few stakes
> Broken and unrepaired, and the tide makes
> A narrow space of level sand thereon,
> Where 'twas our wont to ride while day went down. [29]

The scene was scarcely more cheerful when George Sand
visited the Lido twenty years later. She remarks on the appal-
ling emptiness of the beach and the huge lizards 'which appear
in thousands under your feet and seem to follow you in ever
growing numbers, like part of a nightmare'. In her novel *Leone
Leoni*, she gives a brief image of the lonely Jewish cemetery at
the east end of the island, where Byron began his rides:

> I sat down on one of the graves, which are half-covered
> with grass and fretted incessantly by the raw, salt wind
> from the sea. The moon began to emerge from the mist,
> and the white stones of this huge cemetery stood out
> against the dark undergrowth of the Lido. [30]

By the time Gautier followed in Sand's footsteps, the Lido was already being used as a bathing resort by the Italians, but the couple of open-air taverns had done little to enliven the place. He, too, gives a few melancholy lines to the Jewish cemetery:

> Sand covers it, weeds invade it, and children think nothing of trampling and dancing on the broken and disordered graves. When one chides their irreverence, the children answer quite simply: 'They're Jews.'[31]

Gautier was among the last of the literary visitors to record impressions of a more or less unpeopled Lido. Within a decade or so the changes had begun which were to turn it into the cosmopolitan resort that Aschenbach died in, Lawrence raged against, and thousands of tourists still flock to.

Away from the bathing spots, near the church of San Nicolò, the remaining graves of the old Jewish cemetery can still be seen, protected now by a wall and overgrown with kindlier vegetation.


## SAN MICHELE

On the far side of Venice steamers leave the Fondamente Nuove for the islands of the north. Dominating the prospects from the quay is the cemetery island of San Michele. Stravinsky, Diaghilev, and Ezra Pound all have their graves here. Before them Frederick Rolfe, Baron Corvo, had been buried here in 1913. It was not his first visit. On 8 November 1909 he wrote to his friend Charles Masson Fox:

> . . . But last Monday and Tuesday were great days here. All Saints and All Souls. So I went across the lagoon on the bridge of boats to the cemetery at Sanmichele. All Venice was there with candles and flowers and lamps, decorating the graves of their dead. You never saw such gorgeousness of a garden. And the crowd! Well: I was slowly sauntering along a path, rather grim and sad myself being lonely and all that, when I spied Peter and Carlo and Gildo and Giuseppe and four more (one quite

lovely and quite unknown to me, but smallish), quietly and silently kneeling on their wicked knees round the grave of one of their comrades and praying for the repose of his soul. . . . So then I went back to the grave and they shewed me their work with naive pride, which of course I praised. And we walked about to admire the other graves for quite an hour, sometimes one with me, sometimes another, and all of them taking occasion to say to me privately 'Sior when shall we go to Burano for the night?'[32]

A bleaker image of the festival is presented by Malamud in his story of Fidelman, artist, oarsman, and shabby haunter of the streets of Venice:

On All Souls' Day, unable to resist, he rowed after a black-and-silver funeral barge and cortège of draped mourning gondolas moving like silent arrows across the water to San Michele, gloomy cypressed isle of the dead; the corpse of a young girl in white laid stiff in a casket covered with wreaths of hothouse flowers guarded by wooden angels. She waits, whatever she waited for, or sought, or hungered for, no longer. Ah, i poveri morti, though that depends on how you look at it. He had looked too long.[33]

The distance from San Michele to the Fondamente Nuove is short, but it can be perilous – as Casanova found one night while returning from an assignation at a convent on Murano:

We make good progress as far as San Michele, but scarcely have we passed the island before the wind increases with such fury that I see I am in danger of perishing if I go on; for though I was a good swimmer I was sure neither of my own strength nor of the possibility of resisting the current. I order the gondoliers to tie up to the island; but they answer that I am not in the hands of cowards and to have no fear. Knowing the character of our gondoliers I decide to say nothing; but the gusts of wind redoubled, the foaming waves were coming in over the side of the gondola, and my men, despite their strong arms, could not drive it forward.

We were only a hundred paces from the mouth of the Rio dei Gesuiti when a furious gust of wind knocked the man at the poop into the water, but he caught hold of the gondola and had no difficulty getting aboard again. Having lost his oar he took another; but the gondola, going about, had already travelled two hundred paces to my left and broadside on in one minute. The situation was desperate. I shout to them to abandon the *felze* to the sea, throwing a handful of silver pieces on the carpet of the gondola. I was instantly obeyed, whereupon my two hearties, using all their energy, showed Aeolus that his strength must yield to theirs. In less than four minutes we entered the Rio dei Mendicanti, and, praising them, I ordered them to take me to the quay of the Palazzo Bragadin in Santa Marina, where I had no sooner arrived than I got into bed under blankets to recover my natural heat . . .[34]

## MURANO

Casanova's reasons for being on Murano were rather different from those of the average tourist. Effie Ruskin's, on the other hand, were almost identical:

On Saturday we rowed to Murano, an island about 20 minutes sail from here. . . . It is now nearly deserted but the Cathedral is extremely interesting and the island for several centuries has been chiefly celebrated as being the seat of the Manufactories for the famous Venice glass, which amongst other merits broke in pieces when poison was put into it. One Manufactory entirely for beads we went over. . . . All sizes and colours are made but always of the same form. They are cheap. I got an immense bunch of all colours for 2/6 but they were very small ones. I have ordered some red of a peculiar kind and extremely beautiful and much more expensive to make into neck-

laces for Sophie, Alice & Eliza. I will get pretty clasps for
them at Genoa where they work gold so beautifully.[35]

The island had been the home of Venetian glass since the
thirteenth century, when the furnaces were moved out there to
avoid the danger of fire. Glass-blowing itself can be interesting
enough to watch but is less exciting to read about. This is not
something that visitors to Murano have been quick to grasp.
The literature on the subject is vast and tedious. It is to
Coryate's credit that he does little to add to it. In fact, he seems
to have found Murano more notable for its oysters than its
glass: 'Here did I eate the best Oysters that ever I did in all my
life. They were indeede but little, something lesse then our
Wainflete Oysters about London, but as green as a leeke, and
gratissimi saporis & succi.'[36]

Coryate's priorities were not altogether eccentric at a time
when Murano was also an island of villas and pleasure gardens
for the Venetian nobility; but his indifference to the main
business of the place would hardly have suited James Howell,
who was the steward of a glassware factory in London.
Howell had come to Venice in 1621 for professional reasons.
On 30 May he wrote home to his patron and employer Sir
Robert Mansell: 'I was, since I came hither, in *Murano*, a little
island about the distance of *Lambeth* from *London*, where
Crystal-Glass is made; and 'tis a rare sight to see a whole Street
[the Fondamenta dei Vereri], where on the one side there are
twenty Furnaces together at work.'[37] Howell goes on to
explain that the beauty and lustre of the glass, which cannot be
reproduced elsewhere, is imputed by some 'to the quality of
the circumnambient Air that Lay over the Place, which is
purify'd and attenuated by the concurrence of so many Fires
that are in those Furnaces Night and Day perpetually . . .'[38]

Later Howell refers to the property of Murano glass, noted
by Effie Ruskin, 'to admit no poison'. But this claim was
already under suspicion. Within a few years Sir Thomas
Browne was remarking sceptically, 'Though it be said that
poison will break a Venetian glass, yet have we not met with
any of that nature.' It might have been a useful feature of this
otherwise unappealing product.

Those who prefer not to risk getting trapped at one of the factories by insistent vendors will perhaps settle for this description by Dr John Moore, who visited Murano in the later years of the eighteenth century:

> The island is said to contain 20,000 inhabitants [i.e. well over twice the present population]. The great manufactories of looking-glasses are the only inducements which strangers have to visit this place. I saw one very fine plate, for a mirror, made in the presence of the Archduke in a few minutes. . . . Instead of being cast, as in France and England, the Murano mirrors are all blown in the manner of bottles. It is astonishing to see with what dexterity the workman wields a long hollow cylinder of melted glass, at the end of an iron tube, which, when he has extended as much as possible, by blowing, and every other means his art suggests, he slits with a sharp instrument, removing the two extremities from each other, and folding back the sides: the cylinder now appears a large sheet of glass, which being once more introduced into the furnace, is brought out a clear, finished plate.[39]

Venice put a high value on its glass-workers, and in earlier times any who left the city without permission were liable to sentence of death. As long as they remained, they enjoyed considerable licence. Just before he was caught in the storm near San Michele, Casanova had been pacing the empty quay at Murano in a freezing night-wind, worrying about the purse of gold he had with him:

> I had reason to fear the robbers of Murano, very dangerous and determined cutthroats who enjoy and abuse a number of privileges which the policy of the government grants them in return for the work they do in the glass factories with which the island abounds; to keep them from emigrating the government grants all of them Venetian citizenship. I expected to encounter a pair of them, who would have stripped me to my shirt, for I did not even have in my pocket the usual knife which all honest men in Venice carry to defend their lives.[40]

The business which had brought Casanova to Murano was a complicated affair, involving a couple of nuns and the French ambassador. It is an intrigue which spreads itself across Volumes Three and Four of his memoirs and prompts some of his most attractive sketches of Venetian life. For any who wish to make the pilgrimage, the convent at the centre of the story has been tentatively identified as Santa Maria degli Angeli on the eastern edge of the island.

More commonplace interests will take the tourist to the fine cathedral of San Donato, whose undulating floor is inset with beautiful designs in coloured marble. While here, you should take the opportunity to see the bones of a dragon killed by San Donato himself. These hang, somewhat surprisingly, behind the high altar.

## BURANO

Of the two main outer islands Burano is the one to make for first. The colourful home of fishermen and lacemakers is an agreeable prelude to a visit to Torcello, but to go there afterwards can be an anti-climax. Henry James paid it a visit in the summer of 1881 and was left with a happy impression of 'bright-coloured hovels, of bathing in stagnant canals, of young girls . . . with splendid heads of hair and complexions smeared with powder'.[41] Burano's literary associations are few. Corvo came here for sex with his gondoliers ('As for his rod – lawks!' etc.), but otherwise we must look to the eighteenth-century composer Baldassare Galuppi, who gave his name to the island's main street. Esteemed in his day as Venice's foremost composer, Galuppi visited England in the early 1740s. It was a distant echo of this visit that inspired Browning's poem 'A Toccata of Galuppi's', in which an Englishman reflects on the exotic images called to mind by Galuppi's music:

Here you come with your old music, and here's all the
good it brings.

> What, they lived once thus at Venice where the
>     merchants were the kings,
> Where Saint Mark's is, where the Doges used to wed the
>     sea with rings?
> Ay, because the sea's the street there; and 'tis arched by
>     . . . what you call
> . . . Shylock's bridge with houses on it, where they kept
>     the carnival:
> I was never out of England – it's as if I saw it all.
>
> Did young people take their pleasure when the sea was
>     warm in May?
> Balls and masques begun at midnight, burning ever to
>     mid-day,
> When they made up fresh adventures for the morrow,
>     do you say? . . .

The intriguing, evanescent world that emerges from the paintings of Francesco Guardi and Pietro Longhi, from the memoirs of Casanova and the plays of Goldoni could scarcely ask for a more fitting epigraph than Browning's lines later in the poem:

> As for Venice and her people, merely born to bloom and
>     drop,
> Here on earth they bore their fruitage, mirth and folly
>     were the crop:
> What of soul was left, I wonder, when the kidding had
>     to stop?

With the help of a time-table, it should be possible to spend an hour or so strolling round the pleasant streets of Galuppi's island before the returning steamer leaves for Torcello.

## Torcello

*Torcello, about 6m (2 hrs) N.E. of Venice (2 gondoliers necessary, make a bargain), now an unhealthy island, containing only a few inhabitants.* This is the unpromising introduction to Murray's piece on Torcello in the 1877 *Handbook*. The island's period of grandeur was already many centuries in the past. It had become more or less what we see today – a lonely island with a few relics of Byzantine Christianity. And also one of the most beautiful places in the lagoon.

If you can get here on a morning in early spring, before the tourist season has destroyed its peace, there is still much of the atmosphere that George Sand found on the island a century and a half ago. Leaving her lover to doze on Attila's chair, she wandered alone, picking flowers in the Torcello lanes:

> A profusion of brilliant convolvulus clung to the hedges, stretching here and there above the path to form a more graceful and sumptuous arbour than the hand of man could have achieved. Eight or ten dwellings, twenty at most, scattered among the orchards, house the entire population of the islands. All their occupants had already gone fishing. . . . Butterflies skimmed over the carpet of flowers stretched out under my feet . . . and alighted on the posy I was holding in my hand. Torcello is a reclaimed wilderness. Through copses of water-willow and hibiscus bushes run salt-water streams where petrel and teal delight to stalk. Here and there a marble capital, a fragment of Lower Empire sculpture or a lovely, shattered Greek cross emerges from the long grass. Nature's eternal youth smiles in the midst of these ruins. The air was balmy and only the song of the cicadas disturbed the religious hush of the morning. [42]

Among the encroachments of nature the cathedral remains a powerful monument to the faith of the men who built it almost a thousand years ago. The remote, austere piety of its mosaics drew an apt response from Henry James:

> The interior is rich in grimly mystical mosaics of the twelfth century and the patchwork of precious fragments in the pavement not inferior to that of St. Mark's. But the terribly distinct Apostles are ranged against their dead gold backgrounds as stiffly as grenadiers presenting arms – intensely personal sentinels of a personal Deity. Their stony stare seems to wait forever for some visible revival

of primitive orthodoxy, and one may well wonder whether it finds much beguilement in idly-gazing troops of Western heretics – passionless even in their heresy. [43]

Characteristically, William Beckford had turned from the 'quaint forms of the apostles' to the font near the west door:

> The figures of horned imps cling around its sides; more devilish, more Egyptian, than any I ever beheld. The dragons on old china are not more whimsical: I longed to have filled it with bats' blood, and to have sent it by way of present to the sabbath. I can assure you, it would have done honour to their witcheries. [44]

While Beckford studies the church, his dinner is being prepared at a neighbouring convent. Allured by the sound of his party's flutes and oboes, the nuns 'peeped out of their cells, and shewed themselves by dozens at the grate.' Beckford stays till the sun is low before being rowed back across the rippling lagoon.

It was over half a century later that Ruskin, still a schoolboy, first set eyes on Venice. In his voluminous writings on the city, Torcello occupies a special place; nowhere else do his words quite so completely take possession of their subject. After describing the dreary outline of the island, he launches into this celebrated evocation of Venetian light and space:

> On this mound is built a rude brick campanile, of the commonest Lombardic type, which if we ascend towards evening (and there are none to hinder us, the door of its ruinous staircase swinging idly on its hinges), we may command from it one of the most notable scenes in this wide world of ours. Far as the eye can reach, a waste of wild sea moor, of a lurid ashen grey; not like our northern moors with their jet-black pools and purple heath, but lifeless, the colour of sackcloth, with the corrupted sea-water soaking through the roots of its acrid weeds, and gleaming hither and thither through its snaky channels. No gathering of fantastic mists, nor coursing of clouds across it; but melancholy clearness of space in the warm

sunset, oppressive, reaching to the horizon of its level gloom. [45]

After these sombre periods it is a relief to catch a glimpse of Ruskin in less familiar character. A letter from Effie to her mother on 24 February 1850 gives this account of an outing with her friend Charlotte Ker, Ruskin, and an Austrian officer:

> The day was cloudy but we were afraid to put off the day in case another opportunity should not occur again; the sun broke forth warmly and the afternoon was charming. Charlotte & I ran into the quiet churchyard to see if the violets were yet in flower but we were still a little too soon and only found a quantity of fresh leaves. At three o'clock we sat down in the same place as before, leaning against the old Monastery of the Brothers of Torcello now filled with slag; a black lizard roused by the sun's heat fell from above on my shoulder but was gone before I hardly saw it. George laid out the cloth upon which he spread cold fowls, Parmesan cheese, Italian bread, beef, cakes, Muscat & Champagne Wines – and a copper vessel full of cold water from the draw well completed our bill of fare. John & Paulizza were in the greatest spirits and nothing could be merrier than the two. After dinner, to show us that the Champagne which they certainly did not take much of, had not gone into their heads, they ran races round the old buildings and so fast that one could hardly see them. [46]

'A beautiful place to picnic,' the current *Blue Guide* remarks incautiously. It is so partly because the enduring impression left by Torcello is of a place overtaken by time. From the lagoon you see only wastes of reed and marsh, inhabited by sea-birds and marked out by a campanile and a few scattered buildings. It was from this that Venice arose and to this, in Shelley's vision of the future, that she will return. Long after the city has crumbled away, the fishermen of the island will still be going about their business:

> Sun-girt City, thou hast been
> Ocean's child, and then his queen;
> Now is come a darker day,

And thou soon must be his prey.
The fisher on his watery way,
Wandering at the close of day,
Will spread his sail and seize his oar
Till he pass the gloomy shore,
Lest thy dead should, from their sleep
Bursting o'er the starlight deep,
Lead a rapid masque of death
O'er the waters of his path. [47]

The wild flowers and broken stones of Torcello draw one's thoughts insistently in this direction.

It was here that the story of Venice began. As the water-taxi ferries us away from the city and the towers and palaces fade behind us, we turn again to this lonely island at the edge of the lagoon, which has remained through the centuries an unheeded presence beside its triumphant neighbour. Ruskin's final, elegiac image reminds us of their inevitable kinship:

Thirteen hundred years ago, the grey moorland looked as it does this day, and the purple mountains stood as radiantly in the deep distances of evening; but on the line of the horizon, there were strange fires mixed with the light of sunset, and the lament of many human voices mixed with the fretting of the waves on their ridges of sand. The flames rose from the ruins of Altinum; the lament from the multitude of its people, seeking, like Israel of old, a refuge from the sword in the paths of the sea.

The cattle are feeding and resting upon the site of the city that they left; the mower's scythe swept this day at dawn over the chief street of the city that they built, and the swathes of soft grass are now sending up their scent into the night air, the only incense that fills the temple of their ancient worship. [48]

# REFERENCES

Many of the works cited have gone through numerous editions. To avoid confusion I have tried, where practicable, to identify extracts by the chapter or section of the book in which they appear rather than by page number. Translations are by me unless otherwise stated.

In one way or another I am indebted to all the books that are listed below, but among the more recent ones I should mention in particular J. G. Links, *Venice for Pleasure* (1966) and *Travellers in Europe* (1980), John Julius Norwich, *Venice, the Greatness and the Fall* (1977–81), Michael Marqusee, *Venice, an illustrated anthology* (1988) and James Lees-Milne, *Venetian Evenings* (1988).

## DORSODURO

1 Quoted in Giulio Lorenzetti, *Venice and its Lagoon* (1926), trans. John Guthrie, Trieste, 1975, p. 538.
2 Henry James, 'The Grand Canal' (1892), reprinted in *Italian Hours*, 1909.
3 Théophile Gautier, *Voyage en Italie*, 1852, ch. 7.
4 Horatio Brown, *Life on the Lagoons*, 1884, 'The Madonna della Salute'.
5 John Addington Symonds, *Sketches and Studies in Italy and Greece*, 1898, 'A Venetian Medley', Pt. IX.
6 Henri de Régnier, *Esquisses vénitiennes*, revised edn. 1920, 'La Commedia'.
7 Ibid., 'Le Stratagème'.
8 Charles Eliot Norton, 'Rawdon Brown and the Gravestone of "Banish'd Norfolk"', *Atlantic Monthly*, June 1889.
9 All *pensioni* have now been recategorized as hotels, so before long the evocative term will presumably fall into disuse.
10 The Cini cultural organization, based on the island of San Giorgio Maggiore, was founded by Count Vittorio Cini in 1951 in memory of his son.

11 Frederick Rolfe, 'On Canoading into the Canal', *Blackwood's Magazine*, July 1913.
12 W. D. Howells, *Venetian Life*, 1866, ch. 11.
13 Théophile Gautier, *Voyage en Italie*, 1852, ch. 19.
14 Quoted in E. V. Lucas, *A Wanderer in Venice*, 1914, ch. 16.
15 Ibid.
16 John Moore, *A View of Society and Manners in Italy*, 1781, Letter 6.
17 Horatio Brown, *In and Around Venice*, 1905, 'Venice'.
18 See Brian Pullan, *Rich and Poor in Renaissance Venice*, Oxford, 1971.
19 Quoted in Ibid., p. 265.
20 Frederick Rolfe, *The Desire and Pursuit of the Whole*, 1934, ch. 21.
21 Adrian Stokes, *Venice: An Aspect of Art*, London, 1945, p. 39.
22 Ibid., p. 40. Only patches of the brick now emerge, where the covering of plaster has chipped off.
23 Henry James, 'Two Old Houses and Three Young Women' (1899), Section 1, reprinted in *Italian Hours*, 1909.
24 George Gordon, Lord Byron, *Beppo*, 1818.
25 *Cook's Tourist's Handbook for Northern Italy*, 1875, p. 114.
26 Frederick Rolfe, *The Desire and Pursuit of the Whole*, 1934, ch. 11.
27 Ezra Pound, *The Cantos*, 1954, Canto XXVI, ll. 1–10.
28 Giuseppe Tassini, *Curiosità Veneziane* (1863), ninth edition, Venice, 1988, p. 141.
29 Hugh A. Douglas, *Venice on Foot*, 1906, Walk II.
30 Henry James, 'The Grand Canal' (1892), reprinted in *Italian Hours*, 1909.
31 Henry James, Letter to Alice James, 6 June 1890.
32 W. D. Howells, *Venetian Life*, 1866, ch. 22.
33 Ibid.
34 Giacomo Casanova, *History of My Life*, trans. Willard R. Trask, 1967, Vol. II, ch. 7.
35 John Pudney, *The Thomas Cook Story*, London, 1954, p. 43.
36 Sean O'Faolain, *A Summer in Italy*, 1949, 'A Lavish City'.
37 W. D. Howells, *Venetian Life*, 1866, ch. 20.
38 George Sand, *Lettres d'un voyageur* (1837), Letter 2, trans. Sacha Rabinovitch and Patricia Thomson, Harmondsworth, 1987.
39 Frederick Rolfe, *Venice Letters*, ed. Cecil Woolf, London, 1974, p. 27.
40 Max Beerbohm, 'A Stranger in Venice' (1906), reprinted in *A Variety of Things*, 1928.

## San Polo

1 Horatio Brown, *Life on the Lagoons*, 1884, 'Floods in the City'.
2 Bernard Malamud, *Pictures of Fidelman*, 1969, ch. 6.
3 Carlo Goldoni, *Memoirs* (1787), trans. J. Black, 1926, Pt. I, ch. 1.
4 John Ruskin, *Works*, ed. E. T. Cook and Alexander Wedderburn, London, 1904, Vol. XI, p. 379.

5 Giuseppe Tassini, *Curiosità Veneziane* (1863), ninth edition, Venice, 1988, p. 75.

6 John Ruskin, Letter to his father, 24 September 1845. See *Ruskin in Italy*, ed. Harold Shapiro, Oxford, 1972, pp. 211–2.

7 Henry James, 'Venice' (1882), Section 6, reprinted in *Italian Hours*, 1909.

8 John Ruskin, *Works*, ed. E. T. Cook and Alexander Wedderburn, London, 1904, Vol. XXIV, pp. 170–1.

9 Giuseppe Tassini, *Curiosità Veneziane* (1863), ninth edition, Venice, 1988, p. 336.

10 Desiderius Erasmus, 'Opulentia Sordida', *Colloquies*, Vol. II, trans. N. Bailey, London, 1878.

11 John Evelyn, *Diaries*, ed. E. S. De Beer, Oxford, 1955, Vol. II, pp. 473–4.

12 Hugh A. Douglas, *Venice on Foot*, 1906, Walk IX.

13 Giacomo Casanova, *History of My Life*, trans. Willard R. Trask, 1967, Vol. II, ch. 7.

14 The assassin was to be paid four thousand gold florins, with a pension of a hundred florins to him and his heirs in perpetuity; he was to enjoy amnesty for all offences and to exercise full civic rights; he was provided exemption from taxes, the privilege of carrying arms with two attendants in the whole domain of Florence, and the prerogative of restoring ten outlaws at his choice. If he captured Lorenzino and brought him alive to Florence, the reward would be doubled in each item.

15 John Addington Symonds, *Renaissance in Italy*, 1886, 'The Catholic Reaction', Pt. I, ch. 6.

16 Ibid.

17 Frederick Rolfe, *Venice Letters*, ed. Cecil Woolf, London, 1974, p. 25.

18 Ibid., p. 41.

19 Carlo Gozzi, *The Memoirs* (1797), trans. J. A. Symonds, London, 1890, Vol. II, pp. 38–9.

20 George Sand, *Lettres d'un voyageur* (1837), Letter 2, trans. Sacha Rabinovitch and Patricia Thomson, Harmondsworth, 1987.

21 Pero Tafur, *Travels and Adventures, 1435–1439*, trans. Malcolm Letts, London, 1926, p. 32.

22 Samuel Sharp, *Letters from Italy*, 1767, Letter 11.

23 Fynes Moryson, *An Itinerary* (1617), Glasgow, 1907, pp. 190–1.

24 Elizabeth David, *Italian Food* (1954), Harmondsworth, 1963, p. 169. Quoted in Milton Grundy, *Venice Recorded*, 1971, ch. 6.

25 Thomas Coryate, *Coryat's Crudities*, 1611, 'Observations of Venice'.

26 See *Francis Mortoft: His Book*, ed. Malcolm Letts, London, 1925, p. 138.

27 Thomas Coryate, *Coryat's Crudities*, 1611, 'Observations of Venice'.

28 Ibid.

29 This was not a specifically Venetian concern. Visiting Padua in 1609, William Lithgow remarks that 'beastly Sodomy' is 'as rife here as in *Rome; Naples, Florence, Bullogna, Venice, Ferrara, Genoa, Parma* not being exempted, nor yet the smallest village of Italy: A monstrous filthiness,

and yet to them a pleasant pastime, making Songs, and singing Sonnets of the beauty and pleasure of their *Bardassi*, or buggered boys.'

30 Carlo Gozzi, *The Memoirs* (1797), trans. J. A. Symonds, London, 1890, Vol. I, pp. 279–80.

31 John Ruskin, *Works*, ed. E. T. Cook and Alexander Wedderburn, London, 1904, Vol. X, p. 145.

32 Giuseppe Tassini, *Curiosità Veneziane* (1863), ninth edition, Venice, 1988, p. 125.

33 L. P. Hartley, *Eustace and Hilda*, 1947, ch. 12.

34 Henry James, *The Aspern Papers*, 1888, ch. 1.

35 Gabriele d'Annunzio, *Il Fuoco*, 1900, trans. K. Vivaria, *The Flame of Life*, London, 1900, p. 131.

## CENTRAL VENICE

1 Gore Vidal, *Venice*, London, 1985, p. 148.

2 George Gordon, Lord Byron, Letter to Thomas Moore, 17 November 1816. See *Byron's Letters and Journals*, ed. Leslie A. Marchand, London, 1976.

3 Ibid., Letter to Thomas Moore, 28 January 1817.

4 Pompeo Molmenti, *La Storia di Venezia nella vita privata*, trans. Horatio Brown as *Venice: Its Individual Growth from the Earliest Beginnings to the Fall of the Republic*, London, 1906–8, Pt. III, Vol. I, p. 171.

5 Lorenzo da Ponte, *Memoirs*, trans. L. A. Sheppard, London, 1929, pp. 46–7.

6 Ibid., p. 54.

7 L. P. Hartley, *Eustace and Hilda*, 1947, ch. 8.

8 Sean O'Faolain, *Summer in Italy*, 1949, 'Dissolving Antinomies'.

9 The anonymous denunciation seems to have come from the husband of a woman da Ponte had seduced. The investigators clearly found evidence to support it, since da Ponte was banished from Venetian territory for fifteen years.

10 Pompeo Molmenti, *La Storia di Venezia nella vita privata*, trans. Horatio Brown as *Venice: Its Individual Growth from the Earliest Beginnings to the Fall of the Republic*, London, 1906–8, Pt. III, Vol. I, p. 7.

11 Charles de Brosses, *Lettres familières sur l'Italie*, Letter 14, 13 August 1739.

12 Quoted in Maurice Andrieux, *Daily Life in Venice in the Time of Casanova*, Paris, 1969, trans. Mary Fitton, London, 1972, pp. 48–9.

13 Théophile Gautier, *Voyage en Italie*, 1852, ch. 12.

14 Ibid., ch. 15.

15 Henry James, 'Venice' (1882), Section 8, reprinted in *Italian Hours*, 1909.

16 Henry James, *The Aspern Papers*, 1888, ch. 9.

17 Effie Ruskin, Letter of 28 December 1851. See *Effie in Venice*, ed. Mary Lutyens, London, 1965.

18 George Sand, Preface (written April 1851) to a new edition of *André*, Paris, 1869.

19 Samuel Sharp, *Letters from Italy*, 1767, Letter 5, September 1765.

20 George Gordon, Lord Byron, Letter to James Cam Hobhouse, 3 October 1819. See *Byron's Letters and Journals*, ed. Leslie A. Marchand, London, 1976.

21 John James Ruskin, Letter of 27 November 1849. Quoted in Jeanne Clegg, *Ruskin and Venice*, London, 1981, p. 93.

22 Giuseppe Tassini, *Curiosità Veneziane* (1863), ninth edition, Venice, 1988, p. 416.

23 Quoted in Archibald Colquhoun, *Manzoni and his Times*, London, 1954, p. 54.

24 Ernest Hemingway, *Across the River and Into the Trees*, 1950, ch. 6.

25 Henry James, *The Wings of the Dove*, 1902, Book VII, Section 3.

26 Ibid., Book 7, Section 4.

27 Marcel Brion, *Venice, The Masque of Italy*, trans. Neil Mann, London, 1962, pp. 139–40.

28 Percy Bysshe Shelley, Letter to Thomas Love Peacock, 17/18 December 1818. See *The Letters of Percy Bysshe Shelley*, ed. Frederick L. Jones, Oxford, 1964.

29 George Gordon, Lord Byron, Letter to John Murray, 1 August 1819. See *Byron's Letters and Journals*, ed. Leslie A. Marchand, London, 1976.

30 Ibid.

31 Lady Mary Wortley Montagu, Letter to Lady Pomfret, March 1740. See *The Complete Letters of Lady Mary Wortley Montagu*, ed. Robert Halsband, Oxford, 1966.

32 Giacomo Casanova, *History of My Life*, trans. Willard R. Trask, 1967, Vol. II, ch. 7.

33 W. D. Howells, *Venetian Life*, 1866, ch. 11.

34 Marcel Proust, *A la recherche du temps perdu, La Prisonnière* (1923), trans. C. K. Scott Moncrieff, *The Captive* (1929), London, 1957, Pt. II, p. 260.

35 Henry Wadsworth Longfellow, Letter to his mother, 20 December 1828.

36 Sir John Reresby, *Memoirs and Travels of Sir John Reresby*, London, 1904, p. 6.

37 Johann Wolfgang von Goethe, *Italienische Reise* (1816–29), trans. W. H. Auden and E. Mayer, London, 1962, pp. 85–6.

38 Quoted in Maurice Andrieux, *Daily Life in Venice in the Time of Casanova* (1969), trans. Mary Fitton, London, 1972, p. 166.

39 L. P. Hartley, *Eustace and Hilda*, 1947, ch. 4.

40 W. D. Howells, *Venetian Life*, 1866, ch. 4.

41 George Sand, *Histoire de ma vie*, 1848–54, Pt. V, ch. 3.

42 Giuseppe Tassini, *Curiosità Veneziane* (1863), ninth edition, Venice, 1988, p. 62.

43 John Evelyn, *Diaries*, ed. E. S. De Beer, Oxford, 1955, Vol. II, p. 434.

44 Thomas Coryate, *Coryat's Crudities*, 1611, 'Observations of Venice'.

45 Théophile Gautier, *Voyage en Italie*, 1852, ch. 16.
46 Johann Wolfgang von Goethe, *Italienische Reise* (1816–29), trans. W. H. Auden and E. Mayer, London, 1962, p. 58.

## PIAZZA SAN MARCO

1 Max Beerbohm, 'A Stranger in Venice' (1906), reprinted in *A Variety of Things*, 1928.
2 Thomas Coryate, *Coryat's Crudities*, 1611, 'Observations of Venice'.
3 Effie Ruskin, Letter of 13 November 1849. See *Effie in Venice*, ed. Mary Lutyens, London, 1965.
4 Henry James, *The Aspern Papers*, 1888, ch. 5.
5 Théophile Gautier, *Voyage en Italie*, 1857, ch. 15.
6 John Ruskin, *Works*, ed. E. T. Cook and Alexander Wedderburn, London, 1904, Vol. X, pp. 84–5.
7 Ibid., Vol. XI, pp. 231–2.
8 Michel Butor, *Description de San Marco*, Paris, 1963, p. 14.
9 Augustus Hare, *Cities of Northern Italy*, 1883, ch. 21.
10 Théophile Gautier, *Voyage en Italie*, 1852, ch. 7. Translated in H. Neville Maugham, *Book of Italian Travel (1580–1900)*, London, 1903.
11 John Ruskin, *Works*, ed. E. T. Cook and Alexander Wedderburn, London, 1904, Vol. X, p. 363.
12 John Evelyn, *Diaries*, ed. E. S. De Beer, Oxford, 1955, Vol. II, pp. 441–2.
13 Oscar Wilde, *The Picture of Dorian Gray*, 1891, ch. 14.
14 Elizabeth Barrett Browning. Quoted in Michael Marqusee, *Venice, an illustrated anthology*, London, 1988, p. 89.
15 Thomas Coryate, *Coryat's Crudities*, 1611, 'Observations of Venice'.
16 *The Times*, 26 July 1902.
17 Osbert Sitwell, *Winters of Content*, London, 1932, pp. 39–40.
18 Horatio Brown, *In and Around Venice*, 1905, Pt. II, ch. 1.
19 William Lithgow, *The Rare Adventures and Painefull Peregrinations*, 1614, 'Comments upon Italy'.
20 Ibid.
21 George Ayscough, *Letters from an Officer in the Guards*, 1778, Letter 26.
22 Henry James, 'Venice' (1882), Section 6, reprinted in *Italian Hours*, 1909.
23 Those who do reach the great Sala del Maggior Consiglio should think twice before imitating Boswell's eccentric tribute to Otway, noted in his Journal for 2 July 1765: 'In council room roared out, "Cursed be your Senate!" &c. Had sad headache.'
24 William Beckford, *Dreams, Waking Thoughts, and Incidents*, 1783, Letter 8.
25 John Ruskin, *Works*, ed. E. T. Cook and Alexander Wedderburn, London, 1904, Vol. XI, p. 433.

26 Quoted in Maurice Andrieux, *Daily Life in Venice in the Time of Casanova* (1969), trans. Mary Fitton, London, 1972, p. 221.

27 Honoré de Balzac, *Oeuvres complètes*, ed. Bouteron and Longnon, Paris, 1952, Vol. XXIII, p. 780.

28 Quoted in Giacomo Casanova, *History of My Life*, trans. Willard R. Trask, 1967, Vol. IV, Appendix.

29 Charles Dickens, 'An Italian Dream', *Pictures from Italy*, 1846. The Canale Orfano lies between the islands of San Giorgio and San Servolo. According to James Morris, the death sentence specifically stated that the prisoner should be taken out to the Canale Orfano, weighted, and there drowned with his hands tied behind his back. Fishing hereabouts was forbidden.

30 Mark Twain, *The Innocents Abroad*, 1869, ch. 22.

31 Quoted in J. G. Links, *Venice for Pleasure* (1966), London, 1984, p. 135.

32 Quoted in Alfonso Lowe, *La Serenissima*, London, 1974, p. 15.

33 Hester Piozzi (Thrale), *Observations and Reflections*, 1789, ed. Herbert Barrows, Michigan, 1967, pp. 88–9.

34 John Ruskin, Letter to his father, 5 October 1851. See *Ruskin's Letters from Venice 1851–1852*, ed. John Lewis Bradley, New Haven, 1955.

35 Gilbert Burnet, *Some Letters Containing an account of what seemed most remarkable in Switzerland, Italy &c.*, 1686, Letter 3.

## EASTERN VENICE

1 Henry Wadsworth Longfellow, Letter to his mother, 20 December 1828.

2 Giacomo Casanova, *History of My Life*, trans. Willard R. Trask, 1967, Vol. III, ch. 13.

3 George B. Parks, *The English Traveller to Italy*, Rome, 1954, p. 377.

4 John Ruskin, *Works*, ed. E. T. Cook and Alexander Wedderburn, London, 1904, Vol. XXXV, p. 295.

5 See *Effie in Venice*, ed. Mary Lutyens, London, 1965, p. 63.

6 Effie Ruskin, Letter of 13 November 1849. See *Effie in Venice*, ed. Mary Lutyens, London, 1965.

7 Quoted in Annarosa Poli, *L'Italie dans la vie et dans l'oeuvre de George Sand*, Paris, 1960, p. 61.

8 Marcel Proust, Letter to Mme Strauss. Quoted in George Painter, *Marcel Proust, A Biography*, Vol. I, London, 1959, p. 269.

9 Max Beerbohm, 'A Stranger in Venice' (1906), reprinted in *A Variety of Things*, 1928.

10 Ibid.

11 Ibid.

12 John Ruskin, Letter to his father, 28 September 1845. See *Ruskin in Italy*, ed. Harold Shapiro, Oxford, 1972.

13 The punishment of the *corda*, which recurs on several of the minatory

tablets scattered around Venice, was witnessed by Coryate in St Mark's Square: 'The offender having his hands bound behind him, is conveighed into a rope that hangeth in a pully, and after hoysed up in the rope to a great heigth with two severall swinges, where he sustaineth so great torments that his joynts are for the time loosed and pulled asunder; besides such abundance of bloud is gathered into his hands and face, that for the time he is in the torture, his face and hands doe looke as red as fire.'

14  Henry James, Preface (1906–8) to *The Portrait of a Lady*, 1881.

15  Francesco Petrarch, Letter to Francesco Bruni, 9 April 1363. Translation quoted from Mrs Oliphant, *Makers of Venice*, 1887, Pt. IV, ch. 7.

16  Pero Tafur, *Travels and Adventures, 1435–1439*, trans. Malcolm Letts, London, 1926, pp. 170–1.

17  Thomas Coryate, *Coryat's Crudities*, 1611, 'Observations of Venice'.

18  Cosima Wagner, *The Diaries*, Vol. II, ed. Martin Gregor-Dellin and Dietrich Mack, 1977, trans. Geoffrey Skelton, 1980, entry for Thursday, 12 October 1882.

19  W. D. Howells, *Venetian Life*, 1866, ch. 21.

20  John Ruskin, *Works*, ed. E. T. Cook and Alexander Wedderburn, London, 1904, Vol. XXIV, p. 338.

21  Henry James, 'Venice' (1882), Section 7, reprinted in *Italian Hours*, 1909.

22  John Ruskin, *Works*, ed. E. T. Cook and Alexander Wedderburn, London, 1904, Vol. XXIV, p. 339.

23  Roger Ascham, *The Scholemaster*, 1570, Bk. I, 'Teachyng the brynging up of Youth'.

24  Charles de Brosses, *Lettres familières sur l'Italie*, Letter 14, 13 August 1739.

25  One of Casola's companions on this visit was Philippe de Commines, the French ambassador at the time, later famous for his *Memoirs*.

26  Pietro Casola, *Canon Pietro Casola's Pilgrimage to Jerusalem in the Year 1494*, trans. M. M. Newett, Manchester, 1907, ch. 18. Quoted in this abridged form in J. G. Links, *Travellers in Europe*, London, 1980, p. 77.

27  Gilbert Burnet, *Some Letters Containing an account of what seemed most remarkable in Switzerland, Italy &c.*, 1686, Letter 3.

28  Augustus Hare, *Cities of Northern Italy*, 1883, ch. 23.

29  Marcel Proust, *A la recherche du temps perdu, Albertine disparue* (1925), trans. C. K. Scott Moncrieff, *The Sweet Cheat Gone* (1930), London, 1957, pp. 317–8.

30  Thomas Mann, *Der Tod in Venedig* (1912), trans. H. T. Lowe-Porter, *Death in Venice*, Harmondsworth, 1975, p. 63.

31  Jan Morris, *A Venetian Bestiary*, London, 1982, pp. 123–4.

32  Pero Tafur, *Travels and Adventures, 1435–1439*, trans. Malcolm Letts, London, 1926, p. 170.

33  See John Julius Norwich, *Venice, The Greatness and the Fall*, London, 1981, Vol. II, p. 234.

34  Augustus Hare, *Cities of Northern Italy*, 1883, ch. 23.

35 W. D. Howells, *Venetian Life*, 1866, ch. 19.
36 Théophile Gautier, *Voyage en Italie*, 1852, ch. 13.
37 Katharine de Kay Bronson, 'Browning in Venice', *Cornhill Magazine*, N.S. Vol. XII, February 1902, p. 163.
38 George Sand, *Lettres d'un voyageur* (1837), Letter 2, trans. Sacha Rabinovitch and Patricia Thomson, Harmondsworth, 1987.
39 Ibid.

## Northern Venice

1 Princess Marie von Thurn und Taxis Hohenlohe, *Memoirs of a Princess*, trans. Nora Wydenbruck, London, 1959, pp. 142–3. I have quoted the translation Nora Wydenbruck gives in her biography, *Rilke, Man and Poet*, New York, 1950, p. 187.
2 Muriel Spark, *Territorial Rights*, London, 1979, pp. 8–9.
3 Augustus Hare, *Cities of Northern Italy*, 1883, ch. 23.
4 John Ruskin, *Works*, ed. E. T. Cook and Alexander Wedderburn, London, 1904, Vol. XI, p. 145.
5 This painting, destroyed by fire in 1867, was reckoned by Hazlitt to be the greatest of Titian's works: 'Most probably, as a picture, it is the finest in the world.'
6 According to John Julius Norwich, the skin was in fact stolen from the Arsenal of Constantinople nine years later by one of the survivors of the siege and returned to Bragadin's sons. See *Venice, The Greatness and the Fall*, London, 1981, Vol. II, p. 220.
7 'The Republic of Venice: its Rise, Decline, and Fall', *Quarterly Review*, Vol. CXXXVII, October 1874, p. 452.
8 Thomas Coryate, *Coryat's Crudities*, 1611, 'Observations of Venice'.
9 John Ruskin, *Works*, ed. E. T. Cook and Alexander Wedderburn, London, 1904, Vol. XI, pp. 113–4.
10 Giorgio Vasari, 'The Life of Andrea del Verrocchio' in *The Lives of the Artists*, 1550, trans. George Bull, 1965.
11 Thomas Coryate, *Coryat's Crudities*, 1611, 'Observations of Venice'.
12 Henry James, *The Aspern Papers*, 1888, ch. 9.
13 Count Alvise Zorzi, 'Ruskin in Venice', *Cornhill Magazine*, N.S. Vol. XXI, September 1906, p. 366.
14 Edmond and Jules de Goncourt, *Italie d'hier*, 1893, 'Venise'.
15 Giacomo Casanova, *History of My Life*, trans. Willard R. Trask, 1967, Vol. IV, ch. 3.
16 W. D. Howells, *Venetian Life*, 1866, ch. 3.
17 John Ruskin, *Works*, ed. E. T. Cook and Alexander Wedderburn, London, 1904, Vol. XI, p. 393.
18 Giuseppe Tassini, *Curiosità Veneziane* (1863), ninth edition, Venice, 1988, p. 416.
19 Henry James, 'Venice' (1882), Section 4, reprinted in *Italian Hours*, 1909.

20 Giuseppe Tassini, *Curiosità Veneziane* (1863), ninth edition, Venice, 1988, pp. 481–2.
21 Pompeo Molmenti, *La Storia di Venezia nella vita privata*, revised edition, Trieste, 1978, Vol. I, ch. 14. (Absent from Horatio Brown's translation.)
22 Thomas Coryate, *Coryat's Crudities*, 1611, 'Observations of Venice'.
23 Thomas Otway, *Venice Preserved* (1682), Act III, Scene ii, 11.161–5.
24 Horatio Brown, *Studies in the History of Venice*, 1907, Vol. I, 'Political Assassination'.
25 Felix Fabri, *The Wanderings of Felix Fabri*, trans. Aubrey Stewart, London, Palestine Pilgrims' Text Society, 1892, Vol. I, Pt. I, pp. 79–80.
26 Rosamund Mitchell, *The Spring Voyage*, London, 1964, p. 49.
27 Quoted in J. G. Links, *Travellers in Europe*, London, 1980, p. 64.
28 *The Book of Ser Marco Polo*, ed. Sir Henry Yule, 3rd edn. London, 1929. p. 5.
29 Ibid., p. 6.
30 Jean-Jacques Rousseau, *The Confessions* (1781), Book VII, trans. J. M. Cohen, Harmondsworth, 1953, pp. 294–5.
31 Joseph Addison, *Remarks on Italy*, 1705, 'Venice'.
32 Arthur Young, *Travels in France and Italy*, 1792, entry for 4 November 1789.
33 Henry James, 'Venice' (1882), Section 7, reprinted in *Italian Hours*, 1909.
34 William Beckford, *Dreams, Waking Thoughts, and Incidents*, 1783, Letter 8.
35 Quoted in Guy Chapman, *Beckford*, New York, 1937, p. 69.
36 Frederick Rolfe, *The Desire and Pursuit of the Whole*, 1934, ch. 13.
37 John Ruskin, Letter to his father, 23 September 1845. See *Ruskin in Italy*, ed. Harold Shapiro, Oxford, 1972.
38 Théophile Gautier, *Voyage en Italie*, 1852, ch. 25.
39 There was a long history of tension between Venice and the Pope, but the immediate cause of the affair was relatively trivial. The Council of Ten, having arrested a couple of miscreant priests, refused to hand them over to the ecclesiastical authorities. Although their clerical status was highly dubious, the Pope unwisely decided to make an issue of it.
40 Quoted in Horatio Brown, *Studies in the History of Venice*, 1907, Vol. II, 'Paolo Sarpi, the Man'.
41 Ibid.
42 Edmond and Jules de Goncourt, *Italie d'hier*, 1893, 'Venise'.
43 Mary McCarthy, *Venice Observed*, 1956, ch. 4.
44 John Ruskin, *Works*, ed. E. T. Cook and Alexander Wedderburn, London, 1904, Vol. XI, p. 396.
45 Quoted in James Lees-Milne, *Venetian Evenings*, London, 1988, p. 80.
46 *The Life and Letters of Sir Henry Wotton*, ed. Logan Pearsall Smith, Oxford, 1907, p. 57.
47 Sir Henry Wotton, Letter to the Early of Salisbury, 31 December 1609.
48 See Francis Marion Crawford, *Gleanings from Venetian History*, 1907, ch. 17.

49 Théophile Gautier, *Voyage en Italie*, 1852, ch. 25.
50 Thomas Coryate, *Coryat's Crudities*, 1611, 'Observations of Venice'.
51 Ibid.
52 William Lithgow, *The Rare Adventures and Painefull Peregrinations*, 1614, 'Comments upon Italy'.
53 Jean-Jacques Rousseau, *The Confessions* (1781), Book VII, trans. J. M. Cohen, Harmondsworth, 1953, pp. 302–3.
54 Sir Thomas Hoby, *A Booke of the Travaile and Lief of Me Thomas Hoby*, ed. Edgar Powell. See *The Camden Miscellany*, 1902, Vol. X, pp. 15–16.

## THE ISLANDS

1 Frederick Rolfe, *The Desire and Pursuit of the Whole*, 1934, ch. 12.
2 Giacomo Casanova, *History of My Life*, trans. Willard R. Trask, 1967, Vol. III, ch. 14.
3 Alfred de Musset, 'Chanson' (1834) in *Poésies Nouvelles*.
4 Théophile Gautier, *Voyage en Italie*, 1852, ch. 22.
5 L. P. Hartley, 'The White Wand' in *The White Wand and Other Stories*, London, 1954.
6 Quoted in J. G. Links, *Venice for Pleasure* (1966), London, 1984, p. 230.
7 See Pompeo Molmenti, *La Storia di Venezia nella vita privata*, trans. Horatio Brown as *Venice: Its Individual Growth from the Earliest Beginnings to the Fall of the Republic*, London, 1906–8, Pt. II, Vol. II, p. 224.
8 L. P. Hartley, *Eustace and Hilda*, 1947, ch. 5.
9 Mary McCarthy, *Venice Observed*, 1956, ch. 8.
10 John Ruskin, *Works*, ed. E. T. Cook and Alexander Wedderburn, London, 1904, Vol. XI, p. 381.
11 Henry James, 'Venice' (1882), Section 4, reprinted in *Italian Hours*, 1909.
12 Sir Henry Wotton, Letter to the Earl of Salisbury, 26 May 1606.
13 Hester Piozzi (Thrale), *Observations and Reflections*, 1789, ed. Herbert Barrows, Michigan, 1967, pp. 87–8.
14 Johann Wolfgang von Goethe, *Italienische Reise* (1816–29), trans. W. H. Auden and E. Mayer, London, 1962, p. 79.
15 Cassiodorus, Letter to the Tribunes of the Maritime Population in 537 AD. This translation is quoted from John Julius Norwich, *Venice, The Greatness and the Fall*, London, 1981, Vol. I, pp. 30–1.
16 William Wordsworth, 'On the Extinction of the Venetian Republic'.
17 Angelo Mengaldo (not Mingaldo, as Byron tended to spell it) was a vainglorious ex-soldier in Napoleon's army whom Byron had met through the English Consul in Venice. Alexander Scott was a Scottish resident of Venice who had become one of Byron's friends.
18 George Gordon, Lord Byron, Letter to James Cam Hobhouse, 25 June 1818. See *Byron's Letters and Journals*, ed. Leslie A. Marchand, London, 1976.
19 Percy Bysshe Shelley, 'Julian and Maddalo', ll.85–111.
20 Ibid., ll.132–40.

21 Théophile Gautier, *Voyage en Italie*, 1852, ch. 21.
22 George Gordon, Lord Byron, Letter to Thomas Moore, 17 November (cont. 5 December) 1816. See *Byron's Letters and Journals*, ed. Leslie A. Marchand, London, 1976.
23 Oscar Wilde, *The Picture of Dorian Gray*, 1891, ch. 14.
24 John Ruskin, *Works*, ed. E. T. Cook and Alexander Wedderburn, London, 1904, Vol. XXVII, p. 328.
25 *Murray's Handbook for Travellers in Northern Italy*, London, 1877, p. 344.
26 E. V. Lucas, *A Wanderer in Venice*, 1914, ch. 25.
27 D. H. Lawrence, *Lady Chatterley's Lover*, 1928, ch. 17.
28 Johann Wolfgang von Goethe, *Italienische Reise* (1816–29), trans. W. H. Auden and E. Mayer, London, 1962, p. 81.
29 Percy Bysshe Shelley, 'Julian and Maddalo', ll. 1–13.
30 George Sand, *Leone Leoni*, 1834, ch. 24.
31 Théophile Gautier, *Voyage en Italie*, 1852, ch. 25.
32 Frederick Rolfe, *Venice Letters*, ed. Cecil Woolf, London, 1974, pp. 21–2.
33 Bernard Malamud, *Pictures of Fidelman*, 1969, ch. 6.
34 Giacomo Casanova, *History of My Life*, trans. Willard R. Trask, 1967, Vol. IV, ch. 6.
35 Effie Ruskin, Letter of 3 December 1849. See *Effie in Venice*, ed. Mary Lutyens, London, 1965.
36 Thomas Coryate, *Coryat's Crudities*, 1611, 'Observations of Venice'.
37 James Howell, *Familiar Letters on important subjects, wrote from the year 1618 to 1650*, Letter of 30 May 1621.
38 Ibid.
39 John Moore, *A View of the Society and Manners in Italy*, 1781, Letter 3.
40 Giacomo Casanova, *History of My Life*, trans. Willard R. Trask, 1967, Vol. IV, ch. 6.
41 Henry James, 'Venice' (1882), Section 8, reprinted in *Italian Hours*, 1909.
42 George Sand, *Lettres d'un voyageur* (1837), Letter 3, trans. Sacha Rabino-vitch and Patricia Thomson, Harmondsworth, 1987.
43 Henry James, 'Venice: An Early Impression' (1872), reprinted in *Italian Hours*, 1909.
44 William Beckford, *Dreams, Waking Thoughts, and Incidents*, 1783, Letter 9.
45 John Ruskin, *Works*, ed. E. T. Cook and Alexander Wedderburn, London, 1904, Vol. X, p. 17.
46 Effie Ruskin, Letter of 24 February 1850. See *Effie in Venice*, ed. Mary Lutyens, London, 1965.
47 Percy Bysshe Shelley, 'Lines Written Among the Euganean Hills', ll. 115–141.
48 John Ruskin, *Works*, ed. E. T. Cook and Alexander Wedderburn, London, 1904, Vol. X, pp. 18–19.

# ACKNOWLEDGEMENTS

Acknowledgement is due to the following for kindly giving permission to reproduce copyright material:

Maurice Andrieux, *Daily Life in Venice in the Time of Casanova*, translated by Mary Fitton, Allen & Unwin, 1972. Three extracts reproduced by permission of Unwin Hyman Ltd; Max Beerbohm, 'A Stranger in Venice' from *A Variety of Things*, William Heinemann, 1953. Three extracts reproduced by permission of Mrs Eva Reichmann; Marcel Brion, *Venice, The Masque of Italy*, translated by Neil Mann, Elek Books, 1962. Copyright © Grafton Books, a division of Harper Collins (Publishers) Ltd; Michel Butor, *Description de San Marco*. Copyright © Editions Gallimard 1963; Giacomo Casanova, *History of My Life*, translated by Willard R. Trask. Translation copyright © Harcourt, Brace & World Inc.; Elizabeth David, *Italian Food*, Macdonald, 1954. Extract reproduced by permission of Penguin Books and Elizabeth David; Hugh A. Douglas, *Venice on Foot*, 1970. Extract reproduced by permission of Methuen & Co.; J. W. von Goethe, *Italian Journey*, translated by W. H. Auden and E. Mayer, William Collins, 1962. Extract reproduced by permission of Curtis Brown Ltd; L. P. Hartley, 'The White Wand' from *The White Wand and Other Stories*, 1954. Extract reproduced by permission of Hamish Hamilton Ltd; L. P. Hartley, *Eustace and Hilda*, Putnam & Co., 1947. Four extracts reproduced by permission of the Estate of L. P. Hartley and The Bodley Head Ltd; Ernest Hemingway, *Across the River and into the Trees*, Scribner (New York) and Jonathan Cape (London), 1950. Copyright © 1950, all rights outside US, Hemingway Foreign Rights Trust. Extract reproduced by permission of Mayer, Brown & Platt Inc.; D. H. Lawrence, *Lady Chatterley's Lover*, Penguin, 1960. Extract reproduced by permission of Lawrence Pollinger Ltd and the Estate of Mrs Frieda Lawrence Ravagli; Mary McCarthy, *Venice Observed*, William Heinemann, 1961. Two extracts reproduced by permission of A. M. Heath Ltd; Bernard Malamud, *Pictures of Fidelman*, Farrar, Strauss, Giroux (New York) and Eyre & Spottiswoode (London), 1969. Extract reproduced by permission of the Estate of Bernard Malamud and

Chatto & Windus Ltd; Thomas Mann, *Death in Venice*, translated by
H. T. Lowe-Porter, Penguin Books, 1975. Extract reproduced by
permission of Martin Secker & Warburg Ltd; Rosamond Mitchell,
*The Spring Voyage*, John Murray, 1964. Extract reproduced by
permission of Peters, Fraser & Dunlop Ltd; Jan Morris, *A Venetian
Bestiary*, 1982. Extract reproduced by permission of Thames &
Hudson Ltd; Sean O'Faolain, *A Summer in Italy*, Eyre & Spottis-
woode, 1949. Two extracts reproduced by permission of A. P. Watt
Ltd; Lorenzo da Ponte, *Memoirs*, translated by L. A. Sheppard, 1929.
Extract reproduced by permission of Routledge Ltd; Ezra Pound,
Canto XXVI of *The Cantos*, James Laughlin (New York) and Faber
& Faber (London), 1948. Extract reproduced by permission of Faber
& Faber Ltd; Marcel Proust, *Albertine disparue*, Paris, 1925. Extract
reproduced by permission of Chatto & Windus Ltd; John Pudney,
*The Thomas Cook Story*, Michael Joseph, 1953. Extract reproduced
by permission of David Higham Associates Ltd; Saint Augustine,
*Confessions*, translated by R. S. Pine-Coffin, 1961. Copyright © R.
S. Pine-Coffin, 1961. Extract reproduced by permission of Penguin
Books Ltd; George Sand, *Lettres d'un voyageur*, translated by Sacha
Rabinovitch and Patricia Thomson, 1987. Copyright © Sacha
Rabinovitch and Patricia Thomson, 1987. Extract reproduced by
permission of Penguin Books Ltd; Osbert Sitwell, *Winters of Content*,
Duckworth, 1932. Extract reproduced by permission of David
Higham Associates Ltd; Logan Pearsall Smith (ed.), Introduction to
*The Life and Letters of Sir Henry Wotton*, Clarendon Press, 1907.
Extract reproduced by permission of Oxford University Press;
Muriel Spark, *Territorial Rights*, Macmillan, 1979. Extract repro-
duced by permission of David Higham Associates Ltd; Adrian
Stokes, *Venice: An Aspect of Art*, 1945. Extract reproduced by
permission of Faber & Faber Ltd; Pero Tafur, *Travels and Adventures*,
translated by Malcolm Letts, 1926. Extract reproduced by permis-
sion of Routledge Ltd; Giorgio Vasari, *The Lives of the Artists*,
translated by George Bull, 1965. Copyright © George Bull, 1965.
Extract reproduced by permission of Penguin Books Ltd; Gore
Vidal, *Vidal in Venice*, 1985. Extract reproduced by permission of
Weidenfeld & Nicolson Ltd; Cosima Wagner, *Diaries*, translated by
Geoffrey Skelton. Translation copyright © Geoffrey Skelton and
Harcourt Brace Jovanovich Inc., 1980.

Every effort has been made to trace copyright holders. In some cases
this has proved impossible. The author and publishers of this book
would be pleased to hear from any copyright holders not acknow-
ledged.

# INDEX